N. G. Round

CAMBRIDGE IBERIAN AND
LATIN AMERICAN STUDIES

GENERAL EDITOR

PROFESSOR P. E. RUSSELL, F.B.A.

EMERITUS PROFESSOR OF SPANISH STUDIES,
UNIVERSITY OF OXFORD

Emilia Pardo Bazán

Photograph of Pardo Bazán taken in 1883 (Instituto Municipal de Historia, Barcelona)

Emilia Pardo Bazán
The Making of a Novelist

MAURICE HEMINGWAY

LECTURER IN SPANISH, UNIVERSITY OF EXETER

CAMBRIDGE UNIVERSITY PRESS

CAMBRIDGE

LONDON   NEW YORK   NEW ROCHELLE

MELBOURNE   SYDNEY

Published by the Press Syndicate of the University of Cambridge
The Pitt Building, Trumpington Street, Cambridge CB2 1RP
32 East 57th Street, New York, NY 10022, USA
296 Beaconsfield Parade, Middle Park, Melbourne 3206, Australia

First published 1983

Printed in Great Britain at the University Press, Cambridge

Library of Congress catalogue card number: 82-14609

British Library cataloguing in publication data
Hemingway, Maurice
Emilia Pardo Bazán.–(Cambridge Iberian and Latin American studies)
1. Pardo Bazán, Emilia – Criticism and interpretation
I. Title
863'.5   PQ6629.A7
ISBN 0 521 24466 8

For Helen Grant, most humane of teachers
And for Christine, always a friend

'Creo, y ésta es mi profesión de fe, que el que tiene disposición para escribir debe hacerlo; empezando por poco para ir a más; errando algunas veces para acertar otras; en estilo florido o severo, alto o bajo, como pueda; de asuntos graves o frívolos, según le dicte su temperamento; sin aspirar a la suma perfección, y sin creerse superior a los demás; respetando el gusto y el decoro, pero con cierta soltura; y sin aguardar para todo ello a formarse un criterio muy exacto, filosófico, estético, etc., que ¡ay! no logrará acaso poseer nunca...' From a letter, dated 19 September 1879, from Emilia Pardo Bazán to Francisco Giner. Quoted by Alberto Jiménez Fraud in 'Jaime, doña Emilia y don Francisco', *Papeles de son armadans*, XXVI (1962), 171–82 (p. 176)

'El comer se *humaniza* cada día más. Ya no es el engullir de la bestia hambrienta. También en la mesa puede el espíritu sobreponerse a lo material.' Emilia Pardo Bazán, *La cocina española moderna* (Madrid, 1916), p. viii

Contents

Acknowledgements

I am grateful to the late doña Natalia Cossío de Jiménez for her generous assistance in the finding of unpublished correspondence of Pardo Bazán and in the locating of her library in the Pazo de Meirás; also to don Dalmiro de la Válgoma and don Luis G. de Valdeavellano for permission to consult the Giner papers in the Real Academia de la Historia; to the Director and staff of the Instituto Municipal de Historia in Barcelona for their efficiency and courtesy and for providing me with photocopies of letters from Pardo Bazán to Narciso Oller and José Yxart; to the Secretary and Librarian of the Real Academia Gallega for help in discovering information about Pardo Bazán in La Coruña; to Professor P. E. Russell for his kindness, encouragement and guidance; to Dr J. D. Rutherford for his stimulating and constructive criticism; to my friends and colleagues Dr J. M. Alberich, Dr R. B. R. F. Hitchcock, Dr W. F. Hunter, Mrs J. L. Whetnall, Dr G. L. Williams and Professor K. Whinnom for their help and support in a variety of ways; to Eric Southworth, of St Peter's College, Oxford, from whose kindness and incomparable intelligence I have benefited greatly; also to Mrs Hazel Govier for so cheerfully and efficiently typing my manuscript and for correcting my spelling.

Note on abbreviations

References to works by Pardo Bazán have been made as far as possible to the three volumes of the Aguilar *Obras completas* and have been included in the text abbreviated to a roman numeral (volume), and arabic numeral (page) and a letter, a or b (column on page). The text of the first two volumes of the *Obras completas* is not always accurate. The more glaring errors have been corrected in accordance with the first edition and/or Pardo Bazán's own *Obras completas*. The references to unpublished correspondence from Pardo Bazán to Narciso Oller are the catalogue numbers of the Instituto Municipal de Historia in Barcelona, i.e. the initials of the recipient followed by a roman numeral and an arabic numeral. References to the Giner papers in the Real Academia de la Historia have been abbreviated to RAH, Giner. *Bulletin of Hispanic Studies* has been abbreviated to *BHS*.

Introduction

Emilia Pardo Bazán (1851–1921) is generally regarded as Spain's leading woman novelist. Always a controversial figure, she first achieved notoriety with the publication of such novels as *La Tribuna* (1883) and *Los pazos de Ulloa* (1886) in which the treatment of urban working-class or rural *mores* caused scandal because of its frankness and the debt it seemed to owe to Emile Zola. She continued publishing novels (nineteen in all) until 1911 and to the end of her life was admired as an astonishingly prolific short-story writer. And yet, despite the ready assent to her stature, her work is little known. With a handful of exceptions, her novels are unavailable in modern editions outside the collected works, and until quite recently have been largely forgotten. This is partly due, no doubt, to changing fashions and the customary decline in a writer's reputation in the years following his or her death. 'A significant writer, yes, but rather dated' is probably a common, though in my view mistaken, opinion. In a sense her early notoriety is to blame because her name has become too closely associated with the polemical issues (notably that red herring Naturalism) which surrounded the publication of her early novels.

The early 1970s saw a minor spate of new works on Pardo Bazán. Of these, Nelly Clémessy's *Emilia Pardo Bazán, romancière (la critique, la théorie, la pratique)* (Paris, 1973) is the most important and extensive (it is well over 300,000 words long), and, as its subtitle indicates, it is comprehensive in its scope. Professor Clémessy possesses both critical intelligence and a wealth of erudition, and her book is clearly the fruit of many years of research and reflection.

The present work is less ambitious: its primary intention is to trace what I believe to be Pardo Bazán's growth into maturity as a novelist in the late 1880s and the 1890s. I do not deal with her novels of the 1900s because I want to draw attention to and concentrate on the four novels published between 1890 and 1896 (*Una cristiana – La prueba, La*

1

piedra angular, *Doña Milagros* and *Memorias de un solterón*). These novels have been almost entirely neglected, and all but the first seem to me to represent Pardo Bazán's work at its best.

In order to clear the ground I have put aside the generally accepted notion that Pardo Bazán was first and foremost a Naturalist, a disciple (albeit with reservations) of Emile Zola. This is not to say that Pardo Bazán was unaffected by Naturalism; as a progressive intellectual she was hardly likely not to have been affected one way or another.

Naturalism was the fruit of certain novelists' response to Positivism, which was one of the most influential schools of thought in nineteenth-century Europe. Positivism's rejection of metaphysical speculation and its concomitant faith in the experimental method implied a confidence in science's ability to explain and regulate all that man may need to have explained or regulated. The Naturalist novel (or 'experimental' novel, as Zola pointedly called it) is conceived as an experiment in which a hypothesis is (ostensibly at least) tested and proved. Behind this experimental conception lies a view of man as determined by forces over which he has no control (heredity, milieu and historical moment) and, moreover, as a creature whose behaviour is explicable and predictable by reference to these forces.

No one would deny that the great achievements and prestige of science in the second half of the nineteenth century impressed Pardo Bazán and that her mentality and sensibility were partly formed by it. But this period was not quite so monolithic as is sometimes thought (one need only consider the proliferation of 'isms', political, philosophical and aesthetic), and it is wrong to suppose that all individuals, novelists included, reposed confidently on the bedrock of scientism. In a recent important study of Baroja, C. A. Longhurst implies that the nineteenth century was an age which entertained 'a single, uncomplicated view of the universe', and he states that 'by and large the nineteenth-century novel reflects a stable world, with man in control of that world'.[1] Such generalisations certainly could not be applied to Pardo Bazán, in either her ideology or her novels. It is sometimes forgotten that Schopenhauer, who was, as Dr Longhurst points out (pp. 11 and 14), one of the fathers of the crisis of the twentieth-century novel, was enormously influential on many of those writers who are commonly classed as Realist or Naturalist. Pardo Bazán herself makes an indirect reference in *Una cristiana – La prueba* to Schopenhauer's belief that the external world is but an illusion of the senses (1, 688b).

In any case, who could suppose that Galdós and Alas, two of the leading Spanish Realists of the 1880s, were writing with a pre-conceived and unshakable view of the world and man's place in it? Equally, how could the same be supposed of Pardo Bazán? The 1880s, when she began her career as a novelist, saw a change in the intellectual climate, with serious doubts being cast on the apparent certainties offered by Positivism, certainties never wholeheartedly accepted by Pardo Bazán. I hope to show in the following pages that among the most important features of her mature work are a sense of the problematic and an awareness of the contradictions in her attitude to life.

Pardo Bazán's novelistic production has usually been divided by critics into two halves, a Naturalistic period and a 'Spiritual' period. Some make the division at *Una cristiana – La prueba* (1890) and others at *La quimera* (1905).[2] Clémessy, in part II, chapter 7 of her work referred to above, has sensibly corrected this discrepancy by seeing in the novels of the 1890s a transition between the Naturalist and Spiritual phases. She points out that after 1891 Pardo Bazán abandoned popular milieux and turned her attention first to the middle classes and then to the upper classes. The novelist, she argues, maintains Realist objectivity and delight in description, but the latter is less marked than in the 1880s. The atmosphere of the novels between *Una cristiana – La prueba* and *Memorias de un solterón* (1896) is still 'prosaïque'. After this, in *El tesoro de Gastón* (1897) and *El saludo de las brujas* (1897), it is more refined; this change Clémessy sees as a step towards the more subjective *modernista* style of Pardo Bazán's last three novels – *La quimera* (1905), *La sirena negra* (1908) and *Dulce dueño* (1911). Her main point about the novels of the 1890s, however, is that they are all idealist.

While I accept the validity of Professor Clémessy's arguments, my own view of Pardo Bazán's development as a novelist is somewhat different. For me, the crucial factor in this development is not a change of milieu or atmosphere, but an increasing interest in psychology, and the turning-point is not *Una cristiana – La prueba*, but the most famous of Pardo Bazán's novels, *Los pazos de Ulloa* (1886). I shall be arguing in chapter 1 below that in *Los pazos de Ulloa* one can detect a decisive change in her view of the novelist's activity; whereas before she saw this as being fundamentally the depiction of the

3

external world, now she saw it as being the dramatisation of human psychology. Although there is no doubt that Pardo Bazán's novels of the 1890s are influenced to a greater or lesser degree by her Catholicism, it seems to me that to describe them as 'spiritual' is to overstate the case and divert attention from the central issue of psychology. Even in her last three (undoubtedly religious) novels a major interest is the psychology of religious experience. (The four novels published between 1896 and 1905 stand out from the rest of Pardo Bazán's *œuvre* as rather lightweight pieces, although the parable, *El tesoro de Gastón* (1897), is not without charm.)

In this move towards psychology Pardo Bazán was, of course, not alone. During the 1880s there was a general renewal of interest amongst French novelists in the mental and emotional lives of their characters. This was due partly to their misgivings over Zola's, as it was thought, reductive view of human personality, partly to their discovery of the works of the Russian novelists as these became available in French translation, and partly to the growing prestige of the relatively new science of experimental psychology. Pardo Bazán could also look to the example of her admired Galdós, and I shall be pointing out in passing certain correspondences between the work of the two novelists. Much more, I am sure, could be said of this.

My discussion of the novels is not constrained by a consistent 'approach', except a fundamental desire to 'get back to the text'. The questions I deal with are those which seem to me to be raised by the works themselves, for example, the different strategies adopted in the dramatisation of psychology, and, in the case of three novels, the first-person narrative method; but, above all, Pardo Bazán's ambivalent attitude towards the moral status of her characters. In the discussion of psychology I have attempted to identify her philosophical and medical sources and to consider her successes and failures in the imaginative use of them. For convenience, I refer to the third-person narrator as 'she'. I do not intend to imply, however, that the voice of the narrator is necessarily to be identified with that of the novelist.

Appendix I contains biographical details of the novelist. Appendix II lists some of the French works in Pardo Bazán's private library, and is intended to complement the discussion in chapter I and elsewhere of French influences on the novelist. I have omitted Zola because Pardo Bazán's comprehensive knowledge of his works is well known.

4

I

The development of Pardo Bazán's ideas on the novel in the 1880s

'She is probably right. Something human should, indeed, be dearer to one than all the topographies of the world.' Ford Madox Ford on Jean Rhys, from her *Tigers Are Better Looking* (London, 1968), p. 149

Discussion of Pardo Bazán's work has tended to concentrate on the extent to which she was influenced by Zola's Naturalism, and such a concentration has obscured the fact that her literary flirtation with the French novelist was brief. More fundamental was her relationship with the French Art-for-Art's-Sake school, a school chiefly represented by the poet Théophile Gautier, but embracing also such novelists as Flaubert and the Goncourt brothers.[1] Pardo Bazán's affiliation to *l'art pour l'art* is evident in her repeated assertions that the primary aim of art is the realisation of beauty. In her early broadside *La cuestión palpitante* she declares, when discussing Zola's didactic pretensions, that 'el artista que se proponga fines distintos de la realización de la belleza, tarde o temprano, con seguridad infalible, verá desmoronarse el edificio que erija' (III, 624a). The criterion of beauty is invoked on other occasions in *La cuestión palpitante*, and indeed throughout the whole of the novelist's career. For example in 1916 she expresses the same sentiment, but more succinctly: 'Como artista antepongo a la utilidad la belleza' (III, 1550a).[2] Such declarations do not, however, take us very far in the practical business of criticism unless we can define with some clarity what she meant by 'beauty'. As her career progressed her understanding of the word changed, but in her early years she followed the ideas of Gautier and the Art-for-Art's-Sake movement.[3]

Because Gautier and his associates were reacting strongly against the use of literature as a weapon of propaganda, they tended to minimise the importance of the content of a work and to emphasise (perhaps exaggerate) the importance of its form or style, that is, the sound and appearance on the page of words and combinations of words themselves, and, in poetry, rhythm and rhyme. And in their defence of the autonomy of form they found an ally in the visual arts, because our enjoyment of a painting, for example, need not depend

5

on our apprehension of any theme the painting may illustrate: we may simply enjoy its representational qualities or its combination of masses and colours. Few people demand, moreover, that a painting be morally improving. Gautier's desire to emphasise the influence of painters and painting on the group of writers to which he belonged is illustrated in the following passage:

Cette immixtation de l'art dans la poésie a été et demeure un des signes caractéristiques de la nouvelle Ecole, et fait comprendre pourquoi ses premiers adeptes se recrutèrent plutôt parmi les artistes que parmi les gens de lettres. Une foule d'objets, d'images, de comparaisons, qu'on croyait irréductibles au verbe, sont entrés dans le langage et y sont restés. La sphère de la littérature s'est élargie et renferme maintenant la sphère de l'art dans son orbe immense.

Telle était la situation de nos esprits; les arts nous sollicitaient par les formes séduisantes qu'ils nous offraient pour réaliser notre rêve de beauté.[4]

It is not easy to grasp, from this passage, the exact nature of the influence of painting on literature, partly because Gautier's remarks are not explicit. What in fact were these objects, images and comparisons which entered the language of poetry? Furthermore, how far is it valid to make a comparison between painting and writing? Clearly the raw materials of the artist and the writer are essentially different. Marble, bronze and pigments, unlike words, do not speak immediately to the intellect; they appeal first to the senses. Yet for Gautier, more concerned with form than content, this was precisely their attraction. 'Trois choses me plaisent', we read in *Mademoiselle de Maupin*, 'l'or, le marbre et la pourpre, éclat, solidité, couleur'.[5] That is, the visual and the palpable. Gautier was attracted to words, just as a painter or sculptor is to his raw materials, for their sensuous qualities ('éclat, solidité, couleur') at least as much as for their meaning. This delight in the sensuous appeal of words has its classic statement in the 'Notice' which Gautier wrote for the 1868 edition of Baudelaire's *Les fleurs du mal*:

Pour le poète, les mots ont, en eux-mêmes et en dehors du sens qu'ils expriment, une beauté et une valeur propre comme des pierres précieuses qui ne sont pas encore taillées et montées en bracelets, en colliers ou en bagues: ils charment le connaisseur qui les regarde et les trie du doigt dans la petite coupe où ils sont mis en réserve, comme ferait un orfèvre méditant un bijou. Il y a des mots diamant, saphir, émeraude, d'autres qui luisent comme du phosphore quand on le frotte, et ce n'est pas un mince travail de les choisir.[6]

The poet's task, then, was not so much to convey meaning, or even feelings, as to create a sensuous artifact out of words, and the activity of the artist, from painter to goldsmith, was an inspiration in the attempt to enrich poetic language by enlarging its sensuous appeal.

Pardo Bazán undoubtedly knew Gautier's 'Notice', as her copy of *Les fleurs du mal* was the 1868 edition (see Appendix II), and she quotes from the 'Notice' in *La cuestión palpitante* to illustrate the sensuous appeal of words (see III, 613a). A comparison of an extract from the *Apuntes autobiográficos*, which prefaced the first edition of *Los pazos de Ulloa* (1886), with the words of Gautier quoted above is revealing. Pardo Bazán describes how in her early years she became increasingly interested in the sensuous qualities of the Castilian language:

descubriéndome sus arcanidades y tesoros, su relieve y numerosa armonía, y convirtiéndome en coleccionista infatigable de vocablos, en cuya sola hechura (aislada del valor que adquieren en el período) noto bellezas sin cuento, color, brillo y aroma propio, bien como el lapidario antes de engarzada la piedra admira su talla, sus luces y sus quilates. (III, 712a)

The similarity between these words and those of Gautier in both the 1868 'Notice' and *Mademoiselle de Maupin* is striking: Gautier's taste for 'éclat, solidité, couleur' is matched by Pardo Bazán's appreciation of the 'color, brillo y aroma' of words. Both writers point out that the beauty of a word is distinct from its meaning, and both use the simile of a jeweller admiring the qualities of precious stones.

Similar descriptions of style in terms of the plastic arts appear frequently in her early criticism and *obiter dicta*. Writing to Giner in 1882 she compares her preferred style to filigree.[7] In the *Apuntes autobiográficos* she describes herself as innately disposed to the cult of beauty and form (III, 710a), and, in a phrase indicative of her artistic aspirations, she tells how she abandoned a projected history of Spanish mystical literature because such a 'beautiful subject' deserved a 'pen of fine gold, encrusted with diamonds' (III, 721a). In a letter to Juan Montalvo written in 1886 she likens the style of one of his works to bronze and alabaster sculptures, and there was obviously no greater compliment she could pay him.[8] Another highly approving reference to Montalvo's style describes his books as cherries; the form of the books is 'the sweet flesh' and the content merely 'the stone'.[9] So the analogy of taste is added to those of touch, sight and smell to express the sensuous appeal of literary form (Pardo Bazán was not particularly musical – see III, 704b).

What this conception of form meant to Pardo Bazán in practical terms is impossible to discuss without reference to the question of Realism. She spent the 1870s, the decade in which Galdós came to prominence, first in travel in Europe and then in the serious study of philosophy, theology, science and literature. Her first publications were of poetry, studies of the eighteenth-century philosopher Feijóo, Darwin, Milton and Dante, and articles on physics. By her own account she dismissed the novel as a trivial form and had never heard of Galdós or Pereda (see III, 711b). She believed the novel to be in any case beyond her capabilities as a writer because she felt it was entirely a product of the imagination (III, 706b). Her conversion was brought about by her reading of Valera, Alarcón, Pereda and Galdós in the late seventies, and of Balzac, Flaubert, Daudet and the Goncourt brothers when taking the waters at Vichy in 1880.[10] From the material gathered at Vichy she wrote her second novel, *Un viaje de novios*, the preface to which is her first major statement of a Realist aesthetic: 'La novela ha dejado de ser mero entretenimiento, modo de engañar gratamente unas cuantas horas, ascendiendo a estudio social, psicológico, histórico – al cabo, estudio –.' (III, 572a)[11] The novel, having incorporated the modern disciplines of sociology, psychology and historiography, was now a form entirely worthy of her serious mind and, moreover, no longer beyond her capabilities as a writer.

But such a serious approach does not imply that Pardo Bazán set about using the novel as a didactic instrument: nothing would have been more contrary to her belief that art exists primarily for its own sake. The modern writer, in the view of novelists such as Flaubert and the Goncourt brothers, should seek to create beauty through the imitation of contemporary reality, and this requires not only literary craftsmanship but also thorough research.[12] Nevertheless, the fruits of such research are tools of and subordinate to the depiction of reality. Pardo Bazán found her initial inspiration for such a depiction of reality in the works of the Goncourt brothers, taking from them the principle that the aim of the Realist writer should be primarily the rendering of the external world, particularly colour, in words.

In chapter 2 of *La cuestión palpitante*, which is given over to the Goncourts, she describes them as 'mis autores predilectos', and explains her devotion to them by referring to her 'temperamento de colorista'. The greater part of this chapter concentrates on the *colorista* aspect of the Goncourts' work, that is, their use of language to produce 'vivid chromatic sensations' (III, 614b). But the concern for colour in her work, inspired by the Goncourts, goes beyond a simple search for brilliance of visual effect for its own sake, and is incorporated into the attempt to reproduce the world as it appears to the eye, that is, *la verdad* and *lo real*. In *La cuestión palpitante* she aligns herself with the Goncourts in the following expression of praise to colour:

¡Cuán bella y deleitable cosa es el color! [. . .] no dejo de creer que el culto de la línea es anterior al del colorido, como la escultura a la pintura; y pienso que las letras, a medida que avanzan, expresan el color con más brío y fuerza y detallan mejor sus matices y delicadísimas transiciones, y que el estudio del color va complicándose lo mismo que se complicó el de la música desde los maestros italianos acá. (III, 614a)

Modern writing aims at richness of colour rather than purity of line. Other references to 'línea', to be found in the *Estudio preliminar* to her translation of Edmond de Goncourt's *Les frères Zemganno* (III, 963b), show that Pardo Bazán associated line with ideal beauty (the fruit of the imagination rather than observation), whereas the most striking quality of observable reality was colour. When she speaks of the 'realismo ideal' of the Russian novelists and the reconciliation which, she believed, they had effected between spirit and matter, poetry and truth, she completes the list of opposing terms with 'la línea y el color' (III, 952a).[13]

A comparison of this standpoint and Zola's famous *écrans* is revealing. Zola regarded different aesthetic standpoints as analogous to screens through which objects are perceived in a more or less distorted form. The Classical screen is 'un verre grandissant qui développe les lignes et arrête les couleurs', while the Romantic screen is 'un prisme, à la réfraction puissante, qui brise tout rayon lumineux et le décompose en un spectre solaire éblouissant'. The Realist screen is 'un simple verre à vitre, très mince, très clair, et qui a la prétention d'être si parfaitement transparent que les images le traversent et se reproduisent ensuite dans leur réalité'.[14] The latter screen, although slightly darkening colour, shows it more clearly as it is in reality than either of the other two. The problem facing the Realist is to create intensity of colour without succumbing, like the Romantic, to the temptation to distort or magnify features of observable reality. It is interesting to note that Pardo Bazán regarded the *colorista* element in Zola's work as his greatest strength and disagreed with him when, looking upon these 'escalas cromáticas y complicados arpegios' as a defect, he aspired to classical simplicity: '¿No será más bien que esas puras y esculturales líneas que Zola ambiciona y todos ambicionamos excluyen la continua ondulación del estilo, el detalle minucioso, pero rico y palpitante de vida, que exige y apetece el público moderno?' (III, 628a) The Realist is trying to create a work 'throbbing with life', and colour is an indispensable means to this end. Looking back at the Goncourt brothers some ten years after she had first read their work, Pardo Bazán esteemed above all their influence in the elaboration of a Realist language:

En cuanto a su influencia indirecta, es forzoso que se deje sentir [. . .] en el estilo literario de todo verdadero artista, que habrá de propender cada día más a reemplazar la pálida abstracción, la nebulosa generalidad, con la palabra gráfica y pintoresca, la intensidad de la sensación y la visión lúcida de las cosas exteriores, que ya no nos parecen materia inerte, que gracias al esfuerzo del arte expresan, hablan y hasta lloran. (III, 962b)

This remarkable statement takes us a long way towards an understanding of Pardo Bazán's early view of language and the representation of reality. That all-important phrase 'la palabra gráfica y pintoresca' denotes not, of course, an ornamental prettiness, but an attempt to render in language 'la intensidad de la sensación y la visión lúcida de las cosas exteriores', that is, a very immediate picture of the external world. The intensity and particularity of such a style are contrasted with 'la pálida abstracción, la nebulosa generalidad' of a previous or still current use of literary language, and it is reasonable to suppose that the contortions of syntax and other deviations from normal usage in Pardo Bazán's early novels are all part of the effort to achieve this intensity and particularity. It should be noted that such a concept of style is entirely unspiritual (in the broadest sense of the word): there is no mention of ideas, ideals, feelings, or psychology. Alas's comment on her early work confirms the view that it is fundamentally 'unspiritual': 'Mira con cierto desdén *los intereses del alma*, prefiriendo siempre la luz de fuera, las formas plásticas, y en el ineludible *argumento*, someras relaciones sociales, y, cuando más, estudios de caracteres sencillos y aun vulgares.'[15]

I do not want to suggest, however, that Pardo Bazán considered the rendering of the external world to be the only possible aim of the novelist. On the contrary, in an early article on Galdós (1880) she writes that there are two paths the novelist can tread, the observation of either the external or the mental world.[16] It may well be that her reading of the Goncourt brothers encouraged her to follow in her early novels the first of these paths. *Un viaje de novios* (1881) was based on her observations at Vichy, where she first came across the Goncourts' novels. This is the story of a girl (Lucía) who marries a man much older than herself, for reasons which have nothing to do with love and much to do with parental ambition. On her way to her honeymoon in Vichy (her husband has been accidentally left behind at the station) she meets a young man (Artegui) with whom she eventually falls in love. After a struggle between love and duty, she returns home and lives a life of Christian resignation to unhappiness.

Now, although the feminist issues raised by this book are undoubtedly intended to be serious, the seriousness is undermined by the melodramatic plot, with its implausible coincidences and hackneyed situations. Moreover, with the possible exception of Lucía's struggle with her passions in chapter 14, the psychological study of the characters is not profound. In the preface to the novel, Pardo Bazán describes it as a 'novela de costumbres' (III, 573a) and tells how she decided to write a novel rather than a travelogue simply to make the impressions of her journey more readable (III, 571a). This recalls Fernán Caballero's view, expressed in the prologue to *La Gaviota* (1849), of the *novela* (story) as no more than a frame for her 'vast picture' of the Spanish people.[17] Each vignette in *Un viaje de novios* is independent, the plot is disjointed, and the composition evinces little concern for organic form.[18] Because the novelist is not committed wholeheartedly to this novel as a novel, but only as a series of pictures, it seems to me that it is best regarded simply as that: as an artist's sketchbook, containing numerous experiments in the use of language for visual effects and for the registering and animating of external reality. Some examples are offered below:

Dentro, era una exhibición de cuantos pormenores componen el tocado íntimo del niño y la mujer. Las camisas presentaban coquetonamente el adornado escote, ocultando la lisa falda; los pantalones estiraban, simétricas y unidas, una y otra pierna; las chambras tendían los brazos, las batas inclinaban el cuerpo con graciosa lasitud. El blanco tomado y ebúrneo de las puntillas contrastaba con el candor de yeso del madapolán. Alguna cofia de mañana, colocada sobre un pie de palo torneado, lanzaba un toque de colores vivos, de seda y oro, entre las alburas que cubrían aquel recinto como una capa de nieve. (I, 102a)

The subject (clothes) could hardly be more prosaic, yet Pardo Bazán is obviously anxious to bring the scene alive. Very typically in this novel, the description consists of a list of objects, or a 'descripción–inventario', as Baquero Goyanes has called it.[19] The slips, trousers and blouses are personified in a half-burlesque manner and all of them are in action. Also present is the attention to colour in the gradations of white and the contrast provided by the occasional bonnet. The second and final sentence of this extract also exemplify a common feature of Pardo Bazán's early style: the isolating of a verb from its object (or a subject from its verb) by adverbs or adjectives. The effect is to highlight the epithets and to create a knotty and deliberately unflowing style, which, through the very awkwardness of the reading process, gives the reader a sense of the density of the world being described. No 'pallid abstractions' or 'nebulous generalities' here.[20]

Pardo Bazán takes every opportunity to try her hand at the kind of still-life just discussed. Here, the heroine, Lucía, is walking ankle-deep through autumn leaves: 'Hojas había muy diferentes entre sí; unas oscuras, en descomposición, vueltas ya casi mantillo; otras secas, quebradizas, encogidas; otras amarillas, o aun algo verdosas, húmedas todavía con los jugos del tronco que las sustentara' (1, 126a). The novelist's eye notes and records the differences in the leaves. The accumulation of adjectives ('secas, quebradizas, encogidas' and 'amarillas, verdosas, húmedas'), giving an increasingly more precise impression, is another characteristic of the style of this novel. The extreme care with which scenes or objects are described can also be seen in this example: 'En efecto, oíase un borboteo extraño, después un silbo agudo, y un chorro de agua hirviente, que despedía intolerable olor sulfuroso, se lanzaba espumante, recto y rápido hasta la cúpula misma del alto cenador.' (1, 123b) We are given first two aural impressions (the gurgling and the high-pitched whistle) and then the smell and the visual impact of the boiling water. Again, the awkward syntax highlights these impressions: the subject of the coordinating clause ('un chorro de agua hirviente') is isolated from its verb by a subordinate clause which gives us the smell of the water, while the verb itself ('se lanzaba') is isolated from the adverbial phrase needed to complete its meaning by the three adjectives ('espumante, recto y rápido'), which by their position and sound give the impression of the water finally bursting up as a triumphant force.

I have suggested that this attention to language derives from the work of the Goncourt brothers. Their influence is seen very clearly in another example. In *La cuestión palpitante* she notes that the Goncourts sometimes repeat the same word to heighten the intensity of a particular sensation (III, 614a). In the second sentence of the following passage, Pardo Bazán experiments in the same way:

Lucía se quedaba pensativa, fija la pupila en las canastillas de flores del parque, que parecían medallones de esmalte prendidos en una falda de raso verde. Formábanlas diversas variedades de colios: los del centro tenían hojas lanceoladas y brillantes, de un morado oscuro, rojo púrpura, rojo ladrillo, rojo de cresta de pavo, rojo rosa. (I, 125a)

Although *Un viaje de novios* is not a good novel, then, if seen as a sketchbook, it is not without interest, if only because it gives us a point of reference in our attempt to follow Pardo Bazán's growth as a novelist.

Her next novel, *La Tribuna* (1883), which describes the lives of women working in a cigarette factory in Marineda (La Coruña) during the period following the 1868 Revolution, is described, like *Un viaje de novios*, as a 'study of local customs', and is fundamentally a series of descriptions of the external world, with the addition of a rudimentary account of the psychology and seduction of the main character, Amparo, the *Tribuna* of the title. Amparo's attitudes and inner feelings are never scrutinised except for her feminine vanity (II, 168b and 176b–7a), and even then she is called 'superficial y vehemente'. Alas wrote of her: '*La Tribuna* se enamora, y no mucho, de un caballero oficial que le dice que se casará con ella, y no se casa. Esta es toda la psicología de *La Tribuna*, amén de una escena de celos mezclados de orgullo, y de varios arranques patrióticos, que no se puede asegurar que sean cosa del alma.'[21]

However, this novel is not the same kind of random picture-gallery as *Un viaje de novios*: all the descriptions contribute to a unified picture of the living and working conditions of lower-class Marineda. The language is still, as in *Un viaje de novios*, directed towards the rendering of the external world, in particular, the oppressive physicality of the cigarette factory, where much of the action is set. When Pardo Bazán called this novel 'tan duro, tan ingrato'[22] she was referring to the subject-matter, but the epithets could well apply to the manner of the telling: the familiar 'descripciones–inventarios' and the unflowing language. She apparently intended the mere recording of life in the cigarette factory to be dramatic, since she compares the factory to Dante's *inferno*.[23] But detailed inventories on such a large scale are unlikely to interest because the effect is, in my view, merely cold and lifeless, whereas the random descriptions of *Un viaje de novios* have a certain charm, if the book is regarded in the way I have suggested.

This adverse judgement on the descriptive element in *La Tribuna*, has, I think, to be made, but for our purposes the interesting fact is that there are some exceptions. In chapter 30 there is a long series of glimpses of everyday life in a working-class suburb, as seen by a passer-by. For example, we are shown a woman suckling a child, another peeling potatoes, and another furtively emptying dirty water into the street. These descriptions are unusual in this novel because they are of people. Pardo Bazán seems to have stumbled upon the obvious fact that in a novel people are more interesting than things. In each of these tiny vignettes there is left unstated a human situation or particular concern. So that when these humble actions are summed up, with a touch of superciliousness, as 'las excrecencias de la vida', we feel a certain resistance: we suspect a certain irony, as if the passer-by who views these events must be an inhabitant of the 'rich suburbs', someone who does not understand the value of either the humble actions or the humble actors.

Another, and shorter, 'descripción–inventario' (this time of a clock) ends the section dealing with the abortive strike in the cigarette factory: 'Mientras, los bandos de mujeres iban saliendo con la cabeza caída – humilladas todas por el ajeno delito –; y el reloj antiguo de pesas, de tosca madera, pintado de color ocre con churriguerescos adornos dorados, que grave y austero como un juez adornaba el zaguán, dio las seis.' (II, 170a) I call this a 'descripción–inventario' because of the enumeration of details about the clock. It is worth noting in passing the dramatic way in which the subject ('el reloj') is isolated from its predicate ('dio las seis') by the descriptive details. A comparison between this description and that of the autumn leaves discussed above reveals a significant difference. There, the description, although loosely related to the physical presence of a character, had no function apart from itself. By contrast, the description of the clock reinforces the statement in the previous sentence about the women's sense of guilt. The austere, yet rather grand, clock has become a judge, and, as it strikes the hour, seems to be passing sentence. It is not clear whether the transformation has taken place in the mind of the observer or of the women. In either case the effect is powerful, but if it is the latter, it represents a psychological insight and, as in the other passage from *La Tribuna* I have discussed, an element of human concern.

My point is that, although in *La Tribuna* the focus is still on external reality – the factory, the poor areas of Marineda – and such psychology as is present is rudimentary, there are nevertheless some signs of Pardo Bazán's shift of interest towards psychology. *La Tribuna* was completed in October 1882, just before Pardo Bazán's essays on Naturalism, *La cuestión palpitante*, began to appear in *La época*. In this work she singles out psychology, which in the 1880 article on Galdós she had given only equal status with the description of the external world, as the most interesting territory for the novelist to explore:

De todos los territorios que puede explorar el novelista realista y reflexivo, el más rico, el más variado e interesante es sin duda el psicológico, y la influencia innegable del cuerpo en el alma, y viceversa, le brinda magnífico tesoro de observaciones y experimentos. (III, 645a)

This is a quite definite commitment to psychology as the central concern of the Realist novelist.

Pardo Bazán's next novel, *El Cisne de Vilamorta*, completed in autumn 1884, shows evidence of such a commitment. It deals with a triangular relationship between Leocadia, a Romantically inclined schoolteacher, Segundo ('El Cisne'), a local hack poet, and Nieves, the wife of a visiting politician, Victoriano. As Pattison has pointed out, the satire of Romantic illusions and the suicide of Leocadia are clearly reminiscent of Flaubert's *Madame Bovary*.[24] In *El Cisne de Vilamorta* Pardo Bazán took a step in the direction of the psychological novel because, unlike *Un viaje de novios* and *La Tribuna*, this novel centres on the lives of the characters rather than their environment. The step is timid though, since the psychological interest is shared between the four different characters just referred to, each of whom is only lightly sketched, and never really seen or understood by the reader or (one suspects) by the writer.[25]

This outline of Pardo Bazán's early activity as a novelist has so far ignored the influence of Zola, but clearly it has to be considered. Despite the fact that a large proportion of criticism has concentrated on this influence, it seems to me that it has been overestimated and, worse, it has produced a false perspective on these novels and, as I shall be arguing later, on those which immediately follow them. 'Hunt the Naturalist' has been a popular but largely fruitless critical activity. All the elements which are attributed by critics to the impact of Zola (documentation, detailed descriptions, risqué subject-matter and the realistic reproduction of the dialogue of the lower classes) could just as easily be attributed to the impact of the Goncourt brothers, whose importance for Pardo Bazán's work has already been established above. D. F. Brown, the critic who argues most strongly for the decisiveness of Zola's influence, himself admits that Zola's only original contribution to the novel form was the use of heredity (p. 18). Pardo Bazán's debt to Flaubert in *El Cisne de Vilamorta* has already been mentioned.

Nevertheless, it can hardly be denied that the novels which followed *El Cisne de Vilamorta* (*Los pazos de Ulloa*, *La madre naturaleza*, *Insolación* and *Morriña*) owe something to Zola's experimental novel. In *La madre naturaleza* (1887), the novel on which Zola's shadow is most obviously cast, a hypothesis is formulated explicitly, then tested, and the behaviour of Perucho and Manuela is clearly shown to be determined by their circumstances and instincts. Moreover, as Brown has demonstrated, the novel's conception and some of its details owe not a little to Zola's *La faute de l'abbé Mouret* (pp. 99–107). *Los pazos de Ulloa* (1886), too, is based on a Naturalistic experiment, involving environment, heredity, the decadence of don Pedro's family line, and human barbarity, but on its simplest level it purports to demonstrate that human beings who are brought up away from the influences of religion and civilisation inevitably behave according to their animal instincts. Also, as Brown has said, there is a study of 'the decay of the old noble houses of Galicia' (p. 83). In *Insolación* (1889) the experiment could scarcely be more explicit, with the hypothesis (that when Spaniards are exposed to the sun they behave like savages) being put forward in chapter 2 and then (apparently) demonstrated in the following chapters.

However, as I shall argue in chapters 2 and 3, the experimental element in *Los pazos de Ulloa* and *Insolación* raises certain doubts. In the former, the experiment is not carried through with conviction, and, in the latter, we are left wondering whether the hypotheses have been proved or not, or even whether they were intended to be proved. In *Morriña*, the idea that Esclavitud's suicide is determined by her racial characteristics ('el sombrío humor de la raza céltica') is specifically discounted in the final paragraph. Esclavitud's sense of being rejected both by society and God is due more to guilt over her origins (she is the offspring of a priest) than Galician melancholy (*morriña*). In this respect the novel's title is misleading. Or it may even be, as the novel's last sentence suggests, an ironic comment on the Naturalist's tendency to account for human behaviour in a generalised, deterministic manner. So, without wishing to dismiss lightly the impact of Zola's work on Pardo Bazán, I want to insist that it is by no means as decisive and unambiguous as is generally believed.

Indeed, the inspiration for these (as it is thought) most Naturalist of Pardo Bazán's works may well come as much from the Russian novelists as from Zola. Pardo Bazán started reading the Russian novelists in 1885 in French (see III, 760b), and in 1887 she delivered three lectures at the Ateneo (published later that year in book form) entitled *La revolución y la novela en Rusia*. It is clear from this important work that in the Russians she discerned a concept of beauty which was entirely contrary to the Art-for-Art's-Sake aesthetic which informed her early works. In Dostoyevsky she notes how beauty is created from ugliness: 'Con él entramos en una estética nueva, donde lo horrible es bello, lo desesperado consuela, lo innoble raya en sublime.' (III, 855b) This paradoxical species of beauty was nothing new: it lies at the heart of Baudelaire's aesthetic and is pointed to by the very title of *Les fleurs du mal*.[26] Yet, as it appears in Dostoyevsky's work, it disturbed Pardo Bazán's preconceptions about the nature of beauty. Having pointed out all his defects, she concludes that none the less his work possesses an overwhelming beauty: 'Pues con todo, digo que es belleza, belleza torturada, retorcida, satánica, pero intensa, grande y dominadora.' (III, 861b) Such intensity is far removed from the calm, detached vision of the *colorista*, the devoted disciple of the Goncourt brothers. And Pardo Bazán was struck above all by the intensity of Dostoyevsky's psychological analysis: 'Por experiencia propia conozco el diabólico poder del análisis psicológico de Dostoyevsky. Sus libros son de los que le ponen a uno enfermo, aunque se pase de sano.' (III, 860a) Turgenev is (amongst other things) a 'perfect landscape artist', whereas Dostoyevsky is a 'rabid psychologist', with almost an aversion to nature and the physical world (III, 862a). 'Una intensidad psíquica' (to quote a phrase she applies to Goncharov's *Oblomov* – III, 854b) stands in contrast to 'la visión lúcida de las cosas exteriores' and 'la intensidad de la sensación', which, as we have already seen, she admired so much in the work of the Goncourt brothers.

However, Pardo Bazán's awed encounter with Dostoyevsky, Tolstoy and others did not lead her to imitate them. Their anarchic 'loose, baggy monsters' were quite alien to her disciplined mind and her ingrained love of exquisite finish and surface colour. *Los pazos de Ulloa* (which was written while she was first reading the Russian novelists) is a hybrid work.[27] As in previous novels there is, particularly in the first half, the familiar attention to the external world and local customs. But *Los pazos de Ulloa* is a more dynamic and complex novel than any of those which precede it. For the first time Pardo Bazán gives her novel a genuinely experimental framework, as already described, and even this is less simple in its inspiration and impact than is generally believed. The study of the decay of the Galician nobility is not just an attempt to demonstrate how don Pedro must inevitably fall into degradation because of 'the final rottenness of the very ideas of his caste' (Brown, p. 94); it also expresses, particularly in chapter 15, 'la tristeza inexplicable de las cosas que se van' (i, 224b), a melancholic sense that past splendours and beauties are coming to an end. Such a sentiment was typical of the Decadent sensibility of the last third of the nineteenth century, typical, that is, of the anguished conviction that Western civilisation was in its death-throes.[28] This fact suggests that at least part of the experiment in *Los pazos de Ulloa* derives as much from Edgar Allan Poe and his disciples as it does from Zola. Indeed there are certain resemblances, which may not be fortuitous, between the beginning of *Los pazos de Ulloa* and the beginning of Poe's *The Fall of the House of Usher*.

More germane to the present argument, however, is the fact that psychology is present in *Los pazos de Ulloa* from the beginning, and becomes increasingly prominent as the novel progresses. It is evident, for example, in the very first sentence:

Por más que el jinete trataba de sofrenarlo agarrándose con todas sus fuerzas a la única rienda de cordel y susurrando palabrillas calmantes y mansas, el peludo rocín seguía empeñándose en bajar la cuesta a un trote cochinero que desencuadernaba los intestinos, cuando no a trancos desigualísimos de loco galope. (i, 167a)

As in earlier examples I have quoted, there is a certain awkwardness of syntax: the short main clause ('el peludo rocín seguía empeñándose en bajar la cuesta') is dwarfed by the adverbial clauses which both precede and follow it, as if the weight of the sentence were being disputed. But in fact such apparent clumsiness reveals on closer examination a concern to convey a concrete visual image. The initial clause and phrases present us with Julián's vain efforts to control the horse; the main clause describes the horse's contrary efforts; then the last part of the sentence, with its accumulation of adverbial expressions, runs away uncontrollably, like the horse. So syntax is used for graphic purposes. However, it should be noted that the structure of this sentence does not simply exemplify 'la visión lúcida de las cosas exteriores': the concrete visual impression also dramatises

Julián's psychological make-up. We see from the outset of the novel his gentle, effeminate personality, as he ineffectually attempts to overcome uncontrollable physical forces. We can also see here a synthesis of the two conceptions of the novel Pardo Bazán had outlined in her 1880 article on Galdós, that is, a study of either the external world or of human psychology. In a more far-reaching way than we have observed in this first sentence, the whole novel exemplifies this synthesis: Pardo Bazán is now no longer choosing between inner and outer worlds, but is instead exploiting the interaction of one on the other. The reader's grim and terrifying vision of Ulloa is Julián's vision, while the fact that he sees it in this way is a means of characterising him. But, more than this, Julián's personality is given life and a measure of complexity, particularly in the novel's second half, by a pointed kind of irony and a concentration on his perception of particular events and of the general situation. The shift in the novel's centre of interest away from the description of the external world towards depiction of psychology (a shift one does not observe in her earlier novels) may suggest that, although Pardo Bazán did not imitate the rambling composition of the novels of Dostoyevsky or Tolstoy, the lesson she learnt from them was not lost on her and hastened a process already, as we have seen, set in motion.

In her next novel, *La madre naturaleza* (1887), psychological analysis is also present but it is less subtle than in *Los pazos de Ulloa*, and the reader's main experience is of the broad sweep of tragic events determined by factors beyond the protagonists' control. The young Perucho and Manuela, unaware of their kinship, fall in love and contract an incestuous union, in a way which is, we are certainly made to feel, inevitable. The depiction of the psychology of the young people has few of the delicate nuances found in that of the character of Julián, and indeed the reader's interest is engaged more by the character of Manuela's uncle, Gabriel Pardo. But, although Gabriel's hopes and disillusionments are presented with a touching delicacy (I am thinking particularly of the recurring image of the elusive butterfly which appears first at the end of *Los pazos de Ulloa*), his very self-knowledge makes him a less promising subject for the novelist's ironic probing than the bewildered, naive Julián. Nevertheless, in this most Naturalist of Pardo Bazán's novels, the interest in psychology is sustained and, as in *Los pazos de Ulloa*, there is an interaction of outer and inner worlds. In *La madre naturaleza*, however, the interaction is

19

EMILIA PARDO BAZÁN

more one-sided. Nature is described, particularly at the novel's climax (chapters 19 and 20), as an overpowering and hypnotic agent precisely because it overpowers and hypnotises Perucho and Manuela.

After two such large-scale works as *Los pazos de Ulloa* and *La madre naturaleza*, Pardo Bazán published in 1889 two short and intriguing novels, in which for the first time she concentrated her efforts on psychological analysis. Moving from a rural setting to the world of upper-class Madrid, she studies in *Insolación* the mental confusion of Asís, a respectable young widow, who finds herself in love for the first time and unable to reconcile her feelings with her notions of what she is and ought to be. The intelligence and subtlety encountered in this study could already be glimpsed in parts of *Los pazos de Ulloa* and, to a lesser extent, in *La madre naturaleza*, but the singlemindedness with which it is achieved here marks a startling development. Although, as I have suggested, there is in the two previous novels a synthesis of inner and outer worlds, the strictly *costumbrista* element is only loosely related to plot and psychology. By contrast, in *Insolación* all three form an impressive whole. The picture of the Fair of San Isidro and Las Ventas del Espíritu Santo are not only brilliantly vital examples of *costumbrismo*, but are also essential to the development both of the plot and of the presentation of Asís's mental confusion and self-awareness.

In *Morriña* Pardo Bazán displays the same sureness of touch as in *Insolación*. Like its companion-piece, it deals with the awakening of sexual passion, this time in a rather immature young man. Despite the fact that the title implies that the central character is the melancholic maid, Esclavitud, the novel is in reality a fairly light sketch of the close relationship between a mother (doña Aurora) and her son (Rogelio). The psychological analysis, although it is not developed to any great extent, is acute, particularly in the exploration of the complex reactions of the astute mother protecting her son's interests, and of the adolescent boy anxious to become a man.[29]

I have suggested that in this move towards psychology the Russian novelists were a general inspiration rather than a precise influence. It should also be noted, however, that the popularity of the Russians from the 1880s onwards was part of a wider reaction against Naturalism and the Positivism on which Naturalism was based. This reaction, sometimes known as Spiritual Naturalism, was a move away from a materialistic view of human nature and a return to the idea of man's possessing a soul (susceptible to supernatural forces)

20

and a complex psychological make-up.[30] An early sign of the rebellion against Zola's Naturalism was a novel published in 1884 by one of his disciples, J.-K. Huysmans, called *A rebours*, where the hero, Des Esseintes, escapes from the reality of the contemporary world into an artificial world of art, history and the occult. At the end, Des Esseintes is left longing for religious belief.

This religious element was central to certain French writers' dissatisfaction with Naturalism. Vogüé, for example, in his influential critical work, *Le roman russe* (1886), attacks Zola's materialism and pessimism for fostering the widespread contemporary sense of despair which accompanied loss of religious faith.[31] On the other hand, he praises Gogol, Dostoyevsky and Tolstoy, because, while not shying away from the suffering and ugliness of life, they approach their subject-matter with a pity and charity which do not degrade, but ennoble and lead to hope. The awareness of the pain and suffering of life and the divinely inspired attitude towards it combined to form what Vogüé called 'la religion de la souffrance'.

Huysmans, who was in his earlier years a faithful follower of Zola, gradually moved towards a mystical conception of life. The opening chapter of his novel *Là-bas* (1891) is an important document in the reaction against Naturalism because of the clarity of its critique of Zola and the concrete nature of its proposals. Huysmans's ideas overlap at many points with Vogüé's, in particular in his advocacy of the supernatural as an essential part of reality. However, his views, as expressed in *Là-bas*, are rather more complex than Vogüé's, being based on a belief in the aristocratic nature of art and a rejection of the modern world. Significantly, and unlike Vogüé, he excepts Flaubert and the Goncourt brothers, all Art-for-Art's-Sake writers, from his strictures on Naturalism. Durtal, who is normally taken to be Huysmans's mouthpiece in this instance, puts forward a formula for a new kind of Realism: 'Il faudrait, en un mot, suivre la grande voie si profondément creusée par Zola, mais il serait nécessaire de tracer en l'air un chemin parallèle, une autre route, en un mot, un naturalisme spiritualiste.' This Spiritual Naturalism would retain 'la véracité du document, la précision du détail, la langue étoffée et nerveuse du réalisme', while at the same time not attempting to explain away mystery by 'les maladies des sens'.[32] In other words, the novel would be Realist in its method of observation and its language, but would not be constrained by the materialistic restrictions of Zola's formula.

A common theme in the many expressions of disenchantment with

Zola was a disillusionment with science. This reaction was greatly strengthened by Ferdinand Brunetière's declaration of 'la banqueroute de la science'.[33] Science, it was felt, had been unable to explain human life and had failed to satisfy man's deeper needs. The result was a new search for faith. This was dramatised in two novels written in 1889, Bourget's *Le disciple* and Edouard Rod's *Le sens de la vie*. In the first, the principles of a distinguished philosopher, usually identified with Taine, are put into practice by a disciple of his, with disastrous effects. At the end of the novel the philosopher is on the road to conversion. In the second, the protagonist's quest for the meaning of life is traced from disillusionment to disillusionment until he finally reaches the threshold of conversion. Huysmans's *En route* (1895) is an account of Durtal, the protagonist of *Là-bas*, in a Trappist monastery, and is a fervent apologia of a Catholicism which does not compromise with the modern world. In this respect Huysmans typified the reactionary position of many writers of the Catholic revival.[34]

Needless to say, Pardo Bazán was not unaware of literary developments in France (as her Russian lectures, prompted by Vogüé's work, demonstrate) and in the late 1880s and early 1890s she wrote on various occasions about writers such as Huysmans, Rod and Bourget. However, although she welcomed Spiritual Naturalism, she was relatively unconcerned about the specifically spiritual aspect of this phenomenon. For example, in *La revolución y la novela en Rusia*, despite a statement to the effect that the spiritual element in the Russian novel was, for her, one of its greatest merits (III, 878a), her comments on particular authors and works refer relatively infrequently to the religious content. As I have already suggested, she was attracted primarily to the intensity of their psychological analysis. In an article published in 1889 on Bourget's *Le disciple* she barely touches on the important religious implications of the novel, and when she does her manner is rather patronising: 'El último libro de Bourget es un eco más de ese *regreso al cristianismo* que se manifiesta como tendencia actual y dominante en algunos de los ingenios más selectos de Francia; en buen hora se diga.'[35] The firmly Catholic Pardo Bazán is unmoved by Bourget's progress along the road to conversion.[36] But the same could not be said of her attitude towards his achievement as a writer, for there is ample evidence of her admiration for his powers of psychological analysis.

That she was well acquainted with Bourget's work is attested to by the comprehensive list of his works in the catalogue of her personal library (see Appendix II). Apart from this evidence, there are various references to Bourget, usually approving, in her critical writings and *obiter dicta*. The first reference I can find is in a letter to Menéndez Pelayo, dated 26 June 1886, where she writes:

Vd. que va teniendo tan amplio criterio, ¿cómo no se toma la molestia de seguir un poco la evolución estética *actual* en Francia? Vería Vd. que quienes la infestan son los perfumados secuaces de Ohnet o Feuillet o Bourget, o Setheuriet, que todos acaban en *et.* Los verdaderos discípulos de Zola, Daudet y Goncourt se cuentan por los dedos.[37]

Here Pardo Bazán regards the work of Bourget and his contemporaries as a new and less scabrous departure from the work of her original models. In *Al pie de la Torre Eiffel* (1889) she introduces Bourget to her Spanish public with a review of *Le disciple*: 'Ayer, en un momento de vagar, leí la última novela de Bourget, el eminente *jeune maître* de la novela francesa.' (p. 274) She regards him as first among his contemporaries and mentions especially his skill at psychological analysis. She makes similar comments in another review of his work published three years later: 'Varias veces he manifestado opiniones muy favorables a Bourget, a quien tengo quizá por el talento más cultivado y robusto de la nueva generación. En su especialidad de relojero del alma [. . .] Bourget no tiene rival ni acaso lo tenga en mucho tiempo.' (III, 1064b) Another remark of the same period is equally flattering:

Pues léase a Pablo Bourget, y nótese en tan eminente artista, hasta cuando traza novelas amorosas o cuadros de tocador, la presencia de la intensa educación filosófica, la perpetua aplicación de los principios, el enlace riguroso de las deducciones, la lógica victoriosa de los caracteres, todo lo que ha servido de fundamento a su reputación de psicólogo. (III, 1037a)

Her admiration for 'el gran psicólogo Bourget' (as she calls him in an essay on Campoamor – III, 1323a) is reflected in fairly frequent references to him.[38]

Now, unlike Pardo Bazán's early novels, those with which the greater part of the present study is concerned were not preceded by an introductory preface, and her comments on them elsewhere are few, so the impact of Bourget on her work cannot be established in the same way as that of the Goncourt brothers and Zola can be on the novels of the 1880s. Indeed it must be said at once that doña Emilia's novels after *Los pazos de Ulloa* differ in various respects from Bourget's. The French writer is almost exclusively interested in the psychology of love. In works such as *L'irréparable*, *Deuxième amour*, *Un crime d'amour* and his *Physiologie de l'amour moderne*, he explores the intricacies of the relationship between the sexes from a viewpoint of extreme pessimism. His work is the antithesis of the Romantic idealisation of love, and love is generally presented as the corruption, even the destruction, of others. Notorious as the apostle of pessimism, he was accused of making a large contribution to the gloom fashionable among young *fin-de-siècle* writers, whose inspiration was Schopenhauer and Hartmann.[39] For Bourget, it seems, a truthful account of life presupposed a pessimistic world-view, an attitude he attributes to the apocryphal *physiologiste* in *Physiologie de l'amour moderne*, who refers to 'le premier devoir de l'observateur, – la misanthropie'.[40] Like many of his contemporaries, Bourget reacted to some extent against this unrelieved pessimism, and *Cruelle énigme* (1885) and *Le disciple* (1889), while still presenting extremely grim human situations, give a hint of the author's move towards Catholicism in the 1890s.

Despite her praise for Bourget, Pardo Bazán was unhappy about the pessimism in his work and refers to the 'excesiva materialidad' of his analysis and his tendency to exaggerate the purely physiological side of love (III, 1066b). She dislikes the way in which Bourget ignores the variety and richness of modifications which sexual instinct undergoes in man, with his rational nature and moral sense: 'En el hombre, *nada es principalmente físico*. Si estudios del género del de Bourget no demuestran esta gran verdad, por entretenidos, sutiles y profundos que sean, dejarán en el ánimo una huella depresiva, como la deja, al fin y al cabo, la *Fisiología del amor moderno*.' (III, 1067a) Now, in Pardo Bazán's novels of the late 1880s and 1890s there *is* a strong element of pessimism about sexual love (or at least a questioning of the Romantic concept of love), but, as we shall see, also an obstinate idealism quite alien to the French writer.

In addition, there is a difference in subject-matter. Bourget deals with love in a setting which is almost exclusively Parisian and aristocratic, and there is an implacable concentration on the psychology of the main characters. Consequently, his novels convey an atmosphere of intense claustrophobia and, with rare exceptions (for example, the concierge and maid in *Le disciple*), they give the impression that the world of normal life and people does not exist. Nothing could be more different from the atmosphere of Pardo Bazán's novels of the 1890s, set, as they are for the most part, in the world of middle-class Galicia, where tragedy combines with comedy, and villainy with goodness. Moreover, these novels, although lacking the long, detailed descriptions of the earlier novels, still give a picture of a definite physical and social context. In this sense Pardo Bazán remains a Realist in the tradition of Balzac, and deviates from Bourget, whose novels pay little attention to physical setting.

Nevertheless, there are general reasons for believing that Bourget exercised a positive influence on Pardo Bazán. The first is that in the article in *Al pie de la Torre Eiffel* she attributes to him the very qualities she found lacking in Zola: 'Bourget ha sustituído a la psicología *externa* de la escuela de Zola una psicología–analítica, tan sutil, delicada y quintaesenciada, que llega a ser dolorosa.' (pp. 279–80) Her comments on Zola and psychology from the 1890s onwards confirm this admiration for Bourget.

In a review of Zola's novel *L'argent* she complains that Zola's characters are mere incarnations of theories and abstract concepts, and insists that life itself is far more complex and inconsistent: 'Tiene sus leyes, no cabe duda, pero secretas, que encubre una apariencia de irregularidad, produciendo lo que suele llamarse misterios del corazón, arcanos del alma, contradicciones que entretejen nuestros actos.' (III, 989b) Writing about Stendhal in 1901 she makes a similar point:

Existe [...] en los movimientos del corazón [...] mucho que siempre resistirá al análisis y no podrá tener explicación satisfactoria. Esto lo advertimos en nosotros mismos: *observamos* que no podemos *observar*, que no acertamos a definir y depurar las causas oscuras ni aun de nuestra sensibilidad propia.[41]

Words such as 'secretas', 'misterios', 'arcanos' and 'causas oscuras' indicate that Pardo Bazán viewed the human mind not only as complex but also mysterious. Again her criticisms of Zola are revealing:

Al profesar el determinismo como consecuencia del método experimental, se confinó en una psicología mecánica, quitándole a la lira infinitas y vibrantes cuerdas. Los caracteres en Zola tienen algo de elemental y rudimentario; no profundizó los arcanos del pensar y del sentir; tomó el instinto, no por raíz honda, sino por ley constante, prestando a la mayoría de sus personajes una vida entre automática y – fuerza es estampar la palabra, empleada por muy certeros críticos – bestial.[42]

Despite the adverse reference to the consequences of materialistic determinism contained in the last word, Pardo Bazán condemns mechanical psychology not so much on grounds of scientific or philosophical truth as of artistic expediency ('quitándole a la lira infinitas y vibrantes cuerdas'). She prefers to explore the secret places ('arcanos') of the mind and to see instinct as 'raíz honda', because that implies mystery. As I hope the rest of the present book will demonstrate, in her novels she becomes increasingly concerned to lay bare the secret motives behind human behaviour.

This concern brings us to the second reason for being persuaded of Bourget's importance for Pardo Bazán. In the article in *Al pie de la Torre Eiffel* (written in 1889, the year of the publication of *Insolación* and *Morriña*) she identified in his subtle psychological analysis precisely this conception of the mind as mysterious territory:

Por manera que las novelas de Bourget ofrecen una complicación de sentimientos y una filigrana o red de detalles íntimos, que hacen de ellas obras maestras de relojería intelectual. Toda rueda del pensamiento de sus héroes, todo microscópico resorte de esos que, sin saberlo nosotros, hacen funcionar nuestro espíritu, determinando las evoluciones, los juicios y los actos humanos, Bourget lo coge con pinzas y lo maneja y lo pone en actividad para que nos demos cuenta de su importancia. (pp. 280–1)

The fact that she talks of no other novelist in this way supports the notion that Bourget was an important source of inspiration for her. More precise evidence will be adduced in chapter 7, where I shall point out reminiscences in *Memorias de un solterón* of Bourget's use of the Unconscious in *L'irréparable*.

The question of influence here is not simply academic; a comparison of the two writers helps us describe more exactly the nature of Pardo Bazán's development as a novelist in the late 1880s and early 1890s. Although she had already learnt from the Russians that the novelist cannot concern himself primarily with the rendering of the external world, their novels were not examples which she could follow. Bourget's disciplined intelligence and minute probings of the human mind were much more attuned to her own sensibility. He confirmed her in her belief that Zola's concept of human psychology was reductive not only in philosophical but also in artistic terms. This does not mean that Pardo Bazán was the Spanish Bourget, any more than she was the Spanish Zola or Dostoyevsky (I have outlined above the important contrasts between Bourget's work and her own work of the 1890s). What it does mean is that, encouraged by Bourget's achievement, she now set her sights on a new kind of exquisite beauty, to be created through an exploration of the mysterious ambiguities of the human mind, heart and spirit.

2

Los pazos de Ulloa: Naturalism and beyond[1]

'Hay en el alma humana algo inclasificable. El hombre no se conoce a sí mismo, y en la libertad y espontaneidad de su psicología reserva sorpresas – capa tras capa, de agua profunda.' *La transición*, p. 330

I suggested in the previous chapter that *Los pazos de Ulloa* is a hybrid work: it has a clear Naturalistic framework, yet at the same time contains psychological analysis rather more subtle than that found in Zola's novels. I want to concentrate on *Los pazos de Ulloa* in this chapter in order to pinpoint what seems to me to be a key moment in Pardo Bazán's novelistic apprenticeship. *La madre naturaleza* also illustrates the hybridity I have mentioned and is at times both delicate and acute, but it does not, I think, possess the profundity of psychological analysis which is present in *Los pazos de Ulloa* and is the hallmark of Pardo Bazán's mature work.

Los pazos deals with the efforts of a priest, Julián, to bring order and civilisation to the savage and degenerate lifestyle at the manor of Ulloa in remote rural Galicia. Encouraged by Julián, don Pedro, the so-called marquis of Ulloa, marries his Santiago cousin, Nucha, and abandons his mistress, Sabel, the daughter of his majordomo. But the attempt to civilise don Pedro is futile: when Nucha bears a daughter and not a son he returns to his former ways. Nucha becomes increasingly anxious for her own safety and that of her daughter and finally pleads with Julián to help her escape. The two are discovered in conference and Julián is sent away. Nucha dies soon after.

I include this plot summary for convenience. But in fact it could reasonably be said to be an arbitrary summary, because it is difficult to decide what kind of a novel *Los pazos de Ulloa* is. In the *Apuntes autobiográficos* which prefaced the first edition of this novel Pardo Bazán described it as a study of 'the Galician countryside, *caciquismo* [local politics based on the influence of a few powerful figures – *caciques*] and the decadence of a noble house' (III, 727b). The *Apuntes autobiográficos* were written some seven months after the completion of the novel so one may regard this comment as either a considered opinion or one clouded by forgetfulness. At first sight, however, Pardo

27

Bazán's description seems reasonable. There certainly is a study of the workings of local politics, especially in chapters 24 and 25, and of the declining Galician aristocracy, in chapter 15 and in the picture given of the dilapidated manor of Ulloa. 'La montaña gallega' I take to refer to Galician life in general, because the description of landscape is reserved for the sequel, *La madre naturaleza*. Some months after completing her novel, then, Pardo Bazán saw it as a study of life in Galicia. I shall be arguing that this is how she initially conceived the novel and probably continued to think of it, even though by the time it was completed it could no longer be accurately described in this way.

It is probable that the Naturalistic framework of *Los pazos de Ulloa* derived originally from the documentary intention: life in the remoter parts of Galicia is barbaric and the action of the novel is designed to demonstrate this. The main hypothesis, that remote rural environments degrade and animalise human beings, is put forward at the end of chapter 2: 'La aldea, cuando se cría uno en ella y no sale de ella jamás, envilece, empobrece y embrutece.' (i, 174a) This hypothesis is tested in the attempt made by Julián to civilise don Pedro by encouraging him to marry and exposing him and his household to the influence of religion and Christian morality. The signal failure of this attempt is intended to prove the hypothesis: neither civilisation nor religion is powerful enough to counteract the degrading effect of a barbaric environment on human beings. The point is conveyed symbolically at the end of the novel when Julián, on returning to Ulloa, encounters the two children Perucho and Manuela. The illegitimate child of nature is dressed almost like a *señorito*, while the legitimate child of civilisation is dressed almost in rags.

However, few readers are likely to be convinced by this experiment, because the representatives of religion and civilisation, Julián and Nucha, have clearly been devised with the express intention of ensuring the failure of the attempt to civilise don Pedro. Both of them have weak bodies and personalities, yet, as we see from the example of Nucha's sister, Rita, whom Pedro rejects as a wife, towns can and do produce robust, strong-willed personalities. Who knows how Rita might have coped with Primitivo and the other inhabitants of Ulloa? But such a question is beside the point. If Rita had married and tamed don Pedro the conclusion to the experiment would have been different, but so would the novel. As I have argued elsewhere, Pardo Bazán conceived the action of *Los pazos de Ulloa* as a tragedy, and the inevitable triumph of evil over good in certain circumstances, although cast in experimental form, is a necessary part of the novel's tragic conception.[2] It was necessary that Nucha should suffer and eventually die and that Julián should fail and be humiliated. However, the gratuitousness of the presence of these characters in the novel – the fact that they have been introduced for the obvious purpose of loading the dice against civilisation – seems to me to undermine the credibility of their tragic situation. Moreover, the action provokes too many nagging questions, some of which have already been mentioned. What would have happened if Julián had been a stronger person? What if Pedro had married Rita instead of Nucha? What if Nucha had given birth to a boy and not a girl? What if Julián had written to Nucha's father to inform him of her situation? The necessity of the tragic outcome is only in the novelist's intention, not in the situation itself. There could, in other words, have been a non-tragic ending.

So I am arguing that *Los pazos de Ulloa* has more than one flaw: the experiment does not convince and the tragic circumstances lack necessity. One might also add that the novelist's original project of documenting Galician life could happily have been abandoned, or at least reduced in scope. As it stands, the most extended *costumbrista* section, the elections episode in chapters 24 to 26 (which are among the longest chapters in the novel), while in itself not lacking in interest, is at this late stage in the novel an irritating distraction from the main events.

However, I want to suggest that despite what *Los pazos de Ulloa* fails to be, it remains interesting because of what it aspires to become; that is, neither a documentary, nor a Naturalist experiment, not even a tragedy, but a study of the mental life of Nucha and Julián. Indeed it may well be that those very characters who were introduced initially as a means to an end increasingly captured the novelist's imagination until they became the main object of her concern.

In the creation of the characters of Nucha and Julián Pardo Bazán drew for the first time on the findings of medical and psychological research (the two categories were not easily distinguishable at that time). The most obvious examples of this are the quasi-technical explanations given at the beginning and end of the dream in chapter 19:

Empezó a soñar con los pazos, con el gran caserón; mas por extraña anomalía, propia del sueño, cuyo fundamento son siempre nociones de lo real, pero barajadas, desquiciadas y revueltas merced al anárquico influjo de la imaginación, no veía la huronera tal cual la había visto siempre. (I, 241b)

Despertó repentinamente, resintiéndose de una punzada dolorosa en la mano derecha, sobre la cual había gravitado el peso del cuerpo todo, al acostarse del lado izquierdo, posición favorable a las pesadillas. (I, 242a)

The second of these extracts is reminiscent of the following passage by one of the most important English psychologists of the time, James Sully (1842–1925):

All of us are familiar with the common forms of nightmare, in which we strive hopelessly to flee from some menacing evil, and this dream experience, it may be presumed, frequently comes from a feeling of strain in the muscles, due to an awkward disposition of the limbs during sleep.[3]

Sully's *Illusions* (1881), from which this extract comes, was translated into French in 1883 and, along with three other works, was the subject of a review article published in the *Revue des deux mondes* of 1885 at the time Pardo Bazán was writing *Los pazos de Ulloa*.[4] As she undoubtedly read this journal and almost certainly made use of another of the works treated in the article (Ribot's *Les maladies de la mémoire*) in *La piedra angular* (see chapter 5 below), it is not impossible that she knew Sully's work.

Against the apparently current view that 'dreams are a grotesque dissolution of all order, a very chaos and whirl of images without any discoverable connection', Sully argues that, on the contrary, dream sequences are tightly structured and usually determined by the law of association, that is, if two ideas have any degree of resemblance, the one may call up the other. This principle can be observed in Julián's dream. The house has become an intimidating medieval fortress and we are told that Julián must have read about or seen a picture of such fortresses (I, 241b). As both the *pazos* and a fortress are intimidating for Julián, in his dream one becomes the other. Moreover, by the same process the details of the coat-of-arms of the *pazos* are associated with Julián's experiences of that evening: the pine tree becomes one of the trees he has heard moaning in the wind, and the two wolves rampant are howling like the dog Julián has heard that evening and whose cry local superstition regards as a premonition of death. Other details of the dream can be linked to Sully's analysis (for example, the changing and coalescing of images, and the fact that Julián can neither move nor shout – see Sully, pp. 163 and 173), but the most important feature is what he calls the 'lyrical element in dreams'. By this he means that 'if any shade of feeling becomes fixed and dominant in the mind, it will tend to control all the images of the time, allowing certain congruous ones to enter, and excluding others' (pp. 164–5). It need hardly be said that all the images in Julián's dream are controlled by his 'fixed and dominant' sense of helplessness and terror. The dizzy chaos of his nightmare has a clear underlying order: each element (and I have mentioned only a few) can be associated with a recent experience, and the whole is bound together by the extreme anxiety of his waking life.[5]

Despite the pedantic intrusion of the narrator in the extracts quoted above, this nightmare is not a lame rehearsal of textbook information, because such information is used by the novelist to convey a very immediate sense of Julián's mental distress and confusion. Moreover, she takes the characteristics of the dream sequence and creates with them a remarkable waking nightmare. When Julián awakes, he finds that reality is just as nightmarish as his dream, and the *pazos* seem as threatening as the castle which he had seen in his dreams. Furthermore, for Nucha, in whose room Julián takes refuge, reality has also become nightmarish. As in Julián's dream, objects are transformed into images of fear. The clothes she has hung up seem like men hanging from a scaffold or corpses leaving their coffins wearing shrouds. At times she sees headless people or ugly faces. The decorations on the screen move and the windows creaking in the wind remind her of moaning ghosts. The sound of the wind in the trees and the images of death refer back to Julián's dream, while the grotesque pictures on the screen prefigure (as I shall note in a moment) a passage in chapter 23. As Julián and Nucha go down to explore the cellars, lightning flashes and Julián invokes St Barbara. As this saint is traditionally invoked for protection against lightning, Julián's invocation is appropriate to the circumstances, but it also serves other purposes. It refers us back to Julián's nightmare, where the *pazos* are transformed not only into a medieval fortress but also into the tower which is the emblem of St Barbara (1, 242a). But, apart from intensifying our sense that Julián's present situation is as horrifying to him as his dream, his ejaculation, given the fact that it is preceded by the following sentence, also throws light on Nucha's circumstances: 'Un relámpago alumbró súbitamente las profundidades de las arcadas del claustro y el rostro de la señorita, que adquirió a la luz verdosa el aspecto trágico de una faz de imagen.' (1, 244ab) The likening of Nucha's face to that of an image of a saint sets off a series of associations, not unlike those in Julián's nightmare: lightning is associated with St Barbara; Nucha is associated with St Barbara as well (as she has already been in Julián's dream); St Barbara was locked in a tower, as Nucha is now trapped in the *pazos*; St Barbara was eventually killed, and her fate suggests a similar fate for Nucha. To pick up these associations the reader must of course be acquainted with the story of St Barbara, but, as I shall be suggesting in chapter 4, most Spanish readers of the nineteenth century would have been well acquainted with the lives of the saints.

In the cellar itself, the nightmarish transformations of reality (by now familiar to the reader) recur, but this time perceived by both Nucha and Julián. The image of a dog which had so alarmed Julián now assails Nucha as she fancies, on opening the cellar door, that she is attacked and bitten by an enormous dog. Then, in the imagination of both, the leg of an old table becomes a mummified arm, the face of a clock becomes a corpse's face, and some old riding boots lying among the rubbish put them in mind of a murder victim lying there. The furious storm sounds to them like a squadron of horses galloping over the roof or a giant casting a huge rock onto the roof (I, 244b–5a). By organising this chapter on a model similar to that she had used for Julián's nightmare (the association and transformation of mental images) Pardo Bazán gives it a nightmarish quality, and manages thereby to maintain and heighten the emotional intensity of an astonishingly intense episode.

But that is not the end of the matter: at the next emotional climax (chapter 23), when Nucha discovers that Perucho is her husband's illegitimate son, reference is again made to the screen, the pictures on which, as we have already been told, she imagines coming to life in a nightmarish manner. In another fine dramatic moment, the novelist presents us with two contrasting images, the first of Nucha's horror and Julián's dismay as the secret of Perucho's birth is revealed, and the second of the happiness of the unsuspecting children as they bathe together. The second of these images is followed by a fairly long description of the screen in the room. Such a description is apparently gratuitous, but in fact it helps to convey the duration of Nucha's stupor before her sudden and violent reaction at the end of the paragraph. But apart from this, the metamorphoses which we are told exist in the pictures on the screen (trees are like lettuces, mountains like cheeses, clouds like loaves of bread) recall the metamorphoses of chapters 19 and 20. The point is clear enough: for

Nucha the existence and presence of the illegitimate child and the threat to her daughter he unwittingly presents is one more (perhaps the worst) aspect of her nightmarish circumstances.

There is one final twist: the only time the word *metamorfosis* appears in the novel is in the first sentence of the chapter (24) following the one I have just been commenting on. The narrator refers to the metamorphosis which the election campaign produced in the 'sleepy and lethargic' life of the *pazos* (I, 253a). This is ironic indeed, because the impression we have just been given of life at the *pazos* through the terror-stricken imaginations of Julián and Nucha is anything but 'sleepy and lethargic'.

Pardo Bazán used contemporary notions about dreams, then, to dramatise a situation which is, to say the least, stressful for Julián and Nucha, and, paradoxically, she created out of the fruits of scientific investigation a Poe-like phantasmagoria. But in a more far-reaching way contemporary notions about human psychology provided her with a point of departure for the total conception of the characters of Nucha and Julián. When Pardo Bazán categorised them both as 'temperamentos linfático–nerviosos' (I, 167a, 174b, 236a) she was using standard nineteenth-century psychological terminology. Although doctors and psychologists no longer subscribed to the traditional theory of the humours, they continued to categorise people in a comparable way according to temperaments, that is, the lymphatic (characterised by pale or pink skin, sluggishness and physical weakness), the sanguine (characterised by a ruddy countenance and a robust constitution), and the nervous (characterised by flabby muscles, abrupt impulsive reactions and mobile features). These temperaments could exist in individuals either singly or in a combination of two, for example, the nervous–lymphatic.[6]

Nucha and Julián are explicitly categorised as nervous–lymphatic in the portions of the text just referred to, and Pardo Bazán leaves us in no doubt that she is using authentic technical terminology by making the doctor, Máximo Juncal, comment on the unhealthy upbringing of women in towns, and complain that sedentary urban life creates in them an excess of lymph at the expense of blood (I, 227b). Moreover, in chapter 17 he places Nucha amongst 'las linfático–nerviosas' (I, 230b–1a).

J.-L. Brachet, in his important *Traité de l'hystérie* (1847), states that the nervous–lymphatic temperament was the one most predisposed to hysteria. The essential sign of hysteria for Brachet (distinguishing it from a simple 'crise de nerfs') was 'une boule' moving up the throat.[7] Whether or not Pardo Bazán is drawing either directly on Brachet or on the Goncourt brothers, who used Brachet in the composition of *Germinie Lacerteux* (1864),[8] she certainly seems to be presenting the symptoms of hysteria when she makes Nucha reply to Julián: '"No, no y no; esto no es nada; un poco de ahogo en la garganta. Esto lo . . . noto muchas veces; es como una bola que se me forma allí . . ."' (I, 252a) The 'bola' and the choking sensation it causes clearly recall Brachet's description of the symptoms of hysteria.

But even without this rather esoteric clue the reader is probably aware that Nucha is suffering in the latter part of the novel from a form of hysteria, because of the extreme way she reacts to her situation. When in chapter 19 don Pedro kills the spider, we see her with her eyes closed, leaning against the wall, covering her face with a handkerchief. She is suffering, as she says, understating the case, from 'un poco de llanto nervioso' (I, 241a). In the following chapter we are told that 'to the depression which was normally evident in her gaunt face was added a contraction, a terror, which were signs of great nervous strain' (I, 242b), and her subsequent exploration of the cellars ends in a fit of hysteria (I, 245ab). After the elections she becomes obsessed by the notion that her child's life is in danger, and at one point the way she moves her lips noiselessly at table is described as 'a common phenomenon in people possessed by an *idée fixe*' (I, 269a). So, in delineating the character of Nucha, Pardo Bazán was making a kind of case-study of a nervous–lymphatic temperament suffering, because of stressful circumstances, from a form of convulsive hysteria. This study of Nucha, although energetic and sometimes touching, does not, however, go deep. Her words and actions give us little sense of a complex personality. Yet this is not necessarily a defect in the economy of the whole novel; as I have already indicated, her reactions serve to heighten the emotional intensity of the second half of the novel, and, moreover, to mirror and contrast with the novel's main character, Julián.

Nucha mirrors Julián in that she is of the same temperamental type; she contrasts with him in that her temperament and its manifestations are, rightly or wrongly, more acceptable in a woman than in a man. In her case a nervous–lymphatic temperament does not seem incongruous; in Julián's case it is at times ludicrous. Moreover, whereas with the worsening of her hysterical condition her resolution grows and she begins to dominate Julián, he, on the other hand, is unable to make any decision, so the contrast between his passivity and her resolution makes him seem to be all the more lacking in manly strength of character.

The starting point for my examination of Julián's character is a passage in chapter 3, where the narrator, having told us that chastity came easily to the chaplain, for the very reason that he had kept it intact and had never known the pleasures of sex, goes on to say how he is helped in his triumph over sin by the grace of God and his own weak personality:

A Julián le ayudaba en su triunfo, amén de la gracia de Dios que él solicitaba muy de veras, la endeblez de su temperamento linfático–nervioso, puramente femenino, sin rebeldías, propenso a la ternura, dulce y benigno como las propias malvas, pero no exento en ocasiones de esas energías súbitas que también se observan en la mujer, el ser que posee menos fuerza en estado normal y más cantidad de ella desarrolla en las crisis convulsivas. (I, 174b–5a)

The central phrase of this passage is 'su temperamento linfático–nervioso'. The narrator lists the characteristics of this type – its docility, tenderness and kindness, together with sudden outbursts ('energías súbitas') – and tells us that they are essentially feminine. The point is reiterated later in the novel when Julián's 'valor temblón' is described as 'el breve arranque nervioso de las mujeres' (I, 240b). Now, the listing of the characteristics of a particular psychological case by no means assures the creation of real characters, real, that is, in the sense that they are not abstractions, but come alive as concrete individuals. At times, as I shall suggest below in chapter 6, Pardo Bazán does fall into the trap of presenting characters as a list of symptoms drawn from a textbook or scientific journal. But this is not usually the case with the presentation of the character of Julián. Even in the rather portentous passage at present under discussion there are signs of the way Pardo Bazán brings Julián to life, that is, through irony. I am referring to the words 'a Julián le ayudaba en su triunfo, amén de la gracia de Dios que él solicitaba muy de veras'. Given the fact that we have just been told that chastity came very easily to Julián, the reference to his triumph is surely ironic, as is the idea of his pleading for God's grace to help him in the unequal struggle. The irony conveys to us the chaplain's excessive earnestness and lack of self-knowledge, in short, his engaging naivety. Pardo Bazán is here individualising Julián rather than presenting us with a generalised psychological case; she is giving us a sense of how this particular man's mind works.

A similar use of irony in the characterisation of Julián can be found in the second paragraph of the novel, which describes him on horseback:

Iba el jinete colorado, no como un pimiento, sino como una fresa, encendimiento propio de personas linfáticas. Por ser joven y de miembros delicados, y por no tener pelo de barba, pareciera un niño, a no desmentir la presunción sus trazas sacerdotales. Aunque cubierto del amarillo polvo que levantaba el trote del jaco, bien se advertía que el traje del mozo era de paño negro liso, cortado con la flojedad y poca gracia que distingue a las prendas de ropa de seglar vestidas por clérigos. Los guantes, despellejados ya por la tosca brida, eran asimismo negros y nuevecitos, igual que el hongo, que llevaba calado hasta las cejas, por temor a que los zarandeos de la trotada se lo hiciesen saltar al suelo, que sería el mayor compromiso del mundo. Bajo el cuello del desairado levitín asomaba un dedo de alzacuello, bordado de cuentas de abalorio. Demostraba el jinete escasa maestría hípica: inclinado sobre el arzón, con las piernas encogidas y a dos dedos de salir despedido por las orejas, leíase en su rostro tanto miedo al cuartago como si fuese algún corcel indómito rebosando fiereza y bríos. (I, 167ab)

Until the last sentence of this paragraph, the narrator's tone of voice is rather ambiguous. On the surface it seems as if this is straightforward description, but beneath the surface there are signs of irony. For example, in the first sentence the description of the red colour of Julián's face sounds objective enough, especially as it includes the technical term 'personas linfáticas'. 'That is the colour characteristic of this personality type', it seems to imply. The narrator rejects the standard Spanish simile 'red as a pepper' in favour of the unconventional 'red as a strawberry' in order, apparently, to indicate that the colour of the man's face is not sanguine ruddiness, but lymphatic pinkness. But there is something suspicious about this distinction: are the two fruits really so different in colour? Surely we are intended to register not the colour, but the taste and texture: peppers are hot and crisp, whereas strawberries, like Julián, are sweet and bland. The irony of the comparison is increased when this implied blandness is contrasted with the connotations of 'masterfulness' in the word 'jinete', the subject of tne sentence.

Similar concealed irony can be found in the fourth sentence of the paragraph. Again this is an apparently straightforward description, this time of Julián's gloves and hat. But why is the diminutive 'nuevecitos' rather than 'nuevos' applied to the gloves? It is of course

36

the word he himself uses as he worries about his nice new gloves. The same kind of ironic *style indirect libre* is used with regard to his hat, which he wears pulled down as far as his eyebrows to stop it falling off. When we are told that if it were in fact to fall off this would be a disaster ('el mayor compromiso del mundo'), it can hardly be the narrator who places such exaggerated importance on a trivial event. It must be Julián. This irony confirms the impression given by the use of the word 'nuevecitos' of his fastidiousness and childlike ingenuousness. By the final sentence, the irony is unconcealed. The application of the term 'maestría hípica' (even negatively) to Julián is frankly ridiculous, as is the contrast between his pony and the fiery steed he imagines himself to be riding. So here we are given not only an example of a general psychological phenomenon (the 'persona linfática' of the first sentence) but also, through irony, the workings of an individual's mind.

Despite these examples Julián's personality is generally presented in the first half of the novel in a rather crude way: through the contrast between his feebleness and the barbarity and the cruelty of the inhabitants of Ulloa. The two passages I have discussed are a foretaste of the quality of the novel's second half, where the presentation of Julián is much subtler, being done consistently with a very pointed form of irony. He is in a situation that demands a firm, energetic and cunning character: he must banish don Pedro's mistress and illegitimate child from the house, and fearlessly confront the sinister Primitivo. But Julián, by his nature, is lacking in these qualities. He knows what he ought to do, but cannot do it. Pardo Bazán dramatises his dilemma by giving him a series of outbursts which correspond to the 'sudden outbursts' referred to in chapter 3. For example, in chapter 14 he meditates on the situation in the house, with both the legitimate wife, Nucha, and the mistress, Sabel, living under the same roof, and we are told: 'Al capellán le entraba a veces impulsos de coger una escoba y barrer bien fuerte, bien fuerte, hasta que echase de allí a tan mala ralea. Pero [. . .].' (1, 219a) His feminine personality is thrown into relief by the metaphor he uses – he wants to sweep them all away with a broom, and, as in a previous example, the suggestion of his actual thoughts, conveyed in *style indirect libre* ('bien fuerte, bien fuerte'), places his earnest indignation in an ironic perspective. The 'but' makes the point: he would never be able to remove these undesirable characters with a broom or anything else. The metaphor is used again in chapter 19, this time in direct speech.

Julián is blaming himself for ever returning to Ulloa. He might have known, he thinks to himself, that don Pedro would go back to his old ways: '"Mi poca energía tiene la culpa. Con riesgo de la vida debí barrer esa canalla, si no por buenas, a latigazos. Pero yo no tengo agallas [...]."' (1, 238a) The broom appears again, now followed up by a more suitable weapon, a whip ('a latigazos'). But the increased violence is no less futile, and the outburst is followed by another 'pero'. A final example occurs in chapter 26, where Julián is thinking of the dangers threatening Nucha's baby, to whom he is devoted: 'A veces el cariño le inspiraba ideas feroces, como agarrar un palo y moler las costillas a Primitivo; coger un látigo y dar el mismo trato a Sabel. Pero, ¡ay! [. . .].' (1, 263b) Even greater violence here ('ideas feroces', a club, and a whip), yet still the inevitable 'pero', followed by a disconsolate ' ¡ay!'.

The contrast between the right course of action and Julián's inability to carry it out is seen most clearly when he has finally decided that he must leave Ulloa; he can no longer sanction adultery with his presence. Having firmly resolved to leave, he starts packing his bag, and thinks indignantly about what has happened. But his indignant thoughts are punctuated by references to the clothes he is packing. The narrator interrupts his flow to tell us that as he was saying this he was lining his trunk with socks, and that a certain outraged superlative occurred to him as he was carefully folding his new cassock. Even in a crisis, when most people would be throwing their clothes in unthinkingly, Julián retains his fastidiousness. His diatribe continues, only to be cut short again: 'Llegaba aquí de soliloquio, cuando trataba sin éxito de acomodar el sombrero de canal de modo que la cubierta de la maleta no lo abollase.' (1, 238b) Having ruefully reflected on the power and attraction of sin, he counts out his handkerchiefs and finds that one is missing. This, together with the fact that his hat is getting squashed, makes him decide to put off his departure until . . . *mañana*: 'Al día siguiente le sería fácil colocar mejor su sombrero y resolver la marcha. Por veinticuatro horas más o menos . . .' (1, 238b–9a) So much for his resolution! The unfortunate chaplain means well, but is unequipped to cope with the situation.

The by now firmly established personality of Julián is encapsulated in a telling moment at the end of chapter 24 when he protests at Nucha's denial that there is anything wrong with her and throws himself at her command:

— ¡Por Dios, señorita, no me responda que no! . . . ¡Si lo estoy viendo! Señorita Marcelina . . . ¡Válgame mi patrono San Julián! ¡Que no he de poder yo servirle de algo, prestarle ayuda o consuelo! Soy una persona humilde, inútil; pero con la intención, señorita, soy grande como una montaña. ¡Quisiera, se lo digo con el corazón, que me mandase, que me mandase!

Hacía estas protestas esgrimiendo un paño untado de tiza contra las sacras, cuyo cerco de metal limpiaba con denuedo, sin mirarlo. (I, 258a)

The irony here brings Julián clearly into focus. His vehemence is sincere, but its futility is exposed at almost every point. In the final sentence (which shows him in a similar light to that in which he appears when packing his bags) his would-be boldness is conveyed by the fencing image, yet his weapon is a cleaning-cloth (domestic, like the broom of earlier examples) and the adversary the sacring tablets. 'Sin mirarlo' suggests that he raises his eyes to Nucha, yet he does not stop cleaning, and part of his mind at least is still on the task in hand. At the beginning of the extract, the protestation ' ¡Si lo estoy viendo!' reminds us that he is always the last to see what is patently obvious to others. St Julian, whom the chaplain invokes here, is, we must feel after the description of his bland and effeminate image in chapter 6, unlikely to help him much. The cliché 'soy una persona humilde, inútil' is, in this case, all too true, and if anything, an understatement. But our scorn for Julián's utter ineffectualness cannot withstand the ingenuous sincerity of his declaration 'pero con la intención, señorita, soy grande como una montaña'. Alas, the road to hell is paved with good intentions. When Julián finally does decide, at Nucha's prompting, to help her escape, his proposed actions go against all priestly propriety. He is, in effect, intending to abduct a married woman, but of this he is oblivious.

Now, as I hope will be clear, the irony directed at Julián, although at times making him appear ridiculous, is not malicious. Our exasperation at his pusillanimity is probably tempered by pity, since, belonging as he does to a certain personality type, he cannot help being what he is. We cannot reasonably blame him for lacking those qualities needed to contend with what is in any case an intractable situation. Moreover, our sympathy for Julián is increased as the novel progresses because we are given hints of a personal dilemma which he himself is unaware of. That is, his ambiguous feelings towards Nucha.

From a letter written to Narciso Oller on 7 July 1885 it is clear that Pardo Bazán's conception of Julián included his being in love with

Nucha.[9] Yet in the novel itself Julián's feelings are suggested only indirectly. Why is this? Although Alas, Galdós and Valera had already dealt with the subject of a priest's struggle with illegitimate passions, it was still a delicate issue in pious Restoration Spain, and this is no doubt one reason for Pardo Bazán's reticence. But there may be another reason. Such reticence may also be due to the novelist's fear that her explanation of Julián in terms of his personality type was too glib, and that to state his love for Nucha explicitly would detract from the reader's sense of the complexity, even mysteriousness, of his mental and emotional life. In other words, Pardo Bazán may have been reacting against what she considered to be the schematic psychology of Zola's characters, to one of whom (Serge Mouret) the original conception of Julián owed much.

So Julián's feelings for Nucha are conveyed not overtly but by a series of clues, such as the fervour with which he recommends her to don Pedro as a suitable wife, his paternal sentiments towards her daughter, Manuela, and the fact that when on one occasion Nucha takes his hands in hers he is disturbed 'de un modo inexplicable' (I, 253a). But the most revealing clue is the way Julián sees Nucha as a saint, and in particular the Blessed Virgin Mary, whether as she appears in pictures of the Visitation (I, 225a), or as the image of the *Soledad* (I, 234b) and the *Dolorosa* (I, 272b). In Julián's mind such comparisons express Nucha's purity – even after she becomes pregnant he cannot imagine her undergoing the same physiological processes as other women (I, 218a) – and he regards her as destined to be always immaculate (I, 218b). For the reader, however, these comparisons express Julián's attempt at reconciling his vocation as a priest with his feelings as a man. Since he is a priest, he is permitted to love no woman except one: the Virgin Mary. To her alone can he give his devotion; indeed, he is, like all Catholics, duty-bound to do so. So by a process of transference he makes Nucha into the Virgin Mary to justify his feelings to himself. There is no objective reason given in the novel for regarding her as the ideal being Julián considers her to be, and in fact she herself rejects his description of her as 'un ángel' (I, 272a).[10] Julián, the 'linfático–nervioso', is too ingenuous to understand and too weak to come to terms with his feelings. By the end of the novel, when the situation explodes into violence and he himself is accused of adultery, he has ceased to be comic. The irony disappears and the tragedy of his situation is brought to our attention.

Pardo Bazán has taken a psychological case – 'un temperamento linfático–nervioso' – and made of it an individual. She is not simply saying 'There you are, that's how that kind of psychological phenomenon behaves': she is inviting us to understand what it feels like to be that particular individual, with his own particular conflicts. In doing this, she shows signs of the intelligence and understanding of human deviousness which so notably inform *Insolación* and many of the works which follow it. For the reasons outlined at the beginning of this chapter, it seems to me that *Los pazos de Ulloa* is a flawed novel. But it may well be that in struggling with this work she found her true forte: the ironic observation of the human capacity for delusion and self-deception.

3

Insolación and *Morriña*

'La contradicción, irregularidad e inconsecuencia, el enigma que existe en el hombre.' III, 615a

Insolación and *Morriña* are companion pieces. They were both published in 1889 and later issued together in a single volume. Their subtitle 'dos historias amorosas' possibly explains why for a long time they were regarded as lightweight pieces, a mere diversion punctuating Pardo Bazán's more lengthy and earnest works. In fact, as I shall be arguing, they are both serious novels, exploring some of the major concerns of Pardo Bazán's fiction and representing an important step forward in her development as a novelist.

'INSOLACIÓN'

Insolación, which is set in Madrid, deals with the relationship between the young, respectable Galician widow, Asís, and the raffish Andalusian, Pacheco. Although she scarcely knows him, Asís accepts Pacheco's invitation to visit the Fair of San Isidro, where a combination of the atmosphere, the sun and alcohol causes her to behave in what in her eyes is an unseemly manner. The rest of the novel concerns Asís's attempts to banish Pacheco from her mind. Finally, just as she is about to leave for Galicia, she allows him to sleep with her and they decide to marry.

Insolación has had mixed critical fortunes. At first it was not highly regarded: now it is seen increasingly as 'a little masterpiece'.[1] The two poles are represented by the two most provocative commentators on this novel, Leopoldo Alas and Matías Montes Huidobro. Alas scorned it, while Montes Huidobro describes it as 'una de las mejores novelas del siglo XIX'.[2]

The core of Alas's indictment of *Insolación* is that through a false understanding of Realist impersonality (the notion of the detached narrator) Pardo Bazán has chosen as her subject a vulgar love affair without poetry or feeling. It is, according to Alas, a pointless story of lust in which the novelist is not even trying to convey an idea or a moral. The two main characters are of no interest, either to the writer or to the reader: Pacheco is 'a silly, empty-headed Andalusian' (p. 80), and Asís is 'a nobody' (p. 70). Leaving aside the astonishing comment on Asís, it is tempting to sympathise with this view, because one can see what this greatest of Spanish critics means.

The third-person narrator of *Insolación* (chapters 2 to 8 are told in the first person) is nothing if not elusive. At times she speaks plainly and with superior wisdom, relating Asís's experience to general human experience (see I, 416a, 443a and 463b). Indeed there are moments when she expresses strong personal opinions which seem uncalled for, as when she lampoons the tasteless and pretentious furnishings of Asís's apartment (I, 444b–5a). Elsewhere, however, she confuses us by not making it clear whether certain comments are her own or those of Asís, expressed in *style indirect libre*. For example, are the comments on the tedious social round at the beginning of chapter 15 made by Asís or the narrator? Or, in the following sentence – 'Asís avanzaba protegida por el antuca, pero bañada y animada por el sol, el sol instigador y cómplice de todo aquel enredo sin antecedentes, sin finalidad y sin excusa' (I, 461b) – is the phrase 'sin excusa' the judgement of Asís or the narrator? It is impossible to tell.

One is also struck by the narrator's coy refusal to evaluate Asís's honesty or to commit herself on the likelihood of happiness for the couple at the end. At the beginning of chapter 9 she casts doubts on the veracity of Asís's account of the events at the Fair of San Isidro, but does not positively discredit it. In chapter 21 Gabriel Pardo's scepticism about Pacheco's suitability for marriage is given due weight because it is more than a little substantiated by what we already know of Asís's admirer. We are further inclined to accept Pardo's judgement both of Pacheco's personality and of Asís's behaviour because from this novel, and even more from *La madre naturaleza*, we know him to be an honourable, sensitive man, worthy of respect. Yet his status as a possible mouthpiece for the narrator has been undermined at, for example, the end of chapter 14, where we are told that having discovered, as he believes, that Asís has a lover, he utters the very clichés he scorns in the mouths of others. Moreover, he is not a disinterested observer of Asís's life, because we are told that he admires her and that he had intended to make her a proposal of marriage (I, 417b, 446b and 452a).

The narrator herself appears to stand for conventional morality.

43

For example, in chapter 12 she tells us that it is painful to have to record certain things, but that she must in all honesty do so. However, to avoid scandal she will present them in an indirect way while at the same time disguising her disapproval: 'Así, la implícita desaprobación del novelista se disfraza de habilidad.' (I, 445b) She describes Pardo's liberal views on sex as 'detestables sofismos' and the consolation he offers Asís as 'anestesia de la conciencia, con cloroformo de malas doctrinas' (I, 450b and 451b). Furthermore, the prohibitions of conventional morality are praised as 'principios salvadores, eternos, mal llamados por el comandante clichés' (I, 472b). Yet are we really expected to agree with her (and we cannot as readers entirely forget that Pardo Bazán was a militant feminist) when she applies the phrase 'detestables sofismos' to Pardo's views that women should be judged by the same moral standards as men, and that women should not be condemned for life because of one moral lapse? Moreover, there is a discrepancy between the narrator's apparent condemnation of Asís's behaviour and the sympathy with which her dilemma is presented. It is even more difficult, then, to discover the narrator's moral norms in this novel than in *Los pazos de Ulloa*, where there is an undoubted ambiguity in her attitude to both civilisation and barbarism. Small wonder that *Insolación* drew the exasperated comment from Alas that 'no se sabe qué pensar leyendo aquello' (p. 81).

Alas's dismay at the lack of feeling in the account of the love affair is no less understandable: at crucial moments the narrator deliberately distances us from the couple by irony. For example, when they are alone for the first time after the San Isidro escapade and Asís is leaning her head on Pacheco's shoulder waiting to hear what he will say, the narrator sets the scene: 'En la sala parecía que la varita de algún mágico invisible derramaba silencio apacible y amoroso, y la luz de la lámpara, al través de su celosía de encaje, alumbraba con poética suavidad el recinto.' (I, 444b) The narrator reinforces the irony of the amorous silence and soft lights with the long burlesque description of the room's tasteless furnishings, referred to above. The silence and soft lights reappear at the end of chapter 15 as Asís is awaiting Pacheco's second visit to her apartment, so it is impossible for us to be genuinely moved by either of these amorous encounters.

In their supposedly final meeting at the Ventas del Espíritu Santo we are given an ironic perspective on the couple's potentially sad parting. They are described as two turtle-doves slipping into their dovecote, and the restaurant itself is like a nest hanging from a branch (I, 463ab). At the beginning and end of the episode Asís and Pacheco appear rather ridiculous because we see them from the point of view of a group of inquisitive factory-girls who are cooking a large pot of mutton stew and observing and listening to them through an open window, without their being aware of it. Add to this deflating irony the fact that the 'love-bird' metaphor is extended and applied to the girls, who become a flock of 'pájaros', 'aves' and 'gorrionas', the girls' grotesque dance to the 'odious' and 'horrible' sound of the pianola, and the farcical encounter with the old woman, and there is little room left for sentiment.

Finally, the Epilogue, in which Asís and Pacheco are reconciled and decide to marry, begins with the following comment on the cloying sentimentality of the situation: 'No entremos en el saloncito de Asís mientras dure el tiroteo de explicaciones (¡cosa más empalagosa!), sino cuando la pareja liba la primera miel de las paces (empalagosísima también; pero paciencia).' (I, 471b) A few paragraphs later Pacheco, noticing Asís's tears, tenderly asks: '"Pero ¿qué es eso? ¿Llora mi niña?"' The narrator comments: 'Puede que llorase, en efecto. No debía de ser el reflejo de la lámpara lo que tanto relucía en su mejilla izquierda . . .' (I, 472b) Again the narrator stands aloof and mocks the tender scene between the couple. And the justification she gives for their decision to sleep together deflates them even more by patronising them with the suggestion that they are simply passing through an inevitable process (I, 473a).

What are we to make of this? Is Pardo Bazán's irony sneering and reductive? Is she implying that love is this, no more, no less, a rather absurd business of no great importance? This is certainly Alas's reading of *Insolación*:

Lo más triste de todo es que del conjunto del libro se desprende que la escritora ilustre nos da las aventuras de su viudita como un idilio realista de amor, como diciendo: 'el amor, bueno o malo, es eso; examinado de cerca y con profundidad y franqueza y sin *idealismos*, el amor es ese apetito, no vehemente, pero sí tenaz e invariable, prosaico, soso, frío,' y a pesar de verlo así, no se desespera, ni siquiera encuentra un dejo de amargura en ese amor; no hay pesimismo, no hay sarcasmo implícito en esta historia de aventuras indecentes y frías, sosas y apocadas; hay complacencia, casi alegría; no se sabe qué pensar leyendo aquello. ¡Y esta es la obra por excelencia *amorosa*, de doña Emilia! Esta señora se ha dejado llevar en tal ocasión del prurito de los sectarios imprudentes, vulgares, superficiales, y ha sacrificado a lo que ella cree dogma realista, mucha clase de fueros de la misma dama y de la escritora célebre; por el afán de la impersonalidad, mal entendida, ha llegado a preferir para heroína de su novela de amor un ser repugnante en su insignificancia, baja y deslavazada criatura imaginaria, que nada puede decirnos de lo que el amor, en efecto, haya podido ser para la fantasía y el corazón de la artista; y al pintar tipo tan lejano de su propio modo de ser, no supo darle más vida que la somera y aparente de una observación vulgar, prosaica y fragmentariamente nacida. (pp. 81–2)

I have quoted Alas at length because his remarks put the critical issues very clearly and, if they are just, are a damning indictment of the novel. They imply that the work is trivial since it is informed not by genuine conviction but by a misguided desire on the novelist's part to follow the latest literary fashion. As I have suggested above, Alas's arguments are, on the surface, persuasive. Yet it seems to me that, however intelligent they may be, they fail to take account of the ambiguities in the novel.

In the first place, he does Pardo Bazán less than justice when he suggests that she sacrifices all on the altar of modish Realism. Of course, her detachment is motivated partly by a desire to present events in a dispassionate manner. On the other hand, however, Realist conventions are treated with irony. For example, the narrator gently satirises the gratuitous detail of Realist technique when, anticipating Valéry's scornful parody contained in the words 'la marquise sortit à cinq heures', she tells us that the girls who observe Asís and Pacheco at the *merendero* work in the tobacco factory – 'por lo que pueda importar' (1, 464a). As if it mattered! Later in the same chapter the documentary pretensions of Realism are mocked when we learn that the old woman who pesters Asís and Pacheco is called la señá Donata – 'if the sources are to be trusted' (1, 464b). In chapter 21 we are told that 'Pardo had picked up a newspaper, *La Epoca* I think, and was reading it absentmindedly' (1, 470b), as if the narrator were genuinely trying to remember a scene she had witnessed. And again, does it really matter which newspaper Pardo was reading? So it is unjust to suggest that Pardo Bazán is uncritically following the Realist fashion.

But there remains the more serious charge that she is devaluing love. Although I want to argue that this is not in fact the case, it is strange that Alas should suggest that Pardo Bazán ought of necessity to present love as unequivocally poetic. For her, as for many intellectuals of those times, there was a genuine problem. In the wake of Darwin and Schopenhauer it was difficult to see love as anything more than a mechanism for the continuation of the species. Pardo Bazán, caught up as she was in the scientific adventure, was not unaffected by the problem. It is alluded to at the end of chapter 22 of *Los pazos de Ulloa*, where, in a burlesque idyll, the male hares 'blinded by love and convulsed with desire' risk death to pursue their Dulcinea (I, 249b). Perhaps, it seems to be suggested, we deceive ourselves if we believe that human courtship is any more or less poetic than that of other species. But Pardo Bazán's obstinate Romanticism does not allow the matter to rest there. One might with justice argue (as I shall be doing in the following chapters) that the conflict between Romanticism and Realism, in both the general sense and the precise literary sense of these words, is one of the major concerns of her fiction.

Even in *Insolación*, where the calm, controlled narrator shows little sign of tension, the dilemma can be glimpsed. The evidence provided by the novel suggests that the affair between Asís and Pacheco is trivial and superficial. She is a young, inexperienced widow who falls for his obvious charms. His defects are outlined by Gabriel Pardo in chapter 21: he is a lazy, ignorant womaniser, quite unsuitable as a husband and father (I, 471a). In chapter 2, the duquesa de Sahagún is said to have described him in similar terms (although with less hostility) (I, 421ab) and Pacheco himself admits, not without satisfaction, that he is, 'apart from being dissolute, a layabout and a waster' and that 'he has never done anything worthwhile, nor does he want to' (I, 457a). Yet despite such powerful testimony to the rightness of Pardo's opinion of Asís's suitor, the narrator does not throw her full support behind him. As we have seen, she detaches herself from him by irony and discredits his impartiality. Moreover, at the end of his confidently unfavourable judgement on the love affair, she comments: 'Así meditaba el comandante. ¿Era injusto o sagaz? ¿Obedecía a su costumbre de analizarlo todo o a una puntita de berrinche?' (I, 471b) Is he right or wrong? Is his judgement clouded either by his habit of analysing every issue or by jealousy? No answer is given.

Equally the question is left open in the Epilogue. The couple are sitting opposite each other, they hold hands and their eyes meet:

Con la nueva y victoriosa dulzura de semejante comunicación, Asís sentía que se mezclaba un asombro muy grande. Miraba a Pacheco y creía no haberle visto nunca; descubría en su apostura, en su cara, en sus ojos, algo sublime, que realmente no existía; pero era positivo entonces para la señora, pues así sucede en toda revelación, para que resplandezca su origen superior a la materia inerte y al ciego acaso . . . , y a Asís se le revelaba entonces el amor. Poco a poco, sin conciencia de sus actos, acercaba la mano de Diego a su pecho, ansiosa de apretarla contra el corazón y de calmar así el ahogo suave que le oprimía . . . Sus pupilas se humedecieron, su respiración se apresuró, y corrío por sus vértebras misterioso escalofrío, corriente de aire agitado por las alas del Ideal. (I, 472a)

As in other examples of irony I have referred to, there are two perspectives, Asís's and the narrator's. Asís sees something sublime in Pacheco's appearance which, according to the narrator, 'in reality did not exist'. The suggestion is that passion is blinding her to his true character. But the rest of the sentence, which comments on the nature of revelation, calls in question such hard-headed empiricism. The non-empirical is by its very nature not perceivable by the senses. All higher or spiritual truth is revealed only to its chosen recipient, and to others his vision may seem madness. The dual perspective is also present in the final sentence of the extract. On the one hand, there is a concentration on Asís's physical reactions (her eyes, her breathing, her vertebrae) which points to the merely physical nature of her feelings for Pacheco. On the other hand, the phrases 'misterioso escalofrío', and 'agitado por las alas del Ideal' (which do not seem to me at all ironic) invest her feelings with a certain poetry. 'Ideal' implies that this is not mere lust, but Romantic love.

A similar hint of Romantic Idealism in this apparently pointless love affair appears further on in the Epilogue, when the narrator enigmatically remarks that the interesting point about this otherwise commonplace love-affair is the cause, genesis and rapid development of that most unexpected 'idea', the couple's decision to marry. 'What could have possibly motivated this decision?', the narrator asks, before offering some more or less prosaic answers. There follows a teasingly ambiguous passage, which because of its importance I quote in full:

Que cada cual lo arregle a su gusto y rastree y discurra qué caminos siguieron aquellos espíritus para no reparar en inconvenientes, no recelar de lo futuro, cerrar los ojos a problemas del porvenir y mandar a paseo las sabias advertencias de la razón, que tiembla de espanto ante lo irreparable, lo indisoluble, lo que lleva escrito el letrero medroso: 'Para siempre', y avisa que de malos principios rara vez se sacan buenos fines. Y reconstruya también a su modo los diálogos en que la 'idea' se abrió paso; tímida primero; luego, clara, imperiosa y terminante; después, triunfadora, agasajada por el amor, que, coronado de rosas, empuñando a guisa de cetro la más aguda y emponzoñada de sus flechas, velaba a la puerta del aposento, cerrando el paso a profanos disectores.

Por eso, y porque no gusto de hacer mala obra, líbreme Dios de entrar hasta que el sol alumbre con dorada claridad el saloncito, colándose por la ventana que Asís, despeinada, alegre, más fresca que el amanecer, abre de par en par sin recelo o más bien con orgullo. ¡Ah! Ahora ya se puede subir. Pacheco está allí también, y los dos se asoman, juntos, casi enlazados, como si quisiesen quitar todo sabor clandestino a la entrevista, dar a su amor un baño de claridad solar, y a la vecindad entera parte de boda . . . Diríase que los futuros esposos deseaban cantar un himno a su numen tutelar, el sol, y ofrecerle la primera plegaria matutina. (i, 473ab)

The first sentence lists some good reasons why it would be foolish for Asís and Pacheco to marry, and the epigrammatic comment to the effect that things which begin badly rarely end well casts doubts on their future happiness (as Pardo's comments at the end of chapter 21 have already done). Yet, however clear it may seem that their reasons for marrying are superficial, one cannot help feeling that a love which throws all caution to the wind cannot be entirely trivial. Perhaps Asís's attraction to Pacheco is indeed more than physical. Perhaps Pacheco, despite all his previous philandering, is indeed sincere when he says that he is genuinely in love with her (i, 472b).

The final picture of the sun is the Epilogue's most ambiguous feature. To all appearances its golden light bathes the couple in happiness and hope, and they sing a hymn to their guardian deity ('su numen tutelar'). Yet the suggestion of pagan sun-worship here gives the sun pagan overtones of fertility. Perhaps in their euphoria the couple are unwittingly falling into the eternal trap laid by nature, a nature which cares not one whit for their personal happiness, but only for the propagation of the species. However, it seems to me that we are not called upon to choose one or other of the two interpretations, the optimistic and the pessimistic, because they are held together in a genuine ambiguity. Pardo Bazán cannot present love as unequivocally poetic because she is not convinced that it is. But neither is she convinced that it is valueless. As we read *Insolación* we are asked to scrutinise the characters' experience and ponder questions to which there are no easy answers.

My point is that Pardo Bazán is not simply regarding her subject with modish cold detachment. Her detachment is a serious expression of her sense that love and its effects on people are problematic and mysterious, and therefore immensely difficult to evaluate. The extent of her emotional involvement in this dilemma is evident in her letters to Galdós (written about the time of the publication of *Insolación*)[3] and, as we shall see in the following chapters, the novels of the 1890s.

Our perception of the novelist's sense that human relationships are ultimately mysterious not only challenges Alas's scornful dismissal of *Insolación*, it also undermines the strict Naturalist reading of this novel. The most telling of these readings is that of Montes Huidobro who, in an interesting study, points out that there is a rhythmic alternation of Naturalist theory and practical demonstration in *Insolación*. The theory is provided by Gabriel Pardo during his three appearances, and the action of the novel demonstrates the truth of the theory he expounds. The theory, as set out in chapter 2, is as follows. All Spaniards are fundamentally savages, even the most civilised, and all they need is to be exposed to the sun to ignore the taboos and conventions imposed by society. The best practical demonstration of this theory Montes Huidobro rightly finds in the description of the Fair of San Isidro in chapters 3 to 8, where Asís, accompanied by Pacheco, is affected by the sun and alcohol, and behaves in a most improper way. Montes Huidobro identifies three thematic levels in these chapters: first, the sun, representing the determining forces of nature, secondly, the effect of these natural forces on Asís, and thirdly, her attempts at justifying her behaviour.

In the face of this evidence one can hardly deny the presence of an experimental and therefore deterministic element in *Insolación*. Indeed, a second hypothesis, not mentioned by Montes Huidobro, is formulated and tested. In chapter 14 the novel's theorist, Pardo, attacks society's attitude towards sexual misdemeanours in women, and points out that it can lead them to unhappiness. To avoid dishonour a woman who has committed such a misdemeanour must either enter a convent or contract a loveless marriage. The first possibility has already been demonstrated to Gabriel's satisfaction by his experiences described in *La madre naturaleza* (where his niece entered a convent on discovering that she had unwittingly committed incest), and no doubt the decision to marry taken by Asís and Pacheco in the Epilogue would corroborate the second possibility. If Alas is to be believed, there is no 'true love' (p. 69) in their relationship, and there exist, therefore, solid grounds for believing that Asís is unlikely to find lasting happiness in their union. So both of Pardo's theories are tested and, to all appearances, proved. But in actual fact, neither of them is proved conclusively.

In order to show how Pardo's theory about the effect of the sun on Asís's behaviour is demonstrated by the action of the novel, Montes Huidobro has to restrict his comments to chapters 3 to 8. But there is

more to *Insolación* than the description of the Fair of San Isidro. He
attempts to deal with this fact by blandly stating that his analysis
holds good for the rest of the novel (p. 78). This is not true. The sun is
mentioned on only five more occasions after chapter 8, and on none of
these occasions is it a determining agent. Perhaps it is the very title of
the novel which (perhaps deliberately) misleads by focusing attention
on the effect of the sun on Asís at the Fair of San Isidro and the
Naturalist theory it apparently corroborates, and encouraging the
reader to overlook the rest.

Now, it is obviously true that there is an equivalence between
Pardo's theories and the events in chapters 3 to 8. The sunny spring
weather enters into Asís's decision to accept Pacheco's invitation to
the fair, and the sun and alcohol do indeed affect her behaviour.
Moreover, there is an emphasis throughout the novel on the mutual
relationship between body and soul. However, this is largely not the
effect of the physical on the moral, but the reverse. For example, in
chapter 1, when Asís has found some relief from her physical
discomfort, her qualms of conscience revive this discomfort (1, 416b).
More damaging to the deterministic reading of *Insolación*, though, is
our attitude towards the propounder of these theories, Gabriel Pardo
himself. I have already argued that we are distanced from him to
some extent by irony. As a result it is far from clear that the novelist
intends him, as is sometimes said, to be her mouthpiece.[4] His theory
that the sun brings out Spaniards' animal instincts is partly supported
by what happens at the fair, but Asís herself recognises that she
cannot blame her behaviour completely on the sun, much as she
would like to, and that the responsibility is at least in part her own. In
chapter 1 her conscience tells her that she cannot blame her
behaviour on the sun and in chapter 16 she admits that the sun and
alcohol are poor excuses: 'Mareo, alcohol, insolación . . . ¡Pretextos,
tonterías! . . . Lo que pasa es que me gusta, que me va gustando cada
día un poco más, que me trastorna con su palabrería . . . , y punto
redondo.' (1, 458b) So although there is some truth in Pardo's
hypothesis, it is not the whole truth.

Neither is his second hypothesis, that is, a marriage which follows a
single sexual misdemeanour is likely to be loveless. As we have seen,
the question of whether Asís is contracting a loveless marriage which
is therefore destined to be unhappy is deliberately left open. Indeed,
the tentative, questioning tone of the Epilogue is strangely inappropriate to the conclusion of an experiment. Unlike *Los pazos de*

Ulloa, Insolación does not end with a definitive Q.E.D. In any case, even if Pardo's theory could satisfactorily explain Asís's decision to marry, it could not explain why Pacheco should make such a decision. It is as if the two hypotheses, couched in such generalised terms and so neatly set up, one in each half of the novel, and then tested and apparently proved by subsequent events, are matched against the untidy particularity of individual experience.

This is not to say, however, that Pardo Bazán's treatment of Asís is entirely lacking in the general dimension; characteristically in this novel the perspective is equivocal. Asís is typical of her aristocratic class to the extent that she accepts its moral norms and patterns of behaviour. She is happy with her uneventful life and delights in the fact that she is a respectable, blameless lady who nevertheless moves easily in society. On the other hand, she is set apart from the norm by being a young widow who has had a sheltered upbringing in Galicia and whose emotions have never been deeply stirred either by love, marriage or motherhood (I, 440a). Moreover, she comes to realise that social conventions can militate against her own happiness. On this conflict between her typicality and atypicality is based the presentation of her mental life. The great beauty of *Insolación* is not the conclusive demonstration of a thesis, but the subtlety with which Pardo Bazán shows a respectable Catholic lady attempting to deal with unfamiliar feelings she is not supposed to have.

The first chapter, which deals with Asís's thoughts as she wakes up the morning after her unseemly behaviour at the Fair of San Isidro, is an extraordinarily immediate presentation of her discomfort, moral and physical. She tries to pretend it was all a bad dream, but her conscience reminds her that it was not a dream, and well she knows it. Then she seeks comfort by blaming 'aquello' (as she calls it) on the sun, but again her implacable conscience points out, kindly but firmly, that although admittedly until yesterday she had been, exactly as she would like to be regarded, a respectable widow, yesterday she misbehaved herself. And there is no escaping that fact, sun or no sun. Then the figure of her Jesuit confessor, Padre Urdax, appears in her imagination as a stern reproach, as he does on occasions throughout the novel.

In the next eight chapters, which are in the form of a flashback, we are shown her getting more and more deeply involved in a most improper situation for a lady of her standing, while at the same time convincing herself, or half convincing herself, that there is nothing at all improper in her behaviour. The process of self-deception begins when she allows herself to be persuaded to go to the fair:

La proposición, de repente, empezó a tentarme, recordando el dicho de la Sahagún: 'Vaya usted al Santo, que aquello es muy original y muy famoso.' 'Y realmente, ¡qué mal había en satisfacer mi curiosidad?' – pensaba yo –. Lo mismo se oía misa en la ermita del Santo que en las Pascualas; nada desagradable podía ocurrirme llevando conmigo a Pacheco, y si alguien me veía con él, tampoco sospecharía cosa mala de mí a tales horas y en sitio tan público. Ni era probable que anduviese por allí la sombra de una persona decente ¡en día de carreras y toros!, ¡a las diez de la mañana! La escapatoria no ofrecía riesgo . . . ¡y el tiempo convidaba tanto! . . . En fin, que si Pacheco porfiaba algo más, lo que es yo . . . (I, 422b–3a)

In order to justify a decision she has probably already taken, she cites the advice of the duquesa de Sahagún, a paragon of taste and respectability. The duchess had indeed urged her to go to the fair, but not secretly, and not with the womanising Pacheco. Then she pretends she wants only to satisfy her curiosity. Surely no one could blame her for that. When she meets Pacheco, she is on her way to Mass, but she can just as easily hear Mass at the Hermitage of San Isidro as elsewhere. She would certainly not be putting pleasure before religious duties. She speculates that if anyone were to see her with Pacheco, they would not suspect anything improper, thus indicating that she is well aware of the impropriety of the escapade. But even though she has nothing to hide, it is just as well that everyone would be getting ready to go either to the horse races or to the bull fight, so there would be nobody around to see her anyway. There is no danger, and it is a nice day. She is just waiting to have her arm twisted by Pacheco, who we suspect excites her curiosity considerably more than the Fair of San Isidro. This passage illustrates well the kind of deviousness Asís displays throughout the novel. Her conditioning takes her in one direction and her feelings in another. She is a respectable widow, yet she falls hopelessly for the notorious Pacheco. Hence she seeks endlessly to justify herself.

For example, in chapter 10, we see Asís, on the day after the escapade at the fair, anxious to put herself right with society. So, having scrubbed herself clean with 'fricciones mitad morales, mitad higiénicas' (I, 441a), she goes to dine with her maiden aunts, who are, like the duquesa de Sahagún, two paragons of respectability. In a delightful episode she is at first relieved to find herself treated in exactly the same way as before 'aquello', but then her relief gives way to a terrible boredom. She yawns and fidgets so much that her aunts notice and 'with their wonted kindness' mortify her by offering her a different-shaped chair, the corner of the sofa, a wickerwork seat, a cushion for her back. Time crawls along, not hastened by the jejune conversation and the clock which stopped the day it was bought, forty years before. The figure of Apollo, the Sun-God, which is on top of the clock and whose nakedness has passed unnoticed by the chaste aunts for forty years, pinpoints for the reader, if not for Asís, her vain efforts to pretend that the events of the preceding day (the sun and the sensuality) had not taken place.[5] At last a carriage stops outside the house and Asís's escape is described with a final comic touch as she 'heroically' tells the carriage to wait for a while. The fact is that something has stirred inside Asís, and the society where she was formerly so content and into which she now longs to be received again has lost its charm. Her vital personality (chiefly conveyed by the racy, colloquial language in which her thoughts are expressed)[6] is now suffocated by polite society.

Another example of her deviousness is the conversation she has with Gabriel Pardo as they stroll near the Prado. In chapter 2, at the *tertulia*, she had dismissed his views as eccentric; now she is hanging on his every word. Pardo is attacking the Spanish double standard in morality: one rule for men and another for women. If women commit a sexual peccadillo, they are ruined; if men do not, they are ridiculed. It is impossible to convey the subtle irony of this section (described by Ruth Schmidt as 'Jamesian in its ambiguity')[7] without quoting at length, but the following passage may give some idea: 'Asís oía, oía con toda su alma, pareciéndole que nunca había tenido su paisano momentos tan felices como aquella noche, ni hablado tan discreta y profundamente.' (I, 451b) Pardo's words are intelligent and pro-found, of course, because at this moment they are precisely what she wants to hear. They are music to her ears. The night before she would have been scandalised by such propositions. (As Ruth Schmidt has shown (p. 74), the irony is even more subtle because, although for Asís Pardo's remarks are aimed at her own situation, for him they refer back to the tragic events in *La madre naturaleza*.)

In one scene after another we find Asís's mental confusion dramatised. For example, in chapter 17 she has decided she must leave Madrid for Galicia to escape from Pacheco. That is the sensible step, but it is clearly not the step she wants to take. Consequently, as she makes preparations for the journey she is in a furious temper and finds fault with her maid. Nothing is as it should be, or rather she imagines this to be the case. When Pacheco makes one of his well-timed, unexpected appearances, she gives way. She *will* have lunch with him – secretly – just for the last time. As she seems to be escaping from him, she is in reality drawing closer to him.

In the carriage on the way to the Ventas, the couple do not speak: 'Llevaban las manos cogidas; Asís respiraba frecuentemente el manojo de rosas y miraba y remiraba hacia fuera, porque así creía disminuir la gravedad de aquel contrabando, que en su fuero interno – cosa decidida – llamaba *el último*, y por lo mismo le causaba tristeza, sabiéndole a confite que jamás, jamás había de gustar otra vez.' (I, 462b–3a) Here we see very clearly Asís's self-deception and mixed feelings. Their hands are clasped, but she sniffs her roses, looks out of the carriage, anything to avoid admitting the reality of the situation. She knows well enough that this is an unseemly affair which has to be brought to an end, and yet . . . The 'cosa decidida' is still in fact very much an open question. The mixture of decisiveness and wistful hesitation is highlighted in the dream Asís has after her return from the disastrous lunch at the Ventas. Resting on her bed, she congratulates herself on walking out on Pacheco. The 'historia' (as she dismissively describes it) had to end one way or another, and this was as good a way as any. And, as for her, she certainly does not love a gigolo like Pacheco:

¡Y qué fatuo! Pues, ¡no había querido convencerla de que estaba enamorada de él. ¿Enamorada? No, no, señor; gracias a Dios . . . Conservaría, sí, un recuerdo . . . , un recuerdo de esos que . . . [. . .] ¡Qué tontería! Lo probable es que a Pacheco no volviese a verle nunca más . . . Y esta punzada del corazón, ¿qué será? ¿Será enfermedad, o . . .? Parece que lo aprieta un aro de hierro . . . ¡Jesús, qué cavilaciones más insensatas! (I, 469ab)

Asís bravely attempts to convince herself that this sentimental episode means nothing to her, but the pain inside her cannot be so easily dismissed, not even as 'foolish thoughts'. She then dreams that she is on the train back to Galicia and is crossing the arid plain of Castile. As at the Fair of San Isidro, the sun soaks into her brain and blood, and, as on the previous occasion, she is given only *manzanilla* to quench her thirst. She longs for relief from the heat and the dust, and when relief comes as she enters Galicia the image of suffocating heat is replaced by one of overwhelming humidity:

Y aquella lluvia; Asís la siente sobre el corazón, que se lo infiltra, que se lo reblandece, que se lo ensopa, hasta no poder admitir más líquido, hasta que, anegado de tristeza, el corazón empieza también a chorrear agua: primero, gota a gota; luego, a borbotones, con fúnebre ruido de botella que se vacía . . . (I, 470a)

Asís is now drenched in rain rather than sun and has escaped death by burning only to be drowned by the longed-for waters. The sentimental wistfulness which she imagined she felt on the way to the restaurant has now become an intense sorrow.

In this dream, which surely owes little to any medical textbook (its structure seems to follow no source), we are taken back to the Fair of San Isidro where we witnessed a fairly simple case of infatuation, and are shown what we have suspected for some time, that Asís's feelings have been engaged on a deeper level than she cares to admit. Her bluff dismisal of Pacheco before the dream contrasts markedly with her particularly feminine vulnerability at the end of the dream as her heart is softened and drowned by her own tears. She flees in terror from her unacceptable feelings, only to discover that those feelings meet deeper and more pressing needs than her desire for respectability.

She is awoken from her dream by the arrival of Gabriel Pardo, who is closely followed by Pacheco. When the couple are left alone Pacheco is subdued and resigned, and decides to leave at once. Now it is Asís who is constraining *him* to stay. He tells her to think carefully, because, if he stays now, he will stay the whole night. She thinks a moment, all social and religious norms are forgotten, and she tells him to stay (I, 472b).

So Asís has fallen. Gabriel Pardo, anticipating the event slightly, comments on her fall in these terms: ' ¡Cómo escogen las mujeres! En dándoles el puntapié el demonio . . . Indulgencia, Gabriel; no hay mujeres, hay humanidad, y la humanidad es *así* . . .' (I, 471a) Women are all the same, they give way to the slightest temptation. But, no, they cannot be blamed: Asís is simply going the way of all flesh. But how do we as readers react to this supercilious and patronising comment? Surely we are likely to resist its implications and feel that his generalisations do not do anything like justice to the complexity of Asís's feelings and the conflicting impulses in her. She is not just the standard human model ('La humanidad es *así*'); she is not 'like all the others'. We have come to know her as an individual, in her own peculiar circumstances. And that is the measure both of the success of *Insolación* as a psychological novel and of Pardo Bazán's maturity as a novelist.[8]

'MORRIÑA'

In *Morriña*, as in *Insolación*, there is an interaction between Galicia and Madrid. The novel deals with a Galician girl, Esclavitud, the illegitimate daughter of a priest and a woman of easy virtue, who has come to Madrid to escape the shame of her origins. She goes to work as a maid in the house of a widow, doña Aurora, who is also a Galician, and falls in love with doña Aurora's son, Rogelio. The mother discovers what is happening between Esclavitud and her son and, finding the girl a job in another house, takes her son to Galicia for the summer. The night before they leave, Rogelio seduces Esclavitud, and the novel ends with the train's departure for Galicia and Esclavitud's decision to commit suicide.

Now, the obvious pessimism of the novel's ending has inevitably led to *Morriña*'s being described as 'Naturalist': the seduction indicates that sexual instinct triumphs over all laws, whether human or divine, while Esclavitud's suicide shows that she is a victim in the evolutionary struggle for survival. But the novel's obvious Naturalist feature is its experimental structure, that is, the presence of a hypothesis which is tested by the action of the novel. The hypothesis in *Morriña* derives from the Positivist doctrine of the determining influence of race on human behaviour. It proposes that when Galicians are away from their homeland they suffer such anguish – *morriña* – that in certain cases they commit suicide. This hypothesis is not made explicit until the end of the novel, as we shall see, but it is hinted at on various occasions. For example, in chapter 5, when Esclavitud appears for the first time, she tells Aurora that she suffers so much from *morriña* that if she does not leave the house of the Andalusian ladies where she is working, she will either go mad or die. Needless to say, to all appearances her death confirms the hypothesis: Aurora and Rogelio leave for Galicia, while Esclavitud stays in Madrid and dies . . . of *morriña*.

But it is unlikely that such an explanation could satisfy any reader. Is it really true that Esclavitud is led to suicide by a 'nostalgic sickness' in her blood? This is a difficult question to answer because the narrator tells us very little about the maid's feelings. There is no doubt that her depression is partly a symptom of homesickness, otherwise she would not have been so desperate to leave her Andalusian household and find a Galician employer. But this does not mean that her sickness is simply the result of a genetic condition. A

much more important element in her attachment to her native land is
the fact that it is the only affective link she has left: she has nothing else
to fill the emotional abyss of her life. So it is much more plausible to
explain her behaviour in psychological rather than genetic terms.
Indeed this becomes obvious when we read her own description of her
feelings:

Siempre estoy imaginando: 'Esclava, a ti Dios no te puede querer bien.
Nunca buena suerte has de tener, nunca. Ya desde que naciste estás en poder
del enemigo, y buena gana tiene el enemigo de soltar lo que agarra. Por
mucho que te empeñes en ser un ángel, estarás eternamente en pecado mortal.
Ya lo tienes de obligación. Para ti no hay padre, ni madre, ni nada más que
vergüenza cuando te pregunten por ellos. Y así, todo lo que hagas te tiene
que salir del revés, y si te encariñas con una persona, peor, que Dios te ha de
quitar aquel cariño.' (I, 510ab)

However much her Galician blood may have predisposed her to
melancholy, the major cause of her depression is her sense of shame
and guilt over the circumstances of her birth. She believes that God is
punishing her for the sins of her parents and that she will never find
happiness. For a few brief moments, during her innocent relationship
with Rogelio, she experiences affection, but this tenuous happiness
comes to an end when finally she is sent to work in another house.
Moreover, as we already know, the night before Rogelio's departure
for Galicia he seduces her. So she has lost both her love and her
virginity, and is in the same situation as her mother: she is a fallen
woman. We should not be surprised, then, that she commits suicide.
If she believes that she is indeed, as her name suggests, a slave to forces
outside herself, is rejected by God and condemned in advance, what
point is there in living? The obvious course of action is to end her life.
And so she does.

For this reason the Positivist explanation of Esclavitud's suicide is
somewhat simplistic: it does not take account of the complexities of
her moral state. And this is not mere speculation on the part of the
critic, as the narrator herself says as much in the novel's last
paragraph:

Si consultamos sobre este drama a don Gabriel Pardo, que es amigo de
generalidades pedantescas y se paga de malas razones por el afán de
pretender explicarlo todo, nos dirá que el extravío mental que conduce a la
muerte voluntaria es muy propio del sombrío humor de la raza céltica, esa
gran vencida de la historia; como si cada día y en cada provincia de España
no trajese la Prensa suicidios así. (I, 533b)

The narrator openly attacks Pardo's tendency to produce glib answers in his eagerness to account neatly for every phenomenon, and puts pretentious jargon into his mouth, thereby suggesting that the intellectual's abstract generalisations do not penetrate very deeply into the human heart.

My point is that, as in *Insolación*, Pardo Bazán deliberately misleads the reader by setting up an experiment and then, instead of allowing the circumstances of the novel to confirm the hypothesis, shows how the complexities of a human situation cannot be adequately accounted for by such a hypothesis. Her underlying intention is to cast doubt on the certainties which Positivist philosophy claims to offer. In fact, it seems to me that *Morriña* is not so much a novel about Esclavitud's tragic situation as about the difficulty in arriving at judgements about any human situation. There are two sides to every question.

My principal reason for saying this is the ambiguous way in which the narrator presents her characters. For example, doña Aurora, as we first meet her, is an astute, good-humoured and devoted mother, overseeing the health of her immature and not very robust son. Then in chapters 5 to 7 we see her good-heartedness as she warms to the simple-mannered Esclavitud, agrees with Gabriel Pardo that the girl cannot be blamed for the faults of her parents, and welcomes her into her house. This is indeed a charitable act, even, perhaps, a little Romantic. Yet the narrator makes it clear that there is another side to the question, and the other side of the coin of Aurora's goodness is a touch of selfishness. As the narrator tells us, when she does someone a good turn she expects to be rewarded by the sight of that person's happiness, and that in order to be contented herself she needs to be convinced that everyone around her is contented. So her good works do not flow purely from charity; they also answer a personal need. The narrator develops the point as follows:

En su determinación de admitir a Esclavitud habían influido dos móviles: primero, llevar la contraria a aquella antipática de Rita Pardo; segundo, contentar a una chica de tan agradable aspecto como Esclavitud, desempeñando, en cierto modo, papel de Providencia y reconciliándola con el Destino, para ella funesto e implacable desde la hora de nacer. Y este segundo generoso propósito se lo malograba, porque la chica no quería levantar cabeza ni abrir el alma a la buena suerte. (I, 495b)

Here we glimpse two not entirely altruistic motives for her kindness towards Esclavitud. The first is a rather childish desire to prove

Gabriel Pardo's sister, Rita, wrong in her assessment of Esclavitud; the second, described by the narrator as 'generous', is her desire to assume the role of Providence. But her impetuous generosity has its corresponding defects: self-dramatisation and impatience. Melodramatic words such as 'destino', 'funesto', and 'implacable' imply that Esclavitud's fate reminds Aurora of a Romantic tragedy in which she wants to play the part of redeemer or 'redentorista' (to use a key term in one of Pardo Bazán's next novels, *La piedra angular*). She regards herself as an instrument of Providence; but Providence is patient, Aurora is not. She wants the difficult task of reconciling Esclavitud to her destiny to be completed overnight and is anxious that the girl should be grateful. She cannot bear the thought that her plan to redeem Esclavitud has not been entirely successful.

This dual perspective on her good-heartedness was already evident in the previous chapter (8) when the narrator tells us that Aurora, despite her resolve to remain silent, cannot resist telling Rogelio about Esclavitud's past. She cannot deprive herself of the pleasure of recounting her triumph over Rita Pardo (who had refused to tell her Esclavitud's secret) and of telling a moving story. The narrator comments in the following passage on our delight in confronting grave problems in other people's lives without being called upon to solve them:

Hay un placer, cuyo origen no se define, pero a cuyo atractivo cede casi todo el mundo, en referir esos dramas hondos de la vida humana, que de rechazo nos tocan a todos, que tienen el don de interesarnos porque despiertan nuestros sentimientos de compasión y justicia, y al par nos ponen frente a graves problemas, sin obligarnos a resolverlos, sino sólo a considerarlos como consideramos en el teatro el argumento de una tragedia engendradora de terror y piedad. (I, 494a)

Here it is difficult to pin the narrator down because she detaches herself from her character with a general comment. But it is clear that the feelings of compassion that Esclavitud has awoken in Aurora are pleasurable. On the other hand, the reader cannot condemn her completely because, as the narrator insinuates, he too is deriving pleasure from Esclavitud's story.

At the beginning of the novel, then, we see in Aurora goodness tinged with selfishness. At the end this is reversed and we see in her selfishness tinged with goodness. However sincere her concern for Esclavitud, once she realises that her own interests are at stake, she takes measures to get rid of her. Yet the narrator does not want to leave us with an unduly negative impression of Aurora:

Así y todo, la señora no podía reprimir cierta desazón, cierta amargura íntima, una lástima inmensa, que despúes tradujo por doloroso presentimiento. 'Mire usted que compadecerla cuando estoy tan segura de que le he proporcionado lo que más podía desear una muchacha de su clase ...' Y así lo creía en efecto la señora de Pardiñas. Como les sucede a muchas personas bondadosas, incapaces de odiar y hacer daño, no quería reconocer que miraba ante todo a la conveniencia de su hijo ... (I, 532b)

The narrator is characteristically objective here, showing us both the good and the bad in Aurora. The good-hearted woman deceives herself so as not to face up to her real motives. But the phrase 'que despúes tradujo por doloroso presentimiento' warns us that when she learns of Esclavitud's death she will feel genuine remorse.

Although the presentation of her son, Rogelio, is less complex, he too is seen in an equivocal light. He is young and immature, and when he first meets Esclavitud he is wounded because she regards him as a child. Consequently, when he learns that his coldness towards her has upset her, he feels flattered. But as well as gratifying him, Esclavitud's discomfort moves him to pity:

[Esclavitud] le pareció muy demacrada, muy descolorida y más lánguida que un sauce. Al convencerse de esto, su noble alma juvenil se inundó de piedad; pero su orgullo, juvenil también, se estremeció dulcemente. (I, 497a)

To underline this ambiguity the narrator refers a little further on to the boy's 'excellent nature'; but this excellence does not stop him seducing and abandoning Esclavitud at the end, thereby contributing to her suicide.

This sense of the difficulty involved in evaluating certain actions and attitudes informs the presentation of almost all the characters in the novel. For example, the dual perspective on Gabriel Pardo, which is fundamental to a reading of *Insolación*, reappears briefly here. In chapter 7, when Gabriel tells Aurora about Esclavitud's past, he gives the impression of being an honest and compassionate person. But at the same time we are aware that his motives for defending Esclavitud against his sister, Rita, may not be entirely what they seem. First, we register the obvious antipathy which he feels for his sister and we cannot help suspecting that he contradicts her simply to annoy her. Moreover, if we remember his experiences described in *La madre naturaleza* and mentioned in passing in *Insolación*, we know that his opinions on social attitudes towards women are not disinterested. At the end of *Morriña*, as we have seen, the narrator turns on him: he is partial to pedantic generalisations and glib explanations of human behaviour. So, as in the case of Aurora, our initial sympathy for Gabriel is undermined by certain doubts.

In the case of Rita the reverse process is at work. At the beginning, in chapters 6 and 7, she is pretentious and malicious. She alludes darkly to Esclavitud's past but refuses to give details. She describes her brother's defence of Esclavitud as 'Romantic' and warns Aurora about the dangers of employing the girl in her house. The narrator's personal animus towards her is obvious when, for example, she comments that Rita interrupts a remark with a 'cackle of impertinent laughter from the most evil part of her soul' (I, 492b). Yet towards the end it seems to Aurora that Rita was indeed right: 'Aquella falsona de Rita Pardo decía bien ... Conviene mirar mucho a quien mete uno en su casa.' (I, 529a) Perhaps her reaction to Esclavitud had indeed been foolishly Romantic.

The apparent triumph of rebarbative cynicism is evident also in the character of Nicanor Candás, one of Aurora's acquaintances. There is no doubt about the narrator's dislike of him. He is 'asturiano, malicioso y presumido a fuer de buen ovetense; listo como una pimienta y más atravesado que una espina' (I, 480a) (a comment on the detested *Clarín*?). His coarseness and cynicism are contrasted with the noble integrity of Prudencio Rojas, another acquaintance of Aurora's, and it is he who maliciously suggests to Aurora that there is something going on between Rogelio and Esclavitud. Now although at the time his hints seem unjustified because we are fully aware of the innocent nature of the relationship between the two young people, the final seduction does seem to prove him right. Certainly towards the end of the novel Aurora refers approvingly to Candás's superior worldly wisdom. On the other hand, neither his nor Rita Pardo's interpretation of the situation is endorsed by the narrator herself. Esclavitud is not a hypocritical, scheming vixen (any doubt about that is dispelled by her suicide) and when she gives herself to Rogelio it is passively and almost with resignation.

This continual invitation to look at both sides of every issue extends beyond the characters to Galicia itself. For nearly all Aurora's friends it is a country with a mild climate, delicious food, affectionate people and beautiful landscape. For Rogelio it is a paradise lost, the mere mention of which fills his room with country smells such as mint and new-mown grass (I, 514b). On the other hand, for Candás Galicia is a country of untrustworthy, mean good-for-nothings. His well-known cynicism might vitiate his testimony, but Aurora herself admits that

Galicians are not to be trusted: '"A lo mejor te venden amistad mientras te clavan el cuchillo hasta el mango. La verdad se ha de decir: por allá no somos así . . . , francotes y leales, como los castellanos viejos."' (I, 482b) Even the question of domestic servants is seen from this dual perspective. At first Aurora is delighted with her Galician maid because she is so different from the sluttish Madrid maids (I, 487b). But her enthusiasm quickly changes to irritation when Esclavitud refuses to tell her why she is unhappy: 'La muchacha tiene las buenas cualidades de nuestro país, pero no le faltan los defectos. Es humilde, modosa y callada: pero también es algo zorrita, y no hay modo de saber lo que piensa ni lo que le pasa.' (I, 496a) But both the fact that Aurora's judgement is influenced by her constant desire to dominate and our knowledge of Esclavitud's exceptional situation disincline us to accept the unfavourable generalisation on Galicians. It is one more cliché, one more example of the human tendency to rationalise dishonesty with reach-me-down formulas.[9]

CONCLUSION

I have been arguing that *Insolación* and *Morriña* are not, as it is generally thought, examples of Pardo Bazán's supposed Naturalism, but quite the opposite. In both novels Pardo Bazán turns Naturalism on its head. She carefully sets up hypotheses, and then tests and ostensibly proves them in the behaviour of Asís and Esclavitud. Yet these are anything but novels from which one can draw clear and unambiguous conclusions, least of all about the exact mechanism of human behaviour and motivation. If one accepts Ian Watt's argument that the novel concerns itself essentially with the particular rather than the general,[10] then Naturalism's tendency towards abstractions, the use of a particular case to demonstrate a general point, is essentially anti-novelistic. It may be that Pardo Bazán was too much of a novelist not to realise this. This is certainly the impression she gives in a remark she made in 1907: 'Nunca conseguirá el mejor artista interesarnos con el *hombre*, sino con *hombres* diversos, mejor cuanto más individualizados.' (III, 1313a) In *Los pazos de Ulloa* she hesitates and allows the general and the particular to rub shoulders uneasily. In *Insolación* and *Morriña* she challenges the general with the particular, but without entirely discrediting it. Such ambiguity provides, as I shall be arguing in the following chapters, the creative impulse for her mature work.

4

Una cristiana-La prueba

'Todo el romanticismo es acaso una false concepción de la vida y no otra cosa, y el gran romántico Don Quijote, como sabemos, confirma plenamente esta calificación.' *El lirismo*, p. 341

Una cristiana and *La prueba* are sequel novels which I shall refer to as one. It centres on the relationship between Salustio, an engineering student, and Carmen, the young wife of his uncle, Felipe. When Salustio visits Galicia for the wedding he falls in love with Carmen, and thereafter he is obsessed with the question of why she is marrying his repulsive uncle. Eventually he discovers that her motive is to escape from the house of her father, whose immoral conduct she cannot condone. Back in Madrid, Salustio goes to live with Felipe and Carmen and takes every opportunity of observing the latter's reactions both to her husband and to himself. At the end of *Una cristiana* Salustio falls ill and Carmen's devoted attention suggests that she loves him. *La prueba* traces the development of Carmen's feelings towards her husband from repugnance to love. He contracts leprosy and she nurses the dying man with tenderness and heroism. The novel ends with Salustio in a state of intellectual and moral confusion.

After the subtlety and detached scrutiny of *Insolación* and *Morriña*, *Una cristiana-La prueba* is a great disappointment. Pardo Bazán's initial motive for writing about an exemplary Catholic woman was, to judge from her comment to Galdós, apparently trivial: 'Por el camino he pensado una novela, pero no se titula El Hombre; se tiene que titular (a ver si te gusta) *Titi Carmen*. Es la historia de una señora virtuosa e intachable; hay que variar la nota, no se canse el público de tanta cascabelera.'[1] With one eye on public response, Pardo Bazán apparently decided that, after the supposedly risqué content of her previous novels, it was time for a change.

Another possible motive was equally inimical to the realisation of a novel with feeling and conviction. At Christmas of 1887 she had visited Rome, where she had had an audience and apparently got on well with Pope Leo XIII, and in July of 1889 she was awarded the decoration of Pro Ecclesia et Pontifice by the Holy Father.[2] One cannot help wondering whether, having been thus honoured, doña Emilia decided to abandon (albeit temporarily) her sense of the complexity of life to preach openly a rather extreme form of the Catholic party-line. For Fr Moreno (the spokesman for Catholicism in *Una cristiana—La prueba*) issues are as cut and dried as they are for Salustio (the spokesman for Positivism). The project of casting doubts on contemporary Positivism leads on from similar projects in *Insolación* and *Morriña*, and there is no reason in principle why it should not be just as telling. But in the earlier novels Pardo Bazán did not attempt to replace one dogma with another, as she does in *Una cristiana—La prueba*. In the following examination of three aspects of this novel (psychology, the first-person narrative and the religious content) it will, I hope, become clear how her temporary lapse into didacticism illustrates her own point that the novelist attempts to preach at his or her peril.

THE PSYCHOLOGICAL NOVEL

In October of 1889 a Galician newspaper reported that Pardo Bazán 'lleva muy adelantada una novela de costumbres – un estudio psicológico más bien – que se titulará probablemente *Una cristiana*',[3] from which we may deduce that in the novelist's mind *Una cristiana—La prueba* was primarily a psychological novel. The exact meaning of the term 'psychological novel', as discussed in chapter 1 above, is indicated by the narrator, Salustio, when he remarks that although on the surface his story is monotonous and trivial, it is rich in inner details (I, 643b). The novelist is abandoning the conventional reliance on plot and is now attempting to create interest by exploring psychic phenomena. Such an attempt was made possible by a rejection of Zola's schematic psychology, which saw personality as explicable in terms of heredity and environment, in favour of a belief in the essential mysteriousness of human personality.

In the case of *Una cristiana—La prueba* this mysteriousness lies in the concept of the Unconscious, as developed by Schopenhauer and Hartmann.[4] The Unconscious has various meanings, ranging from a simple description of any bodily activity which takes place within an organism without that organ's awareness (for example, digestion) to Schopenhauer's Will as universal force throughout nature,[5] but at both extremes it is an impersonal force which in Eoff's words sets up 'a contrast between the non-rational, embracing the concept of instinct and its relation to the species as a whole, and the rebellious self-consciousness, with which are associated intellect and the sense of personality'.[6] Hartmann identified the Unconscious more particularly with instinct. For him, the realm of instinct was the 'inmost core of every being',[7] whereas the conscious life of the intelligence was a mere accessory.[8]

It is difficult to say whether Pardo Bazán actually read Schopenhauer and Hartmann but, as Whyte and Eoff have shown, their influence in the last third of the nineteenth century was extensive.[9] As we shall see, Pardo Bazán refers to them, directly or indirectly, and the concept of the Unconscious certainly plays an important part in some of her novels from *Una cristiana* to *Memorias de un solterón*.

In *Una cristiana–La prueba* there is an explicit rejection of materialistic psychology when Salustio, in contradiction to those who believe that psychology is as empirical as the natural sciences, points to the fundamental incomprehensibility of human behaviour:

Pero la repugnancia misteriosa, la sublevación de las profundidades de nuestro ser, ésa no acaba, ni se extirpa, ni se transforma; contra la sinrazón ho hay raciocinio, ni lógica contra el instinto, el cual obra en nosotros como la Naturaleza, intuitivamente, en virtud de leyes cuya esencia es y será para nosotros, por los siglos de los siglos, indescifrable arcano. (I, 612a)

It is easy to see how the rich source of mystery perceived by the novelist in irrational instinct should provide material as promising as that found in any cloak-and-dagger tale or detective thriller.

The story of Salustio's relationship with Carmen is in fact structured upon a series of enigmas, each one, as it is solved, leading to another. His first question concerns Carmen's motive for marrying his disagreeable uncle. Does she love him? (I, 567a) When he discovers that she does not love his uncle, there is left 'la eterna pregunta', why is she marrying him? (I, 580a) To this is added the question: 'Is there an illicit relationship between Carmen and Fr Moreno?' Both of these questions are answered when Salustio overhears the conversation of Carmen and the priest, but then the question is raised of Carmen's feelings in her dreadful situation (I, 593b). After the marriage, Salustio tries to discover whether Carmen loves her husband or not, and whether she is happy (I, 605ab, 610a). Then there is the major question of whether Carmen loves Salustio himself (I, 612b). It is this last question which motivates Salustio's investigations for most of *La prueba*, and until the end the answers are pleasing to him. Carmen hates her husband, is obviously wretched, and loves Salustio. But by the end of the novel, so great is the change in Carmen that the answer to each of these questions has been reversed (she loves her husband, is happy, and feels no passion for Salustio), and Salustio, unlike the classic detective, is left in total confusion.

This is the basic mechanism of the novel and as such it seems perfectly acceptable: the novelist uses a highly motivated narrator to delve into the psychic depths of a woman in a potentially interesting situation and attempts to hold the reader's attention with a series of enigmas. Yet few readers are likely to dispute that the mechanism, as used by Pardo Bazán, fails to interest. Why is this so? The answer surely lies in the character and situation of Carmen herself. In the passage referred to above, in which Salustio refers to the power of irrational instinct, he addresses himself to those dramatists who produce 'espeluznantes creaciones' and asks them 'decidme si hay conflicto más tremendo que aquél cuyas peripecias se desarrollan en el fondo del alma de una mujer unida, sujeta, enlazada día y noche al hombre cuya presencia basta para estremecer de horror todas sus fibras' (I, 611b). Such a project (to study the feelings of a woman married to a man who is repugnant to her) is indeed full of possibilities, but in this work Pardo Bazán fails to realise the potential of Carmen's situation as here described. Salustio is certainly fascinated by her plight but little attempt is made to arouse the reader's interest in it independently of his, or make him search for and ponder the clues along with the detective. As I argue below, when I consider Carmen as a saint-figure, she is never established as a concrete presence in the book and her plight is never presented to us in a concrete way.

There is, moreover, an uneasy duality in the novel which arises from the fact that Salustio, the detective, is more of a psychological mystery than the mystery itself. How is Salustio's psychology presented? Not in the way, for example, Julián's is in *Los pazos de Ulloa*, by an ironic view of his reaction to events: with the exception of the political episode in *La prueba*, little happens to characterise him. The novelist rather imparts to us at the beginning of the novel the basic contradiction in Salustio and this contradiction is then developed through his contact with other characters.

The contradiction lies in the fact that Salustio is, on the one hand, a Rationalist, a radical and a religious sceptic and, on the other a Romantic, a traditionalist and a would-be Catholic. This contradiction is explained, rather unexpectedly, by the idea of the Unconscious: unexpectedly, because it would no doubt have surprised Schopenhauer and Hartmann. The explanation centres on the suggestion that there exists in Spaniards a residue of instinctual attitudes which are autonomous of conscious reason. For example, to begin with the Romantic/Rationalist antinomy, when describing in chapter 1 of *Una cristiana* his fellow boarders in doña Pepa's guesthouse, Salustio compares their lack of common-sense with his own hardheadedness – he is 'más formal y positivo' (I, 542a). This prepares the way for the description in chapter 11 of his enlightened Rationalism. However, despite his sense of superiority over his fellows, he sees that he too shares their Romanticism because it is present in his Spanish blood (I, 542a). Now this is a case of racial heredity familiar in Positivist thinking and by itself makes no allusion to the Unconscious. Nevertheless, Salustio's Romanticism is often associated, particularly by his friend, Luis, with his other anti-Rationalist and reactionary urges, and these are undeniably explained in terms of instinct.

If we take the strong anti-semitism from which his antipathy towards Felipe springs, we find that his rational, Positivistic, progressive formation battles in vain against this 'sinrazón de una antipatía instintiva'.[10] He reflects: 'Extraña cosa [. . .] que lo más íntimo de nuestro ser resista a la voluntad y a los dictados del entendimiento, y que exista en nosotros, a despecho de nosotros, un fondo autónomo, instintivo, donde reina la tradición y triunfa el pasado.' (I, 548a) The words 'un fondo autónomo, instintivo' strongly recall Hartmann's concept of unconscious instinct.

Salustio's attraction to Catholic values is accounted for in the same way: 'Unicamente se explica mi extraña aquiescencia a las palabras del padre Moreno suponiendo que existe en el fondo de nuestro espíritu una tendencia perpetua a la abnegación, a la renunciación, por decirlo así, tendencia que se deriva del subsuelo cristiano sobre el cual reposa nuestro racionalismo superficial.' (I, 593b) Scratch a Spaniard, the novelist is suggesting, and you find a Romantic, a traditionalist and a Catholic. The same idea is later put into the mouth of Salustio's friend, Luis (I, 601b). It is of course a considerable step from stating the commonplace that Spaniards are essentially ('en el fondo') conservative, to postulating the existence of a traditionalist Unconscious peculiar to Spain, but this is precisely what Pardo Bazán is here doing. This idiosyncratic adaptation of the concept of unconscious instinct seems to be based on the following (rather dubious) line of argument. Man's inmost core (to use Hartmann's words) is instinct; now, the Spaniard's inmost core is Romantic, traditionalist and Catholic; therefore these traits are instinctive.

The psychological study of Salustio is based, then, on a contradiction inside him. The technique the novelist uses to present this is to surround Salustio with other characters who bring out in him one or other side of the paradox. So his fellow boarders, don Julián, Botello, Trinidad and Dolfos, bring out the Romantic side in him, and Luis Portal the rational side; Belén the liberated and sensual side, Carmen the moral and spiritual. Luis and Carmen are the most important characters in this respect. The intensity of Salustio's attraction to Carmen's virtue and heroism conveys the intensity of his Romantic yearnings. It also conveys the element of madness or 'quijotismo' contained in his Romanticism. So in reply to Luis's charge that in loving Carmen he is mad and unbalanced he says: '"Déjame a mí. Cada loco con su tema. [. . .] Mi gloria consiste en una quimera, ya lo sé, y quimera extravagante . . ."' (I, 627a) But if Carmen draws him towards the quixotic, Luis is his Sancho Panza, 'moderador de mi fantasía quijotesca' (I, 609b). Between these two characters and the poles they represent Salustio oscillates throughout the novel.

Now, this psychological situation, like Carmen's, is no doubt potentially interesting, but the study of Salustio, if more detailed than that of Carmen, just as surely fails. It fails in the first place because nothing changes in Salustio's mind until the very end, when his experience of Carmen's transformation by grace causes him to lose faith in both Rationalism and Romanticism. For the greater part of the book, however, there is no development. We are told at the beginning of chapter 3 that the traditionalist side of Salustio's personality is deep beneath the surface, but it is not shown to be hidden nor is it gradually revealed, so there is no sense of a mystery unfolding, as is the case in *Memorias de un solterón*. Secondly, the novel lacks a consistent ironic perspective. In *La piedra angular*, Moragas, who is clearly related to Salustio, is treated with a careful combination of irony and seriousness so that the reader knows exactly how far to identify with him and how far to dissociate himself from him. This is not the case in *Una cristiana–La prueba*. In retrospect we can see that Salustio's values are intended to be judged inadequate, but this is by no means obvious as we read the work. This is partly due to the fact that he is the narrator and therefore tends automatically to gain the reader's sympathy, and partly due to the fact that he is so wise. Pardo Bazán seems to have fallen between two stools: by giving up her position as omniscient narrator, she forgoes the privilege of directly discrediting Salustio in the reader's eyes, but she also fails to let him do this unwittingly himself, so that the discrediting of his attitude to life at the end is unconvincing. Again we must return to Carmen; if she had been made a more concrete presence, her behaviour would have challenged Salustio more effectively and rendered his final defeat more acceptable.

It has to be concluded, then, that the psychological analysis in this novel is not successful. We have seen that Pardo Bazán was working from the conviction that the human mind can be absorbing in itself without a primary reliance on plot. But we have also seen that she failed to cope with the technical problems involved in making the psychology of her characters interesting to her reader. The success of the psychological studies in those novels which I shall be examining in the following chapters is therefore the more noteworthy.

THE FIRST-PERSON NARRATIVE METHOD

Parallel to Pardo Bazán's increasing interest in psychological analysis is her exploration of the possibilities of the first-person narrative method. She had used this in her first novel, *Pascual López* (1879), probably because she was writing consciously in the picaresque tradition, and then in the *novela breve*, *Bucólica* (1884), but did not return to it until the first half of *Insolación*, where it serves to give a very immediate impression of the protagonist's mental confusion. Thereafter, all of those novels, with the exception of *La piedra angular*, which I take to be Pardo Bazán's most important (*Una cristiana*–*La prueba*, *Doña Milagros*, *Memorias de un solterón*, *La quimera*, *La sirena negra* and *Dulce dueño*) are narrated wholly or in part in the first person. It is as if the first-person method was, for her, essential to the kind of psychological novel in which the characters reveal the secrets of their inner lives. Two private comments on *Bucólica* show that early on she was interested in experimenting with this method. On 17 May 1884 she wrote to Yxart: 'Tiene la singularidad de ser una novela *por cartas*, método que ya de puro antiguo se va volviendo nuevo.' On 19 July 1884 she wrote to Oller: 'Es un ensayo de un estilo fácil y sencillo, el epistolar. No sé si he logrado vencer algo la personalidad del escritor para infundirle la vida del héroe: ¡es tan difícil la empresa!'[11] The implication here is that the first-person method is part of the Realist's attempt at self-effacement aimed in this case at giving the character a life independent of the author's. It may be that already in 1884 Pardo Bazán had misgivings about the third-person method and, when she came to concentrate more exclusively on psychology, she largely abandoned it. I shall be examining her various experiments with the first-person narration during the 1890s in the following chapters.[12]

Bertil Romberg in a study of the first-person narration uses the term 'epic situation' to refer to the narrator's situation when he is telling his story and he identifies three main types: (i) the fictitious memoir; (ii) the diary novel; (iii) the epistolary novel.[13] *Una cristiana–La prueba* is a fictional memoir, although the story covers only the narrator's student years. In the 'Final' Salustio tells Luis that he has written 'una especie de novela o de autobiografía' and then confides to the reader that in the writing of this work he had found a pleasant antidote to his arid studies (I, 703b). The actual moment of composition is some little time after the death of his uncle, Felipe. Salustio has quite recently obtained his diploma, presumably in the summer of the year in which Felipe died, and is now performing his first professional duties. The narrator tells his story, then, soon after the events have occurred, when he is still in a state of confusion following his temporary conversion; his last words are (referring to his feelings about Carmen) 'Ignoro lo que siento . . . Necesito analizar mi espíritu' (I, 706b). This has an important effect on the narration. The traditional type of fictional memoir, exemplified by *Lazarillo de Tormes*, *Guzmán de Alfarache* and *El buscón*, is told some time after the events are supposed to have occurred, when the narrator is wiser or at least has the benefit of hindsight. Pardo Bazán's first novel, *Pascual López*, is of this type. In this work there is a marked gap between the mature narrator and the protagonist, his younger self. In *Una cristiana–La prueba* and more particularly in the first-person novels which follow it, Pardo Bazán abandoned this traditional form in order to make of the novel the process of the narrator's own self-discovery. On the whole, the narrator of this novel shows no sign of greater wisdom or hindsight than the protagonist. To take the second chapter as an example: he describes his Rationalist's belief in the natural potential of human life without conveying any sense of the disillusionment with this creed experienced at the end of the novel. In fact the story is told throughout with the kind of youthful, Romantic intensity characteristic of Salustio before his traumatic experience.

The intention seems to have been to trace his spiritual development towards temporary conversion through the novel, an intention which, as we have seen, was never properly realised.

Pardo Bazán handles the various conventions of the first-person narration (e.g. the perfect memory and the relationship between the narrator and reader) fairly competently, but in the central problem of handing the narration over to the narrator, she fails. The problem involves not just Salustio's literary competence, but also his interests and range of knowledge, both of which are important characterising factors. Needless to say, Salustio could not tell his tale with the same tone of voice as that wise, mature and immensely cultured lady who dominates, say, *Los pazos de Ulloa*. One fundamental difference (fundamental, that is, in nineteenth-century Spain) is his sex. Salustio is a man; yet he notices and comments on things which one would expect to interest only a woman. For example, he describes the clothes and jewellery Carmen is given as wedding presents (I, 572ab) and Belén's clothes (I, 695b) with surprising knowledge. He also seems to know about flower arrangement (I, 637b) and perfume (I, 565b–6a), and remarks on male beauty ('la estética varonil' – I, 624a) in a way more characteristic of a woman, particularly a woman with the aesthetic interests of Pardo Bazán.

Another difference is that Salustio is an unbeliever who has never had any interest in religion (I, 547a); indeed Moreno is the first friar he has ever seen (I, 561b). Yet unaccountably he makes reference to the Bible (I, 649b, 667b, 697b) and Christ's passion (I, 637b), uses the technical liturgical term 'estola' (I, 613a) and compares the character of the mother of Luis's friend, *Mo*, to that of an abbess (I, 648b). He is, moreover, a fairly average engineering student who manages to fail his exams, yet he has an extensive knowledge of such things as religious painting and sculpture (I, 645b, 650b, 652b), medieval triptychs (I, 632b), porcelain figures and Eastern ceramics (I, 632b), poetry (I, 668b), Shakespeare (I, 622a), modern psychology (I, 646a) and medicine (I, 642b). In addition, although he is young and lacking in experience (I, 689a), he possesses an enormous store of wisdom about life and human nature. For example, of Luis he confidently states: 'Era visible que mi amigo estaba en ese período en que las naturalezas, más egoístas que altruístas, ceden al sortilegio de creer en el amor y experimentan una plenitud vanidosa que se parece muchísimo al verdadero entusiasmo.' (I, 623a) And of himself: 'La idea de su forzada convivencia con el leproso me infundió esa pureza o frigidez que se desarrolla a la cabecera de un enfermo grave, al pie de un lecho de muerte, en los supremos instantes penosos de nuestra pobre humanidad.' (I, 684a) How many death-beds, one wonders, can Salustio have been present at?[14]

Salustio is certainly a very confusing personality. There is even some doubt about his age. Although he tells us that he is twenty-two (I, 566b), and his behaviour and position as a student confirm this, we learn that he reaches puberty only between the end of *Una cristiana* and the beginning of *La prueba* (I, 624a). Even allowing for the later maturity of nineteenth-century youth, this is highly improbable.

It seems clear that the novelist has not come to terms in this work with the change from the third-person omniscient narration to the first-person method. She is unable to hand her story over to her narrator and let him tell it in a way consistent with his character as established independently in the novel, and persistently allows her own erudite self to intrude. Her muddled narrator may well be the result of a muddled view of the psychological novel, for she was perhaps trying to endow her novel with the kind of intelligence she found so impressive in Bourget. She goes about it, however, in a superficial way (by superimposing intelligent comments on the narrative) and in a way disastrous to the first-person technique. Bourget, it should be remembered, like Henry James, nearly always used a third-person narrator in his psychological novels. It was a serious error on the part of the Spanish novelist, and one which contributes largely to the failure of the novel as a whole: I noted above how Salustio's wisdom makes it difficult for the reader to accept that within the norms of the novel he is wrong. It was an error, however, that she was not to repeat.

THE RELIGIOUS CONTENT

I argued in chapter I that Pardo Bazán was not greatly impressed by the specifically religious aspect of Spiritual Naturalism. For this reason and because there is nothing particularly religious about the four novels (*Los pazos de Ulloa*, *La madre naturaleza*, *Insolación* and *Morriña*) she wrote immediately after reading Tolstoy and Dostoyevsky, it is misleading to speak of a new religious phase in her work.[15] It remains true, however, that in the 1890s she did respond to the trend towards religious subject-matter in the work of certain French novelists. There are religious overtones to both *La piedra angular* and *Doña Milagros*, and *Una cristiana–La prueba* certainly centres on a specifically Christian view of life.

Now, the interest of the French novelists in the 1890s in religious subjects went hand in hand with a return to Catholicism. This was clearly not the case with the lifelong Catholic Pardo Bazán. Indeed, even in her most Naturalistic works, *Los pazos de Ulloa* and *La madre naturaleza*, she maintains a perfectly orthodox view of human nature (though not one necessarily shared by all Catholics). In these Ulloa novels certain characters seem to lack the free will to rise above the animals in their behaviour, but this is because the Church in that area is effectively dead and grace is therefore absent. Pardo Bazán excluded the operation of grace from these novels not because she did not believe in it (on the contrary, its reality is affirmed either explicitly or implicitly), but because she wanted to exploit the tragic possibilities of man in a graceless situation, in a state of unredeemed nature.[16] My point is that she is not testing the (undoubtedly heterodox) hypothesis that nature is *necessarily* a stronger force than grace, but simply that nature will assert itself when grace is absent.

Although there is no external evidence that Pardo Bazán intended *Una cristiana–La prueba* to be complementary to *Los pazos de Ulloa* and *La madre naturaleza*, from the point of view of the picture given of man's relationship to nature, it undoubtedly is. It is difficult not to notice that the divergence of views about man and nature between Salustio and Moreno in *Una cristiana–La prueba* exactly reproduces a similar divergence between Gabriel Pardo and Julián in *La madre naturaleza*. The similarity in the situation in both *Una cristiana–La prueba* and *La madre naturaleza* is equally noticeable, with Salustio corresponding to Perucho, Carmen to Manuela, and Felipe to Gabriel. The difference in the final resolution of the two triangular situations gives a clue to the difference between the two novels as a whole. In *La madre naturaleza*, Perucho and Manuela follow their natural inclinations, Gabriel is excluded, and the result is a moral disaster. In *Una cristiana–La prueba*, Carmen overcomes her natural feelings for Salustio, comes to love her husband, and the result is a moral triumph. The former tests the hypothesis that human beings away from the influence of civilisation and religion behave like the animals, by using the case of two young people who, unaware of their kinship and brought up together close to nature, eventually form an incestuous relationship. The latter tests a similar (only more radical) hypothesis, that, whatever the circumstances, natural feelings will inevitably triumph over the restraints of religion and society. The subject of this experiment is a young woman married to a man she finds repugnant and living in close proximity to a young man she apparently likes. But in this case the experiment fails: Carmen does not surrender to her feelings.

Pattison notes the contrast *Una cristiana–La prueba* presents to earlier novels: 'These novels negate the theme of *Mother Nature* and *Sunstroke* where Nature was the victor over society.'[17] However, in stressing the opposition between nature and society, he ignores the important theological content of *Una cristiana–La prueba*. The social law is certainly an element, but the triumph over nature belongs primarily to the supernatural power of grace.

Gabriel Pardo is the spokesman for nature in *La madre naturaleza*; in *Una cristiana–La prueba* this role is assumed by Salustio. Like Gabriel, he is a rationalist. 'Creo que nací racionalista', he states early in the novel and explains how, although not exactly an atheist, he is a natural sceptic (I, 547a). In addition, he shares with Gabriel a belief in the goodness of human nature, a belief which accounts for Salustio's idealistic optimism, which often recalls Gabriel's. He aspires towards freedom which, he feels, will bring personal fulfilment or, in his words, 'vida, vida completa y digna del ser racional, que no ha de reducirse a vegetar ni a golosear los placeres, sino que debe recorrer toda la escala del pensamiento, del sentimiento y de la acción' (I, 544b). These categories of thought, feeling and action recall Auguste Comte's three categories ('Aimer, Penser, Agir') in his 'Tableau systématique de l'âme'.[18] This, together with the fact that Salustio refers to his own 'positivismo científico' (I, 548b) and that Moreno addresses him as 'señor positivista' (I, 687a), places Salustio firmly in the nineteenth-century Positivist tradition. He has a hopeful view of what human beings can do for themselves, by themselves, without, as he says, being a visionary or a dreamer (I, 544b). Moreover, he confidently asserts that human happiness consists in the realisation of the 'true purpose of life' (I, 640b), by which he seems to mean sexual and emotional fulfilment.

This thoroughly modern conviction is the basis of his opposition to Moreno's uncompromising Catholicism, and of his disapproval (albeit, as we shall see, a highly ambiguous one) of Carmen's self-sacrifice. It is this which leads him to tell Moreno at the wedding reception that the marriage between his uncle and Carmen is 'un puro disparate', which will bring dire consequences (I, 596a). Their union cannot possibly be happy because it is not based on love and mutual sympathy; it goes against nature. His conviction becomes a matter of pride and he looks forward, at the end of *Una cristiana*, to nature asserting itself.

The crux of the matter is the question of human happiness. For Salustio, as we have seen, happiness consists in fulfilling one's natural human impulses; in this belief he is assenting to a nineteenth-century Rationalist orthodoxy. In the novel this orthodoxy is challenged by Moreno's arguments and Carmen's sacrifice. A similar challenge has been presented by Julián in *La madre naturaleza*, but in that novel the alternative to a life lived according to the dictates of nature is singularly negative. The only reply Julián can offer to Gabriel's defence of nature and of Manuela's innocence is a bald theological formula about the fall of man, vitiated nature ('la naturaleza enferma'), and grace and redemption (I, 409ab). By contrast, *Una cristiana–La prueba* presents a far more developed version of the religious view on the discursive level, as well as a concrete illustration in Carmen of the redeemed life.

The religious view is conveyed through Moreno in his discussions with Salustio. The introduction of an ideologue separate from Carmen was necessary because she is unable to defend herself from the arguments of Salustio, to whom she is unwilling to admit even the existence of a problem (see I, 614a and 640a). Moreno and Salustio talk alone four times in the novel, twice in *Una cristiana* (chapters 7 and 17) and twice in *La prueba* (chapters 9 and 16). In the first meeting, on the way to El Tejo, the first doubt is cast on Salustio's world-view when he finds that the friar, although living a life of self-abnegation, does not give the impression of being unhappy or unfulfilled. This doubt is intensified in the second conversation during the wedding breakfast. Salustio's disgust at the excesses of the meal and subsequent monkish thoughts of abnegation allow Moreno to question the generally accepted idea of happiness and to offer an alternative. As we know, happiness for Salustio is fulfilment in natural terms: Moreno tells him that precisely by wishing to abandon such fulfilment he is standing at 'the threshold of wisdom and happiness', and that those who possess what the world calls happiness are to be pitied (I, 595b).

The discussion of happiness is taken a step further when Salustio reverts to type and condemns the wedding as 'un horrible desastre' (I, 597a). Moreno concedes that, humanly speaking, the match is a mistake, but then goes on to postulate the existence of the supernatural power of grace (I, 597b). At this point he has said no more than Julián to Gabriel in *La madre naturaleza*, but now he states that grace brings the positive gift of peace of mind: 'La paz del alma es un bien real entre los muchos bienes falsos que ofrece el mundo.' (I, 597b) So to live in the power of grace is not just to repress one's natural feelings; it is also to find 'that peace which the world cannot give'. Unlike Gabriel listening to Julián, Salustio is, for the moment at least, convinced by these arguments, and whether this is due to their intrinsic merit, to the effects of the wine or to Salustio's frustrated passion, the reader is left with a positive impression of Moreno's views.

After the wedding, Moreno disappears from the novel until chapter 9 of *La prueba*, by which stage Carmen's ordeal is well advanced and her unhappiness, as predicted by Salustio, is evident. The third confrontation of Salustio and Moreno, in which the former's idea of happiness is again questioned, is thus strategically placed. In fact it immediately follows the account of what Salustio calls the 'memorable day' on which his conversation with Carmen had convinced him of her aversion to her husband and her love for him (chapter 8). During this third interview Salustio claims that what he had foretold has indeed come about and that Carmen is now 'unhappy and sick with repulsion' (I, 657a). Moreno challenges this on grounds consistent with his previous definition of happiness as peace of mind: Carmen is happy because her conscience and honour are intact (I, 658a).

The final dialogue of any significance between Moreno and Salustio is in chapter 17, when Carmen is tending the stricken Felipe. Here the importance of the title of the novel's second half – *La prueba* – is finally explained. In Salustio's eyes, the fact that Carmen is now having to care for a repulsive leper vindicates his point of view. Moreno replies by again challenging his idea of human happiness: '"Usted cree que la vida ha de componerse de una serie de dichas y venturas, y en eso se equivoca mucho, porque la vida es una prueba, y a veces una sucesión de pruebas que acaban con la muerte."' He adds that, humanly speaking, he would have preferred to see Carmen happy in this life but, as her confessor, he prefers to see her suffer because 'such suffering enhances her spiritual beauty' (I, 686b). This last phrase points to the positive side of the religious view which I have been trying to emphasise. In opposition to Salustio's faith in human life, Moreno is sceptical of terrestrial joys and believes that suffering is the norm. This belief, however, far from leading the Christian to despair, is a means of transformation. *Desengaño*, he suggests, leads to charity and this, together with grace, transforms us and eradicates our natural repugnance for suffering and death (i, 688b). What Moreno is describing is the doctrine of Redemption or the New Creation which proclaims that man is raised, through grace, from his natural fallen state to a new life, characterised by different perspectives and different ways of relating to others.[19]

With these four conversations, then, Pardo Bazán provides the novel with an ideological framework similar to those found in earlier novels, but with a quite different emphasis.

The friar's arguments, however, are by themselves inconclusive because, unlike the ideological content of earlier novels, they are balanced throughout by an opposite view which may possibly be proved correct. Moreno's arguments need to be corroborated by the evidence of Carmen's final triumph. This triumph is conveyed to Salustio in chapter 19 of *La prueba*, where the change in Carmen illustrates what Moreno has said about the power of grace. The illustration lies both in what she says and in the way she says it. Whereas in all her previous encounters with Salustio she has been defensive and obviously struggling with her own feelings, now she is completely at her ease. Salustio, on the other hand, is baffled and wounded by the description she gives of her transformation and the way she accounts for it. The transformation has taken place in her feelings; she now loves her husband, tends him gladly and no longer regrets marrying him. She explains this phenomenon with a simple inference from experience: '"Cuando Dios nos manda la copa de ajenjo, si la bebemos de buena gana, sabe a almíbar . . . , y si la tomamos con repugnancia, entonces se nota todo el amargor o más aún del amargor que tiene . . ."' (i, 700a) Without using theological terms, Carmen here makes more specific Moreno's theological formulas about the workings of grace, and focuses more clearly on the part played by the human will ('de buena gana' and 'con repugnancia'). She describes her own suffering (the 'copa de ajenjo' of the passage quoted above) and the change in her attitude towards it. Previously she had accepted it with repugnance, out of a sense of obligation. This is the situation dealt with in *Una cristiana* and much of *La prueba*, particularly in the central episode of the yew tree. There Moreno solemnly reminds Carmen that, as a wife, she will be bound to be faithful to her husband, not only in her actions but also in her feelings (I, 587a). Carmen responds with a rather desperate assertion of confidence in her own powers. Whilst paying lip-service to grace, she states emphatically that she herself is strong enough to change her feelings by her own human efforts; but the vehemence of her assertion betrays her self-deception. This deception is clear to the reader until chapter 17 of *La prueba* because, until then, Carmen shows no sign of love for Felipe and many signs of her attachment to Salustio. At the end, as we have seen, she is undeceived. The progression described by Moreno takes place; acceptance of suffering brings love, which in its turn prepares the ground for grace. Through grace, her heart is changed and she comes to love suffering and sickness.[20]

There has indeed taken place in her a New Creation, for, whereas during most of the novel she is acting against her nature by having recourse to duty and obligation, by the end her very nature has changed and to love her husband is no longer to violate her feelings. The sense of freedom she feels contrasts strongly with the way Julián copes with his love for Nucha. In *Los pazos de Ulloa* he deceives himself about the nature of his feelings by thinking of her in terms of the Virgin Mary, and in *La madre naturaleza*, although he has acquired the 'paz de alma' of which Moreno speaks, his melancholy, his daily visits to Nucha's grave and his tight-lipped reticence indicate continual repression rather than the presence of any transforming power in his life. Certainly he does not share Carmen's joy and release, characteristic of the New Creation.

I have examined the opposition between grace and nature in order to establish the exact contrast between *Una cristiana—La prueba* and *Los pazos de Ulloa* and *La madre naturaleza*. The contrast lies in the fact that the Naturalistic experiment in *Una cristiana—La prueba* eventually fails and Carmen does not behave as all the laws of nature decree she must. Her nature is transformed by the supernatural power of grace. But these later novels do not negate, as Pattison says, the earlier ones; on the contrary, the realms of nature and grace, which they dramatise, are complementary. The contrast lies in Pardo Bazán's intention: *Los pazos de Ulloa* and *La madre naturaleza* are tragedies, whereas Carmen's heroic triumph over nature makes *Una cristiana—La prueba* (at least in the novelist's intention) an epic work.

However, the epic heroine herself is singularly elusive. The reason for this, I suggest, is that Pardo Bazán was more concerned with a hagiographical type than a character whom she knows or understands. As Nelly Clémessy's remark that Carmen is 'une sorte de réincarnation de ces saintes de jadis' indicates (p. 584), the hagio-graphical pattern is central to Pardo Bazán's conception of her character.

Salustio refers to Carmen as a saint on various occasions. On the day of the wedding he writes to Luis that she is 'un ángel', 'un serafín', and 'una santa', and that 'es indudable que en una mujer así hay algo que impone veneración, algo de celestial' (I, 588a). In *La prueba* he describes her as 'santa' (I, 641b, 652a), 'mártir' (I, 637b, 651b, 652a) and 'rosa mística' (I, 670b). That he is thinking specifically of the traditional legends of the saints is clear from his reference to the 'leyenda cristiana' (I, 637b) and the *Año cristiano* (I, 652a) which, together with *Don Quixote*, was standard reading for Spanish middle-class families in the nineteenth century.[21] However, Salustio's comparison of Carmen to a medieval saint is most explicit in the 'Final', where Carmen responds to the dying Felipe's call with an impetuous and heroic sign of love:

Ella se precipitó al lecho con el rostro transfigurado, con la expresión angelical de la Santa Isabel de Murillo; se desplomó sobre el leproso, murmurando: 'Felipe, alma, corazón mío, si no me voy!' Y sobre aquellos labios, roídos por el asqueroso mal, con una vehemencia que en otra ocasión me hubiese estremecido de rabia hasta los mismos tuétanos, apoyó su boca firme y largamente, y sonó el beso santo . . . (I, 706a)

The kissing of a leper, together with the reference to St Elizabeth, leaves the reader in no doubt as to Salustio's view of Carmen as a saint figure.

This is his biased opinion of the woman he loves, but it is corroborated by her own behaviour. Carmen, in fact, dismisses the description of herself as a saint figure with the argument that, among other things, the saints used to tend people with repulsive diseases (I, 652b). Moreno uses the same argument but with particular reference to lepers (I, 688b–9a). But these disclaimers are present simply to make clear to the reader that Carmen, by tending a leper (as she does at the end of the novel), is indeed a saint.

This leads us to ask why Pardo Bazán should have been so interested in using a hagiographical model in this novel. The question is particularly important because the novelist consistently drew on hagiography in her writing. Apart from *Una cristiana–La prueba* and *San Francisco de Asís*, it is found in *La piedra angular* (1891), *El tesoro de Gastón* (1897), various short stories, particularly *Cuentos sacro-profanos* (1899), *Cuadros religiosos* (1925, but first published 1900–1), *La quimera*

(1905), *La sirena negra* (1908) and *Dulce dueño* (1911).[22] In *Una cristiana–La prueba* it can be accounted for in various ways.

First, the saint figure offered Pardo Bazán interesting psychological material. This emerges from one of the *Cuadros religiosos*, *Santa Teresa, reina*, where the writer implies that one of her tasks in writing about the saints was to 'desentrañar el drama íntimo de su corazón' (II, 1572b). This language strongly resembles Salustio's manner of talking about Carmen. There is also a similarity in the 'drama íntimo' of this particular *cuadro* and that of *Una cristiana–La prueba*. Apart from the fact that St Teresa's obligation to leave her husband is described as 'la prueba' (II, 1574b), there is the general comment Pardo Bazán makes on this category of saints: 'No se desmiente en los santos la condición humana, y acaso interesan más aquellos en quienes observamos la lucha de las pasiones y de la gracia.' (II, 1574a) This conflict between 'pasiones' and 'gracia' is evident in *Una cristiana–La prueba*, where Carmen is intended to be seen not only as a sublime figure but also as a human being (I, 639a).

Secondly, it may be a sign of the influence of the Russian novel. Although this novel as a whole does not have the fervour of a work by, say, Dostoyevsky, in the emphasis laid on suffering as the norm of human life and in the kissing of the leper, Pardo Bazán may have been trying to incorporate into her novel 'la religion de la souffrance' which Vogüé so admired in the Russian novel. This emotional response to suffering is characteristic of popular Russian spirituality. G. P. Fedotov tells us: 'Yet the Russian people hold to the favourite idea of sanctifying suffering. They create saints from pity, showing that pity is one of the strongest roots of their religious life.'[23] Now, some years later, Pardo Bazán compared this aspect of the Russian novel with a painting by Murillo and, by implication, the Spanish Realist tradition: 'Es el naturalismo del pintor español, que hizo vagar las blancas manos de Santa Isabel sobre la tiña y las costras de la cabeza de un mísero, y no infundió repugnancia.'[24] Pardo Bazán seems to be saying that Murillo's picture evokes the same response of pity as the sight of suffering in the Russian novel. The fact that Carmen's face, as she kisses her leprous husband, is compared to the face in the same Murillo suggests that this act too is intended to evoke feelings of pity.

But there appears to be a confusion here in the novelist's mind about the appeal of the lives of the saints. From the outset, and increasingly in her career, it was to their heroism that she was attracted. We find this in, for example, *San Francisco de Asís*, particularly in the chapter 'San Francisco y la mujer', which recounts the stories of various 'heroínas'. In this respect she was following the Western hagiographical tradition of martyr heroes, often young virgins, being torn limb from limb, but bearing their suffering with fortitude. Rivadeneira's *Flos sanctorum*, for example, begins with a hair-raising catalogue of tortures under the title of 'De los tormentos de los martyres'. The intention is to set the 'heroycas virtudes' and 'hazañas tan gloriosas' of the saints at greater relief.[25] The Russian tradition of hagiography, however, places no emphasis on heroism, and martyrs for faith are forgotten. It is the meek sufferer who is canonised.[26]

Now if, as it seems, Pardo Bazán intended through Carmen's ordeal to incorporate into the novel the emotional impact of suffering for religion's sake found in the Russian novel, she clearly fails. Carmen is no meek sufferer. Salustio refers on two occasions to her 'heroísmo' (1, 609a, 698a), and in the final chapters she appears unambiguously as a spiritual heroine. Her sacrifice does not evoke pity because one cannot pity a triumphant hero. My point is that Pardo Bazán's assimilation of this important aspect of the Russian novel is muddled. She seems unaware that 'la religion de la souffrance' and the idea of sanctity which she was perhaps unwittingly taking from it, are completely at odds with her heroic presentation of the saint figure.

However, if the presentation of Carmen's heroism is quite alien to the Russian hagiographical tradition, the challenge which, as a saint figure, she makes to contemporary society is not. This challenge may well be a major reason for Pardo Bazán's interest in hagiography. I am referring to the Russian tradition of the 'holy fool' or the 'fool for Christ's sake', that is a madman or simpleton, feigned or genuine, whose forthright speech and often indecent behaviour, although attributed to his madness, were a cause of scandal to his fellow Christians.[27]

The obvious link between this phenomenon and this novel is the baffling character of the seminarist, Serafín, who in various ways resembles the holy fool. He is a simpleton in that his looks and behaviour are a mixture of the foolish and the infantile. Yet, the nonsensical conversation of this clown or 'naughty monkey' (as he is called) is spiced with such intelligent comments that Salustio wonders whether Serafín is a madman or a cunning rogue (1, 570b). Although no one takes him seriously, he sees through Felipe and Cándida, Carmen's father's mistress (I, 571b), and Galician politicians (I, 591b); but his role as simpleton speaking the truth is most clear during the wedding breakfast when he harangues the politicians present in a violent condemnation of their Liberalism. His harangue ends in an epileptic fit (I, 594ab) and to this extent he is literally mad. He does, then, share several of the characteristics of the holy fool.

Now, it is perfectly true that Pardo Bazán would not have needed to go to Russian spirituality to find this amalgam of holiness and madness, because she was already familiar with the tradition of 'divine folly' in Western Catholic spirituality. Even Spain had its holy fool in St John of God.[28] It is an important element in her biography of St Francis where, for example, the saint informs his brothers in the newly formed order that God has told him to be a fool and to preach the foolishness of the cross.[29]

However, although 'divine folly' is already present in *San Francisco de Asís*, the character of Serafín has none of the sentimental appeal of St Francis and his fellow friars. Serafín bears much more resemblance to the two holy fool figures Pardo Bazán refers to in *La revolución y la novela en Rusia*. The first of these is the main character in Dostoyevsky's novel *The Idiot*, Prince Myshkin. Like Serafín, he is simple and childlike while possessing wisdom. More significantly, he, like Serafín, is an epileptic. St Francis is mad only in a metaphorical sense. Moreover, Pardo Bazán refers to Myshkin as Dostoyevsky's most important character after Raskolnikov in *Crime and Punishment*, and describes him as 'tipo imitado del *Quijote*, enderezador de entuertos, loco, o, mejor dicho, simple sublime' (III, 863a). So it is the holy fool in Myshkin, as described by Vogüé, which she singles out for remark.[30] Soon after this section on *The Idiot*, in a reference to the Franciscan 'madman', Brother Juniper, Pardo Bazán follows Dostoyevsky and describes the friar as 'Fray Junípero el *Idiota*' (III, 866b), thereby associating the Russian and Western traditions of 'divine folly'.

The second holy fool figure referred to in *La revolución* is Grisha, who apears in chapter 5 of Tolstoy's *Childhood Memories*. Grisha, Pardo Bazán says, recounting Tolstoy's description, is 'un vagabundo tuerto y marcado de viruelas, medio idiota, o por mejor decir simple – uno de esos vasos de barro grosero donde, según la literatura rusa contemporánea, gusta de encerrarse la luz divina –' (III, 867b). Again we see the link between madness ('idiota', 'simple') and holiness.

Now, although Serafín is not a sublime figure like Grisha, he does share his surface unattractiveness and childlikeness.

I have discussed Serafín's relations to the holy fool tradition, whether Russian or Western, because I believe his function in the novel is to point to an important element in Carmen's status as a saint figure. She is, in a sense, a holy fool, insofar as her behaviour is considered offensive and even lunatic. She is not, of course a simpleton or outrageous in her behaviour, but her values entirely contradict those of the world round her.

Luis, the representative of progressive common-sense, can see nothing virtuous in Carmen's decision to marry Felipe (1, 609a), and describes her because of her actions as 'rather mad' (1, 636a). The modern reader will no doubt share this reaction. Yet this charge of madness is taken up and fitted into the whole challenge presented by Catholic theology to Rationalist orthodoxy. At the end of the novel Salustio concludes that one can be led only so far by common-sense and reason, that great miracles need love, and sublime deeds madness (1, 700b–1a). Carmen's 'madness', however, differs from Salustio's 'quijotismo' in that it is based not on Romantic illusions, but on the reality of faith (see 1, 694a).

The centrality of this point is emphasised by the way the novel ends with a reference to Luis's marriage, an event which itself points to the bankruptcy of 'commonsensology'. Luis has lost his faith in reason, and, in marrying *Mo*, turns explicitly to 'locura': '"Si es locura . . . ¡mejor! Alguna locura se ha de hacer en la vida [. . .]. Estoy convencido de que los locos la aciertan más que los cuerdos. Nuestro siglo está enfermo de sensatez."' (1, 703a) Luis's reference to 'nuestro siglo' indicates that 'divina locura' is being used here as a critique of contemporary society. Just as the holy fool condemned and even despised the society of his time, so the hagiographical material enables Pardo Bazán to make of her novel a head-on collision with the values of the Rationalism of her own time. It seems to be this collision which was intended to generate power in the novel in a way comparable to the highly controversial views on marriage in Tolstoy's *The Kreutzer Sonata*, which according to Pardo Bazán's own account were the source of power in that novel.[31]

However, I suggest that where Tolstoy succeeded, Pardo Bazán failed. This is because, as I argued above, the reader is invited to see Carmen as a confusing mixture of meek sufferer and triumphant heroine. Another defect is the way Salustio is used as narrator. As we have seen, Carmen is an enigma to him, and in their few unwitnessed encounters she is deliberately uncommunicative. Consequently, the reader is given only Salustio's conjecture about her thoughts and feelings, and has little direct experience of the struggle between passion and grace inside her. Hence she remains a shadowy figure.[32]

Now, a reliable and well-informed narrator is not essential to the success of the first-person narrative technique; indeed, in later novels, notably the *Adán y Eva* cycle and *La sirena negra*, Pardo Bazán was to use the 'unreliable narrator' to great effect. That she was aware of the problems involved in this particular technique is clear from the way she surrounds both Carmen and Salustio with characters and groups of characters who serve to counterbalance the limitations of narrative viewpoint by giving the reader a clear point of comparison. This is why the novel contains so much secondary material. In the case of Carmen, a contrast is made between her and Belén, *Mo*, and the Barrientos sisters, all of whom represent a certain type of womanhood. Belén is the sensual sinner, *Mo* the woman of the future, and the Barrientos sisters typical *cursi* middle-class Spanish girls. To emphasise the contrast the novelist brings these characters in at strategic points. For example, Salustio visits Belén after the humiliating scene where Carmen's heroism is contrasted with his inability to eat at the same table as Felipe; he visits *Mo* and her family at the height of Carmen's ordeal, when she has resumed conjugal relations with Felipe; Camila Barrientos's elopement with her sister's *novio* is placed at the end of the last chapter proper and before the 'Final'. In each case the different women are intended to compare unfavourably with Carmen.

The disadvantage of this device is that it is negative; we learn what Carmen is not, but she herself is not presented as a sufficiently concrete alternative. As a matter of fact, the other women are rather more successful as fictional characters than she. Belén in particular is a lively and engaging personality, whose impetuosity is well drawn in chapters 6 and 18 of *La prueba*. Even *Mo* and the Barrientos sisters, whilst not sympathetic, are at least made interesting by the ironic light in which they are placed. So from an artistic, if not moral, point of view, Carmen compares unfavourably with the very characters whose function it is to set her at relief.

Apart from this failure in narrative technique, there is the failure in the presentment of Carmen's sanctity. Salustio tells us that she is a saint, but this is not shown to be the case in her behaviour. A comparison with the character of Dorothea in *Middlemarch* may help to illustrate this omission. In this novel George Eliot, like Pardo Bazán, set out to create in her protagonist a modern-day saint. The quality which the writer identifies in the novel's 'Prelude' as the distinguishing trait of 'later-born Theresas' is ardour, and this quality is frequently attributed to Dorothea herself. In a comparable way Salustio describes Carmen on a number of occasions (1, 579a, 654b, 664b, 706a) as 'vehemente' (notably in the final scene where she kisses the leper). There is a difference, however, in the fact that we are not simply told that Dorothea is ardent; she is consistently shown to be such. We see it, for example, in her vehement argument with her sister Celia and consequent regret at being too hasty (chapter 1); in that desire to give entirely of herself which leads her foolishly to marry Casaubon (chapters 3 to 10); or in her generous defence of Lydgate when all Middlemarch is against him (chapter 76). Moreover, George Eliot's use of the omniscient third-person narration allows her to take us inside Dorothea's ardent thoughts. So when Ladislaw sees the object of his love as a saint (chapter 22), we are ready on independent evidence to accept his opinion.

This is not the case with *Una cristiana–La prueba*. Apart from Carmen's championing of Cándida in chapter 12 of *La prueba*, we are given little reason for accepting Salustio's description of her as 'vehemente'. On the contrary, her continual concern with propriety and appearance in the question of her feelings towards her husband and Salustio makes her seem timid and conventional. Furthermore, the specifically theological aspect of sanctity, which is not a feature of George Eliot's work but is central to Pardo Bazán's, is not presented directly to the reader. The fundamental change effected by grace in Carmen takes place, as it were, entirely off-stage somewhere between chapters 14 and 17. As Alas has already put it, 'es lástima que la autora no nos haga asistir al *cómo fue* de la victoria del fraile y de la gracia en el espíritu de Carmen Aldoa'.[33]

So although there is an attempt to dramatise the ideological conflict between grace and nature, the novelist's efforts there are largely neutralised because the subject of the experiment intended to test the rival hypotheses is a confused abstraction. How can the reader feel for, share the triumph of, and accept the lesson of a character whom he scarcely knows?

CONCLUSION

From the point of view of technique, *Una cristiana–La prueba* is a transitional novel, in which Pardo Bazán's use of the first-person narration displays little of the assurance evident in the third-person novels of the late 1880s as well as in *La piedra angular*, the novel she was writing at the same time as *Una cristiana–La prueba*. As far as psychology in the novel is concerned, she rarely goes beyond the telling to the dramatising of the inner lives of her characters. This defect may be traced back to the fact that the glorifying of a simple, if stirring, ideal is more important to the novelist than the complexity of human life. She uses the novel to refute the Positivist dogma, only to replace it with another. As a result this explicitly religious novel paradoxically conveys none of the mystery of life that such a secular novel as *Insolación* does. In the last resort it does not convince.

The content of this novel points back to the novels of the 1880s and forward to Pardo Bazán's last three published novels. It shares the earlier novels' pessimism about human life, but also, like the later works, suggests the possibility of privileged individuals, such as Carmen, rising above the human condition. Salustio is not such an individual, yet he pursues Romantic chimeras all the same, and the provisional nature of the peace of mind offered by Moreno could never satisfy his fervent longings. Nor, one feels, could it satisfy those of Pardo Bazán. In *La revolución y la novela en Rusia* she confides: 'Y por mi parte, he de confesar francamente que me son simpáticas las locuras de carácter especulativo, sueños que sueña la humanidad de cuando en cuando para convencerse de que no le basta el bienestar material, de que aspira dolorosamente a algo que jamás alcanzará en la tierra (así creemos los espiritualistas).' (III, 805a) The ambiguity in her attitude towards Romantic idealism possibly explains her failure to discredit Salustio's 'quijotismo' in the body of the novel; one has the impression that she is secretly sympathising with him, if only because the refusal of Moreno and Carmen to admit to the existence of a problem, however good their intentions, may strike the reader as dishonest. The most telling features of the epigraph to this chapter are the admiration contained in the epithet 'gran' ('el gran romántico Don Quijote') and the reservation in the adverb 'acaso' ('Todo el romanticismo es acaso una falsa concepción de la vida').

Such an ambiguity was already present in Pardo Bazán's early novels. For example, the disillusionment of the tragic figure of

87

Artegui in *Un viaje de novios* is typical of *fin-de-siècle* Neo-Romanticism,[34] yet the detached observation of this novel makes it very self-consciously Realist. Another example is *La madre naturaleza*, where Pardo Bazán studies the conflict between Gabriel Pardo's progressive formation and his latent Romanticism, and shows his life to be blighted by disillusionment at the failure of all his dreams. Although we are invited to dissociate ourselves from these characters' view of life, our admiration for them makes it difficult for us to do so. In these two novels the ambiguity is probably as unintended as it is in *Una cristiana–La prueba*, but, as we have seen, in *Insolación* Pardo Bazán gives us a deliberately ambiguous perspective on the affair between Asís and Pacheco, so that we cannot finally decide whether there is an element of idealism in their love or not. This uncertainty is even more apparent in Pardo Bazán's last three novels (*La quimera*, *La sirena negra* and *Dulce dueño*), where she deals with the Decadent characters of Silvio, Clara, Gaspar and Catalina. Her hesitation is most clear in the 'Sinfonía', which precedes *La quimera*: the chimera of foolish illusions is destroyed, but so is all that inspires man's noblest deeds. In these late novels, however, the novelist found a way out of the impasse and resolved the tension between reason and Romanticism by the use, more singleminded than in *Una cristiana–La prueba*, of the ideal of sanctity.[35]

5

La piedra angular

'La santidad [. . .] es patrimonio de pocos.' 'Prólogo en el cielo', *Doña Milagros*, II, 353a

The plot of *La piedra angular* (1891), which is set in Marineda (La Coruña), revolves round a crime: the brutal murder of a man by his wife and her lover. The centres of interest are not however the crime and the criminals but the public executioner, Juan Rojo, and the philanthropic doctor, don Pelayo Moragas. Moragas, an opponent of capital punishment, sets out to understand Rojo, a man universally despised for his profession and abandoned by his wife, and whose son, Telmo, is rejected and mistreated by the *marinedinos*. The doctor's plan is to prevent the execution of the two criminals by persuading Rojo to refuse to do his duty in return for an education for his son. His plan succeeds, but Rojo, having given up his son and now completely alone, drowns himself.

La piedra angular has provoked various reactions. For one it is Naturalist, for another it is Romantic.[1] For Osborne it represents a complete change from the novel Pardo Bazán was writing at the same time, *Una cristiana–La prueba*.[2] In fact, as I shall be arguing, *La piedra angular* is closely related to *Una cristiana–La prueba*, as well as to the two previous novels, *Insolación* and *Morriña*. It has been regarded as Naturalist because of, for example, the descriptions of Rojo's sordid dwelling and the prison. But these descriptions should not be taken in isolation from the book's main concerns. The fact that Rojo is forced because of his profession to live where he does, despite the fact that the majority support capital punishment, is part of the wider comment on people's hypocrisy. As far as the prison scene is concerned, although one cannot doubt the sincerity of the indignation expressed over prison conditions, the main function of the distasteful sights we are shown is to set at relief the obvious non-criminality of the condemned woman as well as Moragas's Romantic plan to save her. In other words, this material is not only or even primarily documentary. In any case, as the novel has no experimental structure, it is not very helpful to describe it as 'Naturalist'.

Nevertheless, although *La piedra angular* is not an 'experimental novel', there is no doubt that Pardo Bazán is anxious to inform her art with science. I am referring to her use of experimental psychology. In chapters 1 and 5 she probably drew on Ribot's *Les maladies de la mémoire* (1881), in the first case to create suspense as Moragas tries to recall the identity of his unknown patient (Rojo), and in the second to provide us with details about Rojo's past life.[3] She also makes use of Fechner's Psychophysics or 'an exact theory of the functionally dependent relations of body and soul, or, more generally, of the material and mental, and the physical and psychological worlds'.[4] Moragas, we are told, lays great store by the phenomena of consciousness and 'those mysterious psychophysical activities which are irreducible to merely physiological processes' (II, 279a). As a doctor, he sees human beings as a 'harmonic whole' and believes that many physical conditions have a psychological cause and vice versa. It is this belief which sets him off on his investigation into Rojo's moral life. It is not surprising, given Pardo Bazán's misgivings about the materialistic psychology drawn on by Zola and even Bourget, that she should be attracted to Psychophysics. She has already made use of it in *Insolación*, where Asís's state of mind affects her physical state in chapter 1 as well as elsewhere in the novel. She also uses it quite frequently in *La piedra angular* when she points to a relationship between moods and physical phenomena (see, for example, II, 301a, 314ab and 335b).

As for the Romantic reading, it is true that at times the novel is highly charged and that the ending is genuinely tragic. But, with the possible exception of Moragas's baby daughter, who is contrasted at strategic points with Rojo's son, none of the characters is idealised, so 'Romantic' is hardly an appropriate description. Moreover, much of the 'exaggeratedly intense'[5] emotion is Moragas's and we are clearly meant to regard it ironically.

The consensus of critical opinion, however, is that *La piedra angular* is a didactic novel, attacking capital punishment, the 'corner-stone' of the title.[6] It is certainly true that Pardo Bazán had firm views on this topical issue and made these clear in print during or just after the composition of *La piedra angular*. But it would be wrong to assume that she wrote this novel in order to propagate her abolitionist views. In fact, she was so alarmed at reports that her new novel was in some way didactic that she went to the trouble of specifically denying them.[7]

But even if she had not taken this (in the event ineffective) precaution, it is hard to see how this novel could be read as a simple attack on capital punishment. As Varela remarks, three separate views on the issue are expressed (Cáñamo's, Febrero's and Moragas's) and the narrator does not unambiguously endorse any of them.[8] One should also notice that although the hardened advocate of capital punishment, Cáñamo, is treated by the narrator with hostility, little attempt is made to place his opponent, Febrero, in a favourable light (his defence of the accused is badly conceived and disastrously executed) and the philanthropist, Moragas, is treated with irony.

What Pardo Bazán is in fact focusing on is not so much the issue of capital punishment, as people's hypocrisy towards it. For example, in the first sentence of chapter 8 the narrator tells of public reaction to the crime, commenting with light but unmistakable irony on its hypocrisy and on the way the story is changed as it goes round the town: 'Despertóse la capital marinedina comentando, rumiando, desfigurando, iba a decir *saboreando*, la noticia del crimen de la Erbeda, si no me pareciese calumnia, porque, realmente, los marinedinos no son tan ávidos de emociones fuertes como los parisienses, y el malsano gusto de la sangre y del cieno les subleva el paladar.' (II, 306b–7a) The narrator is speaking in her own voice, yet makes her point with characteristically teasing elusiveness. There is an element of mockery in the changing sense of the present participles: 'comentando' and 'rumiando' are perfectly straightforward, 'desfigurando' is slightly disapproving, and 'saboreando' introduces a note of censure. So the *marinedinos'* discussions of the crime are little more than an unhealthy dwelling on unpleasant details. But this impression is immediately neutralised by the clause beginning 'si no me pareciese calumnia'. The message is still not clear, however. The second half of the sentence might be taken as approving the fact that the *marinedinos* are not as depraved in their tastes as the Parisians, a point one would think hardly worth making. Alternatively, it may be taken as a comment on a provincial town which is petty even in its vices.

This reticent irony is continued in the way the news of the crime is personified and changes its form as if it had a life quite independent of the event to which it refers: 'Se esparció, rodó, creció, dio mil vueltas, adquirió más formas que un Proteo y tuvo más versiones que la Biblia, el horrendo y memorable crimen de la Erbeda.' (II, 307ab) The irony is sustained in an enumeration of the different versions of the crime ('según unos', 'según otros'), those of the lower classes being more charitable than those of the middle classes. The narrator distances herself from both by using erudite terms: she describes the views of the lower classes as 'la opinión matutina' and those of the middle classes as 'la opinión vespertina', because of the different time of day at which each group congregates. She finally lights on the discussion at the *Casino de la Amistad*, a club for local professional people, again carefully distancing herself by irony: 'La tardecita del estreno del crimen no bajaría de treinta personas el grupo. Era el *grand complet*. Se discutían las versiones, se depuraban, y se iba cristalizando la definitiva, la que ya no se discute.' (II, 308b) The real attitude of the *contertulianos*, despite their moral posturing, is suggested by 'estreno', which makes of the crime little more than an entertainment, and by the discrepancy between the pretentious vocabulary and the triviality of their discussion. Moreover, it is implied that the validity of people's views is not unaffected by their motives for holding them. For example, it is strongly suggested that ambition, not conviction, leads Cáñamo to defend capital punishment (II, 310b).

The sense of public opinion which the novelist is trying to convey is strengthened by references to the press, which confirms the reports of the crime and gives the news of the lovers' arrest in a special midday supplement. After the account of the different comments on the crime, we are told of a press dispatch to Madrid which sums up public feeling: '"Reina verdadera indignación todas clases sociales. Excitados ánimos, coméntanse detalles horribles."' (II, 308a) The parody of a press headline with its typical oversimplification ('todas clases sociales'), and the contrast between 'verdadera indignación' and the impression we have been given in the first sentence of the chapter that 'coméntanse' ought more properly to read 'saboréanse', exposes press hypocrisy.

After the condemnation of the accused, it is again the press which, on behalf of middle-class public opinion, expresses approval for the empty rhetoric of the prosecutor, Nozales, and no sign of sympathy for the condemned (II, 330a). However, the town which was unanimous in its condemnation quickly becomes unanimous in its sympathy when faced with the prospect of an execution:

Hoy, lo mismo que hace cinco meses, hierve Marineda, y en casas, en cafés, en las fuentes y tabernas – que son los casinos y cafés de la plebe – no se habla sino de una mujer y de un hombre ... Mas ¡cómo ha variado el acento con que los nombres de la pareja se pronuncian! ¡Cuán diversas las palabras que

los califican! ¡Qué vuelta tan rápida ha dado la veleta de la voluntad! ¡Qué
inconciliables los impulsos de antes y los de ahora! (II, 340a)

In the light of what has gone before, the list of the different levels of
society in Marineda ('casas', 'cafés', 'fuentes', 'tabernas'), parallel
to that in chapter 8, and the apparent ingenuousness of the
exclamations (which makes the more damaging the irony of 'the
weather-cock of public feeling') point to the superficiality of public
moral indignation. The population look not for justice, but a topic to
savour and be indignant about. Before, it was the criminals and their
appalling crime; now, it is unbending justice and its refusal to grant a
reprieve. Once more the narrator makes the point by focusing on the
press, with its high-minded clichés and readiness to fill its pages with
versified pleas for clemency by local hacks. The reversal of opinion is
complete when Moragas overhears Marineda's chief upholder of
capital punishment, Cáñamo, sending a plea for mercy to the
Minister.[9]

It is as if Pardo Bazán is saying that whatever the rights or wrongs
of the death-penalty, the argument is irredeemably obfuscated by
people's muddle-headedness and bad faith with regard to the issue.
Or, to put it another way, the abstract question of capital punishment
necessarily involves the very concrete and ugly phenomena of
executions and executioners, and people would do well to face up to
that fact.

But capital punishment and attitudes towards it are not in any case
Pardo Bazán's main concern. This emerges from a letter she wrote to
Giner just after publication: 'En mi intención la novela es el verdugo,
no la pena de muerte. Huí sin embargo de insistir en *el individuo*, por
ser él quien es (o era, pues ya murió).'[10] So her concern is not capital
punishment, but the person of the executioner. Yet even the novelist's
stated intention does not quite sum up what this novel is about. As
with *Morriña*, there is a difficulty for the reader in deciding what the
real subject of *La piedra angular* is. Is it, in fact, Juan Rojo? Pardo
Bazán's rather obscure comment suggests that she was aware that she
had not dealt with him as fully as she might have. The difficulty lies in
the fact that Rojo's interest as a character is almost entirely in his past
life, which we are merely told about in chapters 5, 10 and 11. Apart
from his reactions to the *marinedinos'* hostility and his moral dilemma
at the end, his situation is not enacted in the present time of the novel.
He is a thing of the past in the novel as he was in real life when Pardo

93

Bazán was planning the work. Not so Moragas, the model for whom, Ramón Pérez Costales, was a close acquaintance of the novelist.[11] It may be that she was more interested in her doctor and friend than in the distant figure of the executioner. In any case, whatever her intention may have been, the greater part of the novel deals not with Rojo but with Moragas.

Yet, despite the prominence of Moragas, it would be wrong, I think, to describe *him* as the subject of the novel. It seems to me that the central interest is the same as it had been in *Morriña*, that is, not a particular character or set of characters, but the difficulty involved in judging people and evaluating their actions.

We have already seen how Pardo Bazán declines to tell us what we should think about capital punishment. She is equally non-committal throughout the novel. It is true that she quite frequently gives us information about the life and history of Marineda or human nature in general, but such opinions are nearly always uncontroversial (an important exception being her attitude towards Rojo's legalism, which I shall discuss below). When the focus of attention is the action of the novel itself, it is as difficult to pin the narrator down as it is in *Insolación* and *Morriña*. One example of this is our shifting view of Juan Rojo. At first we are invited to regard him with distaste, but as we are given details of the circumstances of his life, this distaste turns to qualified sympathy, until finally he acquires a certain tragic nobility.

He is introduced in the first chapter when he goes to consult Moragas about a liver complaint, and everything in this chapter is directed towards placing him in an unfavourable light. A deliberate contrast is drawn between the innocent vitality of Moragas's young daughter and the shabby, shifty figure of the unknown patient who is ushered into the room. A contrast is also drawn between Moragas's engaging openness and Rojo's cringing defensiveness. The latter, we are told, is like one of those repugnant insects which are always retreating into dark corners (II, 279b). Then our horror on discovering Rojo's identity is heightened by the way the revelation is held back until the end of the chapter. Pardo Bazán does this, as I have already said, by drawing on her knowledge of the psychology of memory.

But having established this negative impression in the reader's mind, the novelist then sets about undermining it. Moragas's reaction to Rojo at the end of chapter 1, when he throws the money Rojo has given him out of the window, is not commented on, and there is no reason for us to dissociate ourselves from his disgust. But in the following chapters Rojo's rejection by the population is made increasingly to seem cruel. In the second chapter we see Rojo's son, Telmo, who, although not the perfect cherub Moragas's daughter is, has a certain roguish charm, and we cannot help feeling for this motherless child who, because his father is the executioner, is admitted neither to the school nor to the company of his peers. In chapter 3 we see him heroically defending himself as the schoolboys stone him. But the narrator still maintains a certain neutrality. The schoolboys' thoughts and actions are reported with hardly a comment, and such comments as there are mitigate their guilt by relating their behaviour to human behaviour in general (II, 286b) or by referring to their qualms of conscience (II, 288b). On the other hand, the narrator distances herself from the obviously sinned-against Telmo by irony (II, 287a). The impression she gives of herself is of an intelligent observer, registering and trying to understand, but never eager to oversimplify with precipitate praise or condemnation.

Chapter 4 takes us back to Rojo as he makes his way slowly home. The picture we are given here of two levels of society does not serve simply to establish a real setting (although it does do that): it also modifies our view of Rojo. Walking down the main street, he encounters a group of notables sitting outside the Casino. He greets them by name but they reply only with murmurs of indignation. Immediately afterwards he comes across a respectable working-class woman with her daughter and the girl recognises him with an exclamation of horror. Now, as this section is told from Rojo's point of view, we are automatically inclined to understand the hurt he suffers. But the narrator does not allow us to identify completely with him: he is slightly drunk and stares insolently at the people outside the Casino. Moreover, his macabre response to the child when he lifts his bony left hand and declares, 'como te libres de la justicia, de mí bien libre estás' (II, 290b), does not endear him to us.

Pardo Bazán holds back the most striking example of Rojo's status as a social pariah, however, until the end of the chapter. Having shown him rejected by both the lower and middle classes, she now shows him scorned by the notorious female drunkard, *La Jarreta*, the lowest of the low. This is one of the few occasions when the narrator does not prevent us from identifying with Rojo. He comes across *La Jarreta* as she lies groaning and cursing, too drunk to move, and approaches her 'solicitously' gently offering to help. But his kindness is rewarded only with a string of insults.

This dual perspective on Rojo, now detached, now sympathetic, continues throughout the novel. In the following chapter (5) his wretchedness at being abandoned by his wife is made clear, but so is his obtuseness at taking a job which was so repugnant to her. In fact, his attitude towards his wife is a clue to his fatal flaw, that is, his legalism or *literalismo*. To establish the importance of such legalism to Pardo Bazán's conception of Rojo one need go no further than the novel's epigraph from St Paul's Epistle to the Romans: '. . . ita ut serviamus in novitate spiritus, et non in vetustate litterae.' For Pardo Bazán, if not for the apostle, these words point to the contrast between two opposed attitudes to life: Rojo's legalism and Moragas's belief in the law of forgiveness.

For Rojo, anything is justified if it is written down in the legal code and, conversely, nothing is justified unless written down (II, 323b–4a). Made morally secure by this principle, he is able to carry out atrocities (such as burning down priests' houses) with a clear conscience, provided his orders are received in writing. By the same token, he rejects charges of 'infamia' and 'vileza' made against him because of his profession, appealing again to the law. He is, he argues, a law-abiding citizen and one, moreover, who fulfils the law more than any other (II, 321b). There can be nothing wrong, then, with killing people if it is within the law.

In this Rojo undoubtedly has logic, at least, on his side and the narrator passes no explicit judgement. However, at the beginning of the section dealing with Telmo (chapter 2), in a rare expression of unambiguous disapproval, she has already made clear how we are intended to evaluate Rojo's legalism. Of Telmo she says: 'De su padre había adquirido la noción escueta y coercitiva del literalismo, de la obediencia a los poderes constituídos, y la practicaba; obedecía sin reverenciar ni temer.' (II, 282b) Telmo obeys his father without understanding the spirit of filial piety. In the same way, his father carries out the law without grasping the fact that the law is an instrument of mercy, designed to protect the welfare of those living in society. This attitude extends beyond the legal issue to other aspects of his life and indeed explains the failure of his marriage. Because of his *literalismo* he regards himself as his wife's owner in a very material sense, a fact which blinds him to her growing coolness towards him: '¡Era su mujer! Le pertenecía a él, a él solo, ¡a Juan Rojo!' (II, 295a) Their married relationship is for him another form of contract with its consequent legal obligations. His profession does not affect the validity of this contract, and it is inconceivable to him that his wife should break it and leave him.

Moragas, on the other hand, does not share Rojo's logical approach to justice. His belief in the law of forgiveness, summed up in the words he addresses to Rojo at the end of chapter 12, places him in the long Christian tradition of casuistry. Despite its popular image as a cynical attempt to justify the breaking of the moral law, casuistry is in theory an approach to moral theology based on the application of general moral principles to the particular circumstances of individual cases. For Moragas moral absolutes or legal codes do not necessarily lead to right judgements. The obvious example of these contrasting attitudes occurs in chapter 16, when Moragas is on his way to see Rojo for the last time. He comes across a group of people surrounding a girl called Orosia, whose wretched condition we have already seen in chapter 4, and who now is dying from the effects of her father's protracted cruelty. This incident is placed where it is, before Moragas's demand that Rojo refrain from carrying out the death-penalty, to sharpen the contrast between the two concepts of justice. For Rojo, justice is to fulfil the letter of the law, and accordingly he invokes the word 'justicia' when resisting Moragas's pressure. Moragas, roused to anger, refers to the corpse of the girl he has just seen and points out that her father, despite having caused her death, is innocent before the law. Moragas's 'spiritual' view of justice is the only aspect of his character which is not treated with irony and there is no doubt that we are intended to share his view and reject Rojo's.

But it should not be thought that the criticism of Rojo's *literalismo* is aimed only at him; it applies equally to those *marinedinos* who condemn him. Towards the end of the novel Rojo goes into a church, kneels for the Rosary and tries to pray. But the women in the church recognise him and point at him with distaste and disapproval (II, 349a). Here, as elsewhere, the narrator takes care to maintain both detachment from and sympathy for the executioner. We know that he is so devoted to the letter of the law that he overlooks its spirit. On the other hand, those who point their fingers at him, unaware of his inner anguish, are at that very moment observing the externals of their religion while forgetting the spirit of mercy and forgiveness which is at its heart. We glimpse here the face of the novelist who became increasingly opposed in the 1890s to religious formalism and fanatical Neo-Catholicism.[12] It is not surprising, then, that Pardo Bazán is concerned not to pass simple judgements on Rojo but to invite us to withhold such judgements and grasp the complexity of this particular human situation.

The same is true, in a rather different way, in the case of Moragas:

whereas with Rojo our detachment becomes tinged with sympathy, with Moragas our sympathy becomes tinged with detachment. In the letter to Giner, quoted above, Pardo Bazán, having said that the real model for Rojo is dead, adds a comment that the model for Moragas is still alive: 'Moragas en cambio existe, y esa mezcla de guasa y filantropía se la he visto emplear. Acaso la verdad no será verosímil, pero es bien verdad todo ello – salvo el final por suicidio, que si no existió para Jorge Meyer (Juan Rojo) acabaría por existir si viviese algo más. Murió de muerte natural.' Here we can see that the ambiguous conception of Moragas was quite conscious and taken from life.

Our initial impression of Moragas is of an attentive father and a conscientious doctor, who informs himself about the latest advances in medical science. The first time we see him, he is reading the latest number of the *Revue de psychiatrie*. His belief in Psychophysics is approved of by the narrator and, as we have seen, put into practice by her. In chapter 6 we learn that his interest in medical research is not only scientific but also imaginative and that he is attracted particularly to those medical questions which involve some metaphysical problem or 'misterio del espíritu', such as hypnotism. We also learn that he has a highly developed imagination or 'fantasía', which in his case takes the form of concerning himself with the lives of others, not out of curiosity but as an expression of his open and generous personality. So when he sees the modest and chaste appearance of the accused woman as she is led off to be questioned, his heart goes out to her. The narrator makes the following comment:

Tenemos o, por mejor decir, tienen las personas del carácter de Moragas, de esos chispazos compasivos que con repentina vehemencia se apoderan del alma. Moragas era lo que en la época de Rousseau se llamó *hombre sensible*, y lo que hoy nuestro endurecimiento nombra, con cierto matiz de desdén, persona impresionable. (II, 300b)

By moving from the first- to the third-personal plural ('tenemos [. . .] tienen') the narrator contrives to give the impression of desiring to be objective, while insinuating that she herself is one of the people 'del carácter de Moragas'. The final phrase, moreover, leaves the narrator's approval of Moragas's 'sparks of compassion' in no doubt. These 'sparks' motivate his actions throughout the novel and lead him frequently from one extreme emotional response to another. This is not always to his credit, but at this stage in the novel we are invited to see it as a thoroughly admirable quality.

Chapter 7, which deals with Moragas's treatment of Rojo's son, gives Pardo Bazán a chance to set out in more detail the mixture of scientist and fantasist in Moragas. As he tries to decide whether to attend to Telmo or not, his moral struggle is informed by his 'half-quixotic, half-philanthropic generosity'. This is presumably the combination of 'filantropía' and 'guasa' that Pardo Bazán had observed in the real model for Moragas. On the one hand, Moragas assumes the role of the modern, enlightened and serious philanthropist, and, on the other, he is absurdly Romantic. He himself describes his Romantic impulses as a 'manía redentorista' and muses that he would have been more at home in the Middle Ages because in the modern age concerning oneself with others' misfortunes is as absurd as don Quixote's knight-errantry (II, 305b). Here we are reminded of the dislike of the Positivist age and the nostalgia for the values of the Christian past found in *Una cristiana–La prueba*. The novelist certainly intends Moragas to be seen as something of a medieval saint, for the way in which his repugnance for Rojo turns to a strange fascination is compared to the vocation of the 'chaste apostle who enters a bawdy-house to convert prostitutes' (II, 305a). Similarly, because of his professional ability to overcome distaste for the most repulsive disease, he is compared to a certain saint who declared that a leper's wounds smell like roses (II, 304b). The parallel with Carmen at the end of *La prueba* is obvious and clearly intended to redound to Moragas's credit. Nevertheless, in this chapter the novelist skilfully sets in motion the process of gradually, though not completely, detaching us from Moragas.

This is done by creating a discrepancy between the reader's and Moragas's reaction to Rojo. The chapter begins with the narrator's sympathetic comments on Rojo's genuine paternal feelings, so that when Moragas looks at him as if he were an 'ugly toad' (II, 304a) and thinks to himself that he is fit only to be crushed like a viper (II, 305b), we cannot share his disgust. Moreover, the comparison of Moragas with a medieval saint is gently deflated at the end of the chapter when he puts a stop to the blessings poured on him by the woman who keeps house for Rojo with a suggestive *piropo*. The ironic contrast is between Moragas the saint and Moragas the man of flesh and blood.

But the novelist's strategy is not to change our perspective on Moragas entirely but to create a double perspective, and this she does by only gradually and partially detaching us from him. Accordingly, in the following chapter, which describes the debate on capital punishment, the hint of irony has all but disappeared. Moragas gains our sympathy both because he is allied with the enlightened and dignified Febrero and also because his opponents, including the fanatical retentionist, Cáñamo, are treated with heavy irony (II, 314a). But immediately in chapter 9 the note of detachment is reintroduced and slightly intensified.

Moragas and Febrero leave the Casino, indignant at the low level of debate. But, although they are allies, their views on capital punishment are not, we learn, identical. Febrero is a Positivist who, eschewing emotion, allows his judgement to be informed only by cool reason. He aspires to be, as he says, a 'thinking iceberg' (II, 317a). His Darwinism leads him to believe that criminals are a throwback to a more primitive stage in man's development and that as individuals they cannot be reformed. So although the death-penalty should be avoided if possible, in some cases it may be necessary. What he is opposed to is the primitive concept of justice as vengeance. Moragas's approach, on the other hand, is informed less by reason than emotion. Febrero picks up rather uncannily, if not improbably, what Moragas has already said of himself in chapter 7. He is a 'redentorista', in that, inspired by emotion and Christian ideas of repentance and redemption, he believes that individuals can be reformed. His opposition to capital punishment is in reality pity for its victim. Moragas insists unapologetically that Febrero is quite wrong to place such emphasis on reason and that without enthusiasm and emotion nothing can be achieved. The younger generation, to which Febrero belongs, is cold, contained, and is not prepared to expose itself to ridicule ('ponerse en ridículo'): it is the *quijotismo* or *redentorismo* of such as him that will bring about change.

Although the narrator does not commit herself to either of these points of view, her treatment of Febrero is slightly hostile. He tends to be supercilious about the *marinedinos* (II, 314b) as well as pedantic (when, for example, he uses the German word *werden* for no obvious good reason), so we are more likely to side with Moragas's less logical but more human approach.

But in fact both of them are seen in an ironical light because of the rather theatrical setting and atmosphere their conversation is given. The moon and evening star are described with Romantic imagery (II, 314b), and references to the calm, magical sea punctuate their comments on various occasions. For example, as Moragas opens his heart to Febrero, he stops, enchanted by the sight of the bay, 'cuya

magia le parecía mayor en aquel instante' (II, 315a). Although the .
narrator is characteristically elusive, it is clear from this example and
others that the Romanticism of the setting does not express her
feelings but those of Febrero and especially of Moragas, and is
intended to be ironic. Indeed, once one gets beneath the substance of
the men's discussion to its presentation, one encounters several
touches of irony. The exaggerated air of conspiracy which surrounds
them as they seek solitude on the jetty and as Moragas whispers to
Febrero 'although nobody could hear them' (II, 315b) arouses our
suspicions. Particularly suspect is this sentence: 'Y se internaron, se
internaron, cual si al avanzar por aquel camino que, señalando la
dirección del Océano, no conducía sino a una luz roja, adelantasen
por el fatigoso y desierto vía crucis del consabido progreso.' (II, 315b)
The overdramatic effect of the repeated main verb suggests a satirical
intention on the narrator's part, and the likening of the jetty to 'the
hard and lonely calvary of progress' seems by its very overstatement
to mock the men's pretensions as apostles of progress.

Having warned us of the element of self-dramatisation in
Moragas's otherwise good intentions, the novelist takes us to the
novel's central section (chapters 10 to 12), where Moragas conceives
and begins to put into effect his plan to save the murderers from the
garrotte and to 'redeem' Rojo and his son. The motive for Moragas's
visit to Rojo is to treat his son but, having examined the boy, he then
proceeds to his more serious purpose, his 'auscultación moral' or
investigation into Rojo's life. He intends to discover the chain of
events which led to Rojo's becoming a public executioner in order to
judge whether or not he is 'redeemable'. The novelist conveys the
ruthless skill of Moragas's interrogation with insistent surgical
imagery, such as 'cortando intrépidamente por lo sano' (II, 320a) or
'por ahí el bisturí; por ahí el termo cauterio' (II, 325a). Little by little,
he extracts the information he wants until 'with superhuman
strength' he obtains Rojo's submission to his will. So the process of
Moragas's comprehending and mastery of his patient is complete and
his success as a psychologist has been demonstrated.

But how is the reader to react to this victory? Is he to stand beside
Moragas, share his excitement as he uncovers the secrets of Rojo's life,
and approve of his tactics? As a simple matter of fact it is impossible
for him to share the doctor's excitement, because he has already been
given most of the information in the account of Rojo's memory
processes in chapter 5. This invests passages such as the following with

a certain melodrama: 'No podía Moragas adivinar qué clase de cadáver dormía en el fondo, pero lo presentía allá, muy abajo, en los últimos senos de un pozo de ignominia, vergüenza y desesperación humana.' (II, 327a) The reader already knows the nature of the 'corpse' and is unlikely to regard Moragas's anticipation and penetrating gaze with anything but amused detachment. Furthermore, it is difficult for the reader to approve of Moragas's ruthless tactics because he cannot easily share his scorn for Rojo. The novelist takes care here and in earlier chapters to create sympathy (even if qualified) for Rojo, which at this point dissociates the reader from Moragas.

Apart from this, although there is no doubting the sincerity of Moragas's philanthropic purpose, his motives are not unmixed, as can be seen in the following passage:

Empezaba a sentir Moragas la generosa fiebre, el ansia de bajar a los infiernos para sacar de ellos un alma . . . , y algo también el gustillo de mostrarle a Febrero que en todo fango, en la ciénaga más inmunda y vil, hay una perla que a fuerza de bondad y de abnegación se encuentra, si se busca bien. (II, 321a)

So there exists in his noble redemptive purpose a puerile desire ('gustillo') to prove Febrero's pessimism about human nature wrong.

Moreover, as this episode progresses, we become increasingly aware of Moragas's delight in his role as 'lay apostle'. For example:

El apóstol laico no quería renunciar a la romántica obra de misericordia. (II, 326b)

El propósito le infundió singular animación y hasta alegría. Aquélla sí que era hazaña bonita, verdadera redención. ¡Salvar una existencia y dignificar un alma! (II, 327b)

The *style indirect libre* in the second quotation conveys Moragas's ingenuous self-satisfaction, and the adjectives 'romántica' and 'bonita', which have similar connotations here, point to the element of self-indulgence in his campaign of redemption. The vanity which is mingled with his genuine feeling is also evident in the way he compares himself to the local priests: ' ¡Ah, si el padre Incienso y el padre Fervorín sintiesen estos pujos redentores que siento yo!' (II, 327a)

Finally, his tactics in mastering Rojo are not above reproach. In fact they are a parody of the worst kind of conversion situation: he humiliates Rojo, induces him to confess his guilt and then offers salvation. And he is not averse to blackmail, because he threatens (unprofessionally) to withhold treatment from Rojo's son if the executioner does not admit that his profession degrades the boy.

In any case, the narrator's irony warns us against taking Moragas's philanthropy or *redentorismo* too seriously. Early in this episode, when Rojo stretches out his hands in gratitude, the doctor feels a repugnance towards him: 'Moragas [...], redentorista y todo, se echó atrás prontamente.' (II, 321a) The gentle irony contained in the phrase 'redentorista y todo' is echoed in Moragas's melodramatic behaviour after he has extracted Rojo's confession: 'Moragas llegó a él, y casi a su oído murmuró, tuteándole por repentina inspiración de su retórica de apóstol: —Yo puedo salvar a tu hijo . . .' (II, 328a) We are left at the end of this long episode, then, with a view of Moragas as being fundamentally on the side of the angels, but also rather cruel and self-indulgent.

The extent to which he falls short of his view of himself as 'lay apostle' is made clear in the following chapter (13). The intense fervour of the previous episode is contrasted with the fact that his philanthropic campaign soon loses momentum when domestic matters, such as summer holidays and his daughter's illness, begin to preoccupy him. The point is tersely made when, rationalising his faint-heartedness, he decides that 'para iniciar la campaña re-dentorista . . . mejor a principios de invierno' (II, 329b). The narrator comments on his inability either to carry out his plan to give Rojo's son an education or to quieten his conscience:

El estado moral de don Pelayo lo conocen y padecen todos cuantos hombres, sin llegar a justos, perfectos ni santos, pueden llamarse buenos, sensibles y altruístas. El santo no sufre: cumple sin temor: su voluntad es de una pieza. El bueno . . . cumple o no cumple, pero siempre le sangra la herida de la piedad. (II, 329b)

Moragas is a good man, but not of the stuff that saints are made of.

The trial takes place, and the man and the woman are condemned to death. But Moragas does nothing, and we are told that it is simply the sunny weather and sudden sympathy for Febrero that makes him accept his friend's invitation to visit the condemned woman in prison (II, 332ab). During this visit we see his *quijotismo* in a more positive light. He feels pity for the simple, frightened woman, takes her hand, and, in a tone of ardour and absolute certainty, assures her that she will not die. Warmth returns to her body and eyes and she is consoled. He has achieved what Febrero was incapable of. Yet he has spoken on impulse and has no grounds for giving her the promise he does:

No se daba don Pelayo cuenta exacta de lo que decía; no hablaba su razón, sino su voluntad, algo que le traía a la boca frases imprudentes de esperanza y consuelo. ¿Cómo podía él impedir que aquella mujer pereciese en el patíbulo? ¿Como? . . . 'Pues no se me antoja que muera. Moraguitas, esta partida hay que ganarla . . . ¡Vergüenza para ti si no la ganases! . . .' (II, 335b)

Again we see the combination of generous intentions and self-indulgent wilfulness.

However, he now finally takes positive action and formulates his plan. He will save the woman's life by striking a bargain with Rojo: if the latter agrees not to carry out the execution, Moragas will give his son an education. Sure of the success of his plan he savours all the frantic efforts of those seeking a reprieve for the condemned prisoners and takes an enormous pride in the fact that he alone can prevent the execution: 'Y una esperanza loca y sin límites, un orgullo delicioso en que flotaba su espíritu como al caer en el éter azul, le incitaron a volverse y mirar, desde la altura, a Marineda tendida a sus pies.' (II, 341b) Here, in what is possibly a parody of the temptations of Christ in the wilderness, Moragas is taken up to a high place and looks down imperiously on Marineda. The peninsula, with its two bays, appears to him like the body of a beautiful damsel whom he promises to save from the distressing spectacle of an execution. So the allusion to don Quixote reappears by implication: he is noble, but suffering from delusions of grandeur.

The effect of the final chapter depends very much on this ambivalent presentation of Moragas. One cannot doubt that his plan is well-meant and cleverly conceived, yet there is something particularly cruel in the way he carries it out, despite the compassion he shows in trying to ease the pain from the wounds he has inflicted. The surgical imagery reappears as he forces Rojo to give up his son by pointing out that in the end shame will drive the boy away as it had his mother. Almost sadistically he sets up a situation where Telmo, offered the possibility of living with Moragas, rejects his father to his face. Moragas, carried away by his role as 'lay apostle', seems deliberately to ignore the hopelessness of Rojo's plight in order not to detract from the success of his 'campaña redentorista'. At one point he speaks to Rojo as if he were granting absolution: '"Ya está redimido su hijo de usted . . . , y usted también, por añadidura. Quedará lavada con esa acción toda la infamia anterior."' (II, 344a)

The suggestion of 'for good measure' in the phrase 'por añadidura' cleverly conveys the narrator's indulgent mockery. Emphasis is again placed on Moragas's self-satisfaction (even megalomania) when he finally leaves Rojo's home taking Telmo with him: 'El filántropo sonreía: orgullo inefable dilataba su corazón; sus pulmones bebían la brisa salitrosa; sus pasos eran elásticos, iguales; no tropezaba en las piedras; creía volar. Más poderoso que el jefe del estado, acababa de indultar a dos seres humanos y de regenerar a otros dos.' (II, 346ab) In the light of the final suicide, the irony of 'el filántropo' and 'y de regenerar a otros dos' is unmistakable. Moragas is, then, as we saw above, a shrewd psychologist and a successful tactician, yet the situation in the end eludes his grasp. The implication is that human beings are too complex to be comprehended and organised and that, despite his undoubted goodness, there is something less than human in Moragas's philanthropy. Rojo asserts his independence, and indeed his dignity, by fulfilling his part of the bargain while refusing to accept regeneration on Moragas's terms. Pattison's view is that 'Rojo's sense of duty [. . .] is so strong that, rather than simply refusing his task, he drowns himself'.[13] This is surely an oversimplification; by the end of the last chapter, where his son's empty bed sums up for him the emptiness of his life, it is clear that Rojo has nothing left to live for. The problem of doing his duty is real, but as important a motive for the suicide is the impossibility of a life without the affection of his son. So the novel ends with the surprising situation of Rojo's having greater moral authority than Moragas. The *verdugo*, the lowest of the low, becomes a tragic figure, while Moragas, the doctor and philanthropist, seems obtuse and slightly comic.

CONCLUSION

Between *Insolación*, *Morriña*, *Una cristiana–La prueba* and *La piedra angular* there is a firm continuity of concerns. As in *Insolación* and *Morriña* we encounter in *La piedra angular* an elusive third-person narrator whose function is to make us aware of the complexity of her character's motives without offering definitive judgements. More specifically, one can see in Moragas a more developed version of doña Aurora in *Morriña*, with her plan to 'redeem' Esclavitud and her mixed motives for wanting to do this. *La piedra angular* looks back to *Una cristiana–La prueba* in various ways. Moragas shares Salustio's latent Romanticism and inherited Christian responses. Like Carmen,

he is compared to a saint, but whereas in her case the comparison is
serious and is rejected by her, in his case it is burlesque and readily
accepted by him. He is almost a parody of her, except that he is
treated too fully and sympathetically to be viewed in a true satirical
light.

As a psychological study, Moragas is far more successful than either
Salustio or Carmen. Like Salustio, he is contradictory: rational yet
quixotic, megalomaniac yet compassionate. But his character has
none of the incoherence which blights that of Salustio. As a burlesque
of a saint, he is much more convincing than Carmen is as the real
thing, if only because the psychology of a saint *manqué* is more
accessible than that of a genuine saint. Carmen is taken straight from
the pages of the *Año cristiano*; Moragas, in a very literal sense, is taken
from real life.

A more important explanation of the superiority of Moragas as a
fictional character is to be found in the narrative method. By using the
third-person technique Pardo Bazán avoided the problem of delegating the narration which so troubled her in *Una cristiana–La prueba*.
Speaking in her own voice, or at least a voice assumed for the purposes
of the novel, she is able to introduce the reader directly to the secrets of
her characters' thoughts and feelings. This she does with a discreet
irony which, in the case of Moragas, lays bare the mixed motives
behind the finest actions. Yet she is not exactly, in Flaubert's words,
'comme Dieu dans l'univers, présent partout, et visible nulle part';[14]
at times, especially in the later part of the novel, she drops her mask of
detachment to reveal her qualified sympathy for Moragas and her
emotional involvement in a 'spiritual' view of justice. This willing-
ness to make herself 'visible' is the mainspring of a considerable
warmth in the novel which tempers the cool detachment of the
impartial observer. This combination represents a step forward from
Insolación and *Morriña* and, for me at least, indicates the maturity of
vision which reappears in the *Adán y Eva* cycle. There is little which is
hostile or aloof in Pardo Bazán's neutrality; on the contrary she gives
the impression of wanting to understand the spirit of a human
situation with sufficient clarity to be able to distinguish betwen
appropriate and inappropriate objects of commitment. In the way
she narrates her novel, then, she practises what she preaches in the
novel, and form and content fuse impressively. This alone should
convince us that *La piedra angular* has real qualities which have not
been recognised, and that the novel scarcely deserves the oblivion to
which it has been relegated.

6

Doña Milagros[1]

'En el amor, como en todo sentimiento cardinal, hay variada y riquísima escala de matices, capaces de interesar en el arte, si con arte se presentan.'
Nuevo teatro crítico, no. 24 (December 1892), 80

'Nada eleva el espíritu como el amor.' *Cartas a Galdós*, p. 17

Like Pardo Bazán's two previous novels, *Doña Milagros* is a psychological novel set in Galicia (in this case Marineda), and like *Una cristiana–La prueba* it is told in the first person. Benicio Neira, a gentle, weak-willed man, is married to the domineering Ilduara (Ilda for short). To their family of nine daughters and one son are added, after a gap of five years, twin girls. Ilduara develops a strong antipathy to their neighbour, doña Milagros, whose help she regards as an intolerable interference. After a stormy scene involving Milagros Ilduara suffers an attack from which she dies. The rest of the novel deals with Benicio's ineffectual attempts to cope with his financial and family problems. His one comfort is the chaste affection of Milagros, whose honour he upholds in the face of calumny. However, on hearing a particularly plausible piece of gossip, he breaks with her, only to be reconciled when Milagros defends her honour, as he sees it, from an attack on the part of her house-servant. When Milagros moves with her husband to Barcelona, Benicio, in a Romantic gesture, expresses his devotion by presenting her with his baby twins.

Doña Milagros is the first of a cycle of novels, the title of which, *Adán y Eva*, indicates the general theme of the attraction of the sexes. Needless to say, this was no new theme, but it was particularly topical in an age influenced by Schopenhauer's view of sexual instinct as destructive of individual happiness or aspirations.[2] His pessimism is certainly present in the affair between Benicio's daughter Tula and a house-painter, and in the unhappy marriage between Benicio and Ilduara. But it is only one element: in this cycle Pardo Bazán is more interested in exploring sophisticated forms of relationships between the sexes, and individual psychological reactions within them. In this chapter I shall examine Pardo Bazán's use of the first-person narration and then the novel's psychological interest.

THE FIRST-PERSON NARRATIVE METHOD

Like *Una cristiana–La prueba, Doña Milagros* is a fictional memoir. The epic situation is established in the prologue ('Prólogo en el cielo'), where Benicio is told at the gates of heaven that for his sins (an ironic comment by the novelist on her chosen profession?) he is to write the story of his life in novel form, for the good of some of his fellow men. It is, at least in appearance, therefore, an exemplary tale which has the form of a confession and sometimes of an apologia to the reader. The confession begins at baptism and ends with the narrator in his prime (or beyond), but in fact is never completed because his friend Mauro Pareja takes over the narration in the other novel in the cycle, *Memorias de un solterón*. This transfer means, curiously enough, that Benicio does not touch on the murder of his daughter's seducer Mejía, which is his greatest sin. Although the novel covers some forty or fifty years, it centres on a fairly short period beginning with Ilda's final pregnancy (announced at the end of chapter 1), so it is really the story of Benicio's relationship with Milagros.

The moment of composition of Benicio's account is some time after the events described, although we do not know exactly how long until the end of *Memorias de un solterón*. However, like Salustio, Benicio does not bring to his story any great measure of hindsight. The solemnity of the epic situation leaves us in no doubt as to his total honesty (the prologue emphasises this with his comic scrupulousness in admitting having written letters to local newspapers). Yet total honesty does not imply total perspicacity. An obvious illustration of this is his attitude to his daughter Feíta. He mocks her feminism in a way the nineteenth-century reader might be expected to sympathise with, but her intelligence, practicality and strength of character (shown, for example, in her care for the new-born twins), together with the fact that her views are always vindicated, suggest that we are not intended to agree with him. Benicio's unreliability as a narrator, however, contributes greatly to the rush of events which gives the second half of the narrative its peculiar energy. There is no sense of Benicio being in control of his story and, although he is ostensibly telling it in retrospect, each episode is recounted with a reaction of surprise which gives the impression of 'instantaneous description'.[3] Events escape his attention and he frequently learns from others things he ought by right to be the first to know. For example, he first learns about the sexual basis of Argos's religious devotion from Milagros (chapter 10), about Clara's decision to become a nun from Fr Incienso (chapter

11), about the gossip surrounding Milagros from Mauro Pareja (chapter 12), about his children's extravagance (chapter 13) and the disorder in his household (chapter 15) from Feíta. His general ignorance of events taking place under his very nose invests his brave reaction to Sobrado's suspected philandering (chapter 8) with considerable irony: 'A mí probablemente me tenía por un memo, un alma de Dios, a quien le pasan las cosas por delante de los ojos sin que se entere.' (II, 395b)

I suggested in my discussion of *Una cristiana–La prueba* that in the major problem of delegating the narration to the narrator Pardo Bazán failed. In *Doña Milagros* she seems much more aware of the difficulty, and in fact alludes to it in the prologue. The hero, alarmed at the prospect of writing a novel, protests that he has never aspired to literary glory and complains to his angelic son that he would not know where to begin. The *angelito* explains: '"Tú no tienes que escribir la novela. Basta con que la inspires. Yo te llevo a casa de un novelista de profesión [Pardo Bazán, as it turns out]; te acercas a su oído y susurras: 'Mire usted: cuando vivía hice esto, aquello y lo otro; pensé así, sentí asado . . .' Y basta. El se encargará del resto."' (II, 354b) So the novelist, according to the fictional device, is a ghost-writer, putting Benicio's memoirs into novel form. Pardo Bazán is of course pointing to the absurdity of novelistic conventions. Such irony is present in the novel itself when Benicio describes something he admits he could not see (the look of scorn on Fr Incienso's face – II, 408a) and describes in chapter 17 a private conversation between the local *beatas* which he could not possibly have witnessed. Behind this Galdosian narrative irony lies the serious point of the tension between novelist and narrator. It is as if Pardo Bazán is indulging herself on these occasions to compensate for her strict self-discipline elsewhere.[4]

The tension is most apparent in descriptive passages such as the *Soledad* procession in chapter 17. Pardo Bazán's problem is not to give a description consistent with Benicio's probable powers of expression, but to present such an immediate picture that when Benicio tells us that the image of the Virgin was 'touching' we can understand why. Unlike similar descriptive passages in *Una cristiana–La prueba*, the description does not jar because, at its position in the novel, it forms an emotional climax (the completion of the Argos story) and is clearly focused on Benicio's feelings as he watches his daughters, particularly Argos, in the procession. In other words, the novelist conceals her presence by diverting attention away from herself.[5]

Apart from this, the process of concealment is much simpler in

Doña Milagros than in *Una cristiana—La prueba* because the narrator has been established much more strongly as an individual distinct from the novelist. In the first place, Benicio impresses himself on the reader by the modesty with which he presents his material. The very decision to name his autobiography *Doña Milagros* rather than, for example, *Memorias de un casado*, is a measure of his characteristic modesty.

This modesty is clear from the opening chapter where Benicio introduces himself. He admits that the values he has inherited from his mother hardly equip him for the modern world and while attempting to explain the development of his personality he makes no claim to particular wisdom. Later in the same chapter he alludes to an ingrained sense of his noble birth without wanting to deceive the reader into thinking too highly of his personality. Another example can be found in the following chapter where Benicio counts himself among the 'poor devils' or mediocre types who 'ni se pueden solazar con las grandes concepciones del arte ni chapuzarse hasta la coronilla en las hondas corrientes de la ciencia, y tampoco han de buscar en el trabajo manual la fatiga que trae la sedación del sueño' (II, 364b). Apart from the modest intention of this remark, the conversational tone ('pobres diablos' and 'chapuzarse hasta la coronilla') reinforces our impression of Benicio's lack of pretensions. At times he is diffident about his own qualities, rather like a child addressing an adult. For example, the discrepancy between the seriousness conveyed by the syntax of the following sentence (the parenthesis and progression of preterites) and the triviality of the offence confessed: 'Este punto era . . . convengo en la puerilidad del caso . . . que yo no quise, no pude, no supe acostumbrarme al pan marinedino.' (II, 364a) Elsewhere Benicio addresses the reader in a conspiratorial manner: 'Ilduara [. . .] (la sinceridad me obliga a no omitirlo . . . , pero no lo repitan ustedes), ¡me puso . . . , me puso en la faz la mano . . . !' (II, 379b) Benicio's modesty and diffidence, then, is one of the ways in which he is rendered credible as a narrator separate from the novelist.

Another factor is the care taken to make his range of interests consistent with his position established in the opening chapter, that is, as an educated man but not an intellectual. For example, the information contained in generalising formulas, which is so out of place in Salustio's mouth, is more acceptable in Benicio's. It is sometimes perfectly ordinary information such as 'one of those old windows which are like deep niches' (II, 358a), or 'many of those

officious types who abound' (II, 392b). But even when these formulas
contain more profound reflections on life (for example, 'that
indifference with which men treat women who do not excite their
unhealthy curiosity' – II, 370a), they do not jar on the reader because
he knows Benicio to be a man in his prime, who, although naive, is not
unintelligent.

Benicio's independent presence is further reinforced by the device
of making him address the reader directly. This creates an increasingly intimate relationship between narrator and reader. The direct
address is used for the first time in the conspiratorial passage quoted
above. On the second occasion it appears its purpose is to involve the
reader in the narration to such an extent that he readily feels able to
predict the way things will turn out: 'Las únicas personas a quienes yo
enteraba de la marcha de los asuntos domésticos fueron – ya lo
supondrás lector – doña Milagros y Feíta.' (II, 390b) The reader has
been taken into Benicio's confidence and can therefore understand his
situation. 'Put yourself in my position, intransigent reader', he
beseeches in chapter 14. In chapter 18 the reader's status as both
judge and confidant is taken for granted: 'Lo único que me
preocupaba en tales momentos era la señora. ¿Lo he de confesar? Sí,
porque ya sé que tú, lector, en el curso de esta historia, habrás
encontrado toda clase de defectos que ponerme . . . , excepto el de
duro e inhumano.' (II, 441b) Finally, on the last page of the novel,
Benicio finds it unnecessary to give the reader any information at all,
so well do they understand one another: 'Si en Marineda armó
alboroto el que se llevase a mis dos niñas doña Milagros, lo dejo a tu
penetración, amigo que esto lees.' (II, 446b) In this way the novelist
conceals her presence by strengthening the reader's impression that
the story is being related directly by Benicio.

Here then are some strategies Pardo Bazán adopts to hand the
narration over to Benicio. The discussion of these strategies has
inevitably led me to consider the question of the language he uses.
The progression 'no quise, no pude, no supe', for example, places his
timorousness, as well as his childlike seriousness. The problem for
Pardo Bazán the ghost-writer is to give her client a voice of his own
while at the same time producing a well-constructed novel by her own
standards. She copes with the problem in various ways.

In telling his story Benecio has recourse fairly frequently to imagery
which not only underlines the point he is making but, in its very
ordinariness, strikes the reader as characteristic. For example:

Me quedé dormido como una marmota. (II, 432b)

Con los nervios como cuerdas de guitarra. (II, 428a)

Salió de casa como un cohete. (II, 425a)

But although Benicio's imagery is nearly always concrete and unpretentious, it is not always so conventional. He shows himself to be inventive within the limits of his experience. At times the comparisons are unexceptional but pointed, particularly when they refer to his wife:

Contemplándola después de su doble parto, me asustó: parecía un cirio. (II, 375a)

Mi mujer se retorcía como pisada culebra. (II, 376a)

El rostro de mi esposa se puso del color de los tomates maduros. (II, 378a)

At other times they are picturesque:

—Nadie se los ha pedido—contestaba Ilda con acento que parecía el ruido de un ascua encendida al caer en el agua. (II, 371b)

Podríase comparar a mi Ilduara con un corsé emballenado y recio, que si se oprime, sostiene. (II, 386a)

The narrator speaks as a family man unashamedly domesticated to an unusual degree, but although the domestic details he draws on are ordinary enough, the use he makes of them indicates a certain sensitivity: he is not just a henpecked husband. This is underscored by the appearance of more sensuous images. For example, he reflects on existence in these terms: 'Hay días – muy contados, es cierto – que parecen tejidos con hilos de luz; en otros diríase que la trama de la vida se enreda y se afea y adquiere negruras de fúnebre crespón Aquél era de estos últimos. ¡Qué día, viven los cielos!' (II, 419b) The delicacy of expression suggests to the reader that although Benicio may be an 'inocente' he is not lacking in sensitivity. This is not an error on the part of the novelist: as we shall see below, the Romantic side of Benicio's personality is essential to the novel, and this particular image of light and darkness is used on several occasions to convey his idealisation of Milagros in opposition to his unhappy relationship with his wife.

Another feature of Benicio's personal language is his continual use of apostrophes and exclamations. The first example is found at the end of the first chapter, when he discovers that Ilda is again pregnant 'Pero ¿es posible, ¡oh Providencia dadivosa!, más bien derrochadora

¡La cuna, la cuna otra vez!' (II, 362a) The rhetorical question, apostrophe and exclamation set the tone for Benicio's reactions of overearnestness and ingenuous surprise, as he finds himself unable to cope with what seems to be an unceasing rush of events.

His excessive earnestness is made plain by a series of solemn apostrophes, the first of which (' ¡oh Providencia dadivosa!') has just been quoted. Other examples include:

¡Oh nombre dulce entre todos [libertad] qué musica misteriosa encerrarán tus tres sílabas, para que así hechices nuestra alma! (II, 364b)

¡Oh caros contertulios, cuánto os ha debido de consuelo mi atribulado espíritu durante los momentos de angustia que sobran en este valle de lágrimas! (II, 365b)

But the most notable example is at the beginning of chapter 13 where the God of all creation is invoked seven times before the rhetoric dissolves into the ironic anti-climax of Benicio's rather pathetic, yet all too understandable, question: ' ¡Oh Dios, autor nuestro! [...] ¿por qué divides a la Humanidad en dos sexos?' (II, 416a)

Hardly less frequent is Benicio's use of exclamations,[6] of which the following are but a few:

¡Ay! ¡Qué desplumado se iba quedando el aguilucho aquel de nuestro blasón! (II, 363b)

¡Qué descansado me quedaba después, y con cuánto alivio subía las escaleras de mi casa! (II, 365b)

¡Qué lenguaje, Dios mío, y cuánto sufrí al escucharlo! (II, 381a)

The accumulation of apostrophes and exclamations conveys not only his ingenuousness and inability to cope with circumstances, but also an emotional personality which sets him apart from the blasé men-of-the-world he associates with in the Sociedad de Amigos. Benicio's voice, then, not only corresponds to his own description of himself in the first chapter, but also contributes largely to his characterisation.

In *Doña Milagros* the problems involved in the first-person narration are dealt with much more successfully than in *Una cristiana–La prueba*. Benicio is a narrator who presents his story throughout with a consistent voice and from a consistent viewpoint. Moreover, the choice of a narrator who is not wholly wise and does not foresee or fully understand events is a source of great energy and irony. As a result the novel has a life and freshness completely absent from *Una cristiana–La prueba*.

Pardo Bazán's continuing interest in psychology is evident in a little-known work published in 1896, *Hombres y mujeres de antaño*.[7] This is a series of psychological studies in the manner of Bourget, who is referred to on p. 164 of the collection. For our purposes these studies are interesting because there is a clear relationship between some of them and the characters in *Doña Milagros*, and between the psychological typology in each. In Philip IV and Sor María Jesús de Agreda there is an inversion of the normal psychological characteristics of the sexes comparable to that in Benicio and Ilda. The king is weak ('blando') while the nun is strong and manly ('varonil'). The portrait of Juana la loca strongly resembles that of Benicio's daughter Argos in this novel (I note below that Argos is compared to Pradilla's picture of doña Juana). Pardo Bazán tells us that doña Juana had that passionate devotion to music usually to be found in 'las almas apasionadas y líricas' (p. 120). The last clause illustrates well the way in which Pardo Bazán sees people as psychological types. Juana, like Argos, is an 'alma apasionada y lírica' and both share a passionate love of music. In addition doña Juana's reaction to the death of her husband is very similar to Argos's reaction to the death of her mother. Doña Juana, we are told 'no hizo extremos ni derramó una sola lágrima. Calma traidora, que, como la del mar en el último viaje, ocultaba la resaca y la impetuosa corriente. [. . .] Poco tardó en estallarse la tormenta. Pasado el período de estupor, despertóse Juana; su primer impulso fué el natural: abrazarse con el cadáver, cubrirlo de apasionados besos . . .' (p. 135) A similar sea image is applied to Argos in a parallel situation (as I shall point out below), but here the similarity ends, because Argos recovers from the trauma (only to fall, of course, into another strange psychological state), whereas doña Juana does not. Nevertheless the extreme, impassioned reaction they share places them in the same psychological category. In the following section I shall attempt to differentiate between Pardo Bazán's success and failure in making psychological types into novelistic characters.

The initial psychological interest of *Doña Milagros* lies in the contrast between the externals of a social situation and its inner reality. As a contemporary critic said, 'la historia de D. Benicio Neira [. . .] no puede ser más vulgar',[8] but beneath the surface of ordinary middle-class family life, there is drama hidden. This approach to psychological analysis is clearly similar to that in *Una cristiana–La prueba* and *La piedra angular*. The novelist's interest centres on three characters, Argos, Benicio and Milagros, each of whom I shall discuss in turn.

The character of Argos shows a conscious importation of specialised medical knowledge to account for a certain manifestation of sexual instinct, that is, hysteria resulting from repressed sexuality in a particularly emotional person. The death of Argos's mother – the event which sets the main part of the novel in action – precipitates a crisis in her. Having already been told of her 'expressive and dramatic character' (II, 362b) in chapter 2, we are shown in chapter 6 and thereafter how such a personality reacts to a traumatic event. The process is dramatised by two crises: the first, a rapid one, following immediately after the mother's death, ends in the scene with the corpse, while the second is the slow process of Argos's religious mania as an expression of her infatuation with Fr Incienso.

That Pardo Bazán was drawing on specifically medical inform-ation is clear both from the description of Argos's symptoms and from the discussion of them by Milagros, Fr Incienso and Moragas. Indeed, Moragas's model, Pardo Bazán's doctor, Ramón Pérez Costales, may have been the novelist's source for such information. Argos's convulsion after her mother's death is described thus: 'Argos se dislocaba, se descoyuntaba, formando su cuerpo arco vibrador, como espinazo de culebra; entre cuatro personas no la podíamos sujetar; tal fuerza desarrollaba bajo el influjo del aura epileptiforme.' (II, 382b) The last word here is probably a reference to J. M. Charcot's term 'epileptiform hysteria', and the 'arco vibrador' of Argos's body corresponds to the 'arc en cercle' he identifies as the major feature of a convulsive attack.[9]

Having recovered from this crisis, Argos begins to show more complex signs of hysteria. Milagros is the first to suggest to Benicio that Argos's religious devotion is motivated by sexual frustration (II, 402ab), and the theme is taken up by Fr Incienso. Expressing agreement with Moragas's psychophysical approach to medicine (with which readers of *La piedra angular* are already familiar), he points out that body and soul are clearly related, and advises that Argos be obliged to moderate her religious practices and occupy herself with domestic tasks (II, 407b–8a). Later Moragas lists the various symptoms of Argos's hysterical condition, placing most emphasis on the fact that she wears a bandage round her head to hide a wound from which she sweats blood. This is not the miraculous imposition of a kind of stigmata, but 'la circulación alterada por los fenómenos histéricos' (II, 414b). Stigmatists have commonly been seen as hysterical cases, as a not infrequent symptom of hysteria is periodic external bleeding.[10]

The relevant critical question is not, however, whether Pardo Bazán's medical information is accurate, but why she should give it such prominence in the novel, and whether the novel gains from it. These issues highlight characteristic weaknesses in Pardo Bazán. One is (as we have seen in *Una cristiana–La prueba*) that she is inclined to confuse her own voice with her narrator's. Although this occurs very rarely in *Doña Milagros*, it can be detected when Benicio implausibly uses the technical term 'epileptiforme' to describe Argos's convulsion. But more important than this slight lapse is the uneasy feeling that Pardo Bazán is including medical information simply to display her erudition. As a Realist, she believed that the novelist should be alive to all sources of knowledge that enlarge his understanding of life and no one is likely to censure her for that. But she is at times naive enough to believe that knowledge by itself constitutes understanding, or so it seems. Who can say that, after reading this novel, he genuinely understands Argos – understands, that is, the conflict and despair she must have undergone during her crisis? There can be little hope of a positive response to this question: Pardo Bazán is so taken up with consolidating her place among the most informed intellectuals of her day that she loses her grip on the novelist's craft. All that she gives us is a simple description of a psychological case along the same lines as the portrait of doña Juana la loca referred to above.

Yet the conception is in itself good. Argos's condition, we are led to believe, is not uncommon among girls of her age and, in a cycle of which the theme is the various forms adopted by sexual instinct, it has a place, if only for the contrast it presents to the other forms examined in the cycle. There is no doubt that it is potentially dramatic and we need not be surprised that Pardo Bazán recognised it as such. On the narrative level, she handles it deftly, keeping the reader's interest in Argos's relationship with the Jesuit by making of her a veritable bomb whose fuse we watch slowly burning down. This is done, as I have said, by submitting Argos to two successive crises. The first ends in a scene of what would be appalling melodrama were it not for the verisimilitude it is lent by Moragas's explanation of her condition. Argos, on the day of her mother's funeral, is 'a perfect and beautiful image of mental disturbance'. She is like a *Dolorosa* or Pradilla's picture of doña Juana la loca, and her whole appearance is 'admirable, worthy of a great tragic actress'. We are shown her lips moving noiselessly, and, in a telling image which is the only attempt to take us inside her, we are shown her breast rising and falling as if it were floating on 'the wave of inconsolable grief' (II, 383a). Milagros's gesture in forcing Argos to kiss her mother's corpse saves the girl from a breakdown, but it also brings the episode to a close with Argos in a violently hysterical state. After this, the reader can hardly doubt that Argos's renewed unbalanced behaviour will issue in a similar explosive scene.

It was possibly to satisfy this justifiable expectation that the novelist got rid of Moragas temporarily and introduced the old-fashioned doctor, don Dioscuro Napelo, to treat Argos. Moragas, for all his science, was helpless on the first occasion (apart from issuing dire warnings) and would probably be the same now. His judicious policy of 'calma, mucha calma' (II, 414b) is no doubt more prudent from a medical point of view (Milagros after all had a ninety-nine-and-a-half per cent chance of sending Argos completely mad), but it does not provide the novelist with dramatic climaxes. The bleeding process, on the other hand, is not only compelling; the outflowing of Argos's black semicoagulated blood is also a powerful metaphor for the purging of her dark, deep-rooted passion.[11]

Of Pardo Bazán's narrative skill, then, there is no question. She is in fact using here the same method of accumulating climaxes as we find in *Los pazos de Ulloa*, but concentrating on one individual rather than a total situation. However, the accumulation of climaxes is unlikely to interest or move the reader unless he is also interested in or moved by the character or characters being presented to him. The creation of a neat, dramatic situation is more suitable for a short story than a novel – indeed, Pardo Bazán based *La novia fiel* from *Cuentos de amor* on medical material similar to that used here.[12] The greater length of the novel demands a correspondingly greater complexity in the analysis of a particular psychological state or process. Such complexity is present in the character of Julián in *Los pazos de Ulloa*, but not here in the character of Argos.

The first-person method hides her thoughts from us and, moreover, we do not, except on rare occasions, hear her speak. The kind of self-deception she indulges in (consciously or not, we never know) by confusing religious devotion with sexual passion makes her a subject as potentially interesting as Julián, but the novelist prefers to leave her as mute and as lifeless, though externally striking, as the statue of *La Soledad* of which we are told she is 'la viva reproducción, la copia fiel' (II, 439a).

That the character of Argos is a failure – and, as we remember from the case of Carmen, a familiar failure – needs to be stated. But the particular interest of this failure lies in the surprising way in which it contrasts with the success of the other main characters, Benicio and doña Milagros (and to a lesser degree Ilda and Feíta). Pardo Bazán's writing here is of a quite different order. Argos's character is delineated in isolation from any other character – she is a psychological case whose symptoms are simply described as they develop. Benicio, Milagros, Ilda and Feíta, on the other hand, cannot be discussed without reference to each other, as their psychology is presented to us by a process of interaction. One of the fruitful limitations of the first-person narration is that the narrator, particularly one as naive as Benicio, is not competent to render psychology fully. The novelist is therefore bound to dramatise rather than describe if the characters are to come alive at all (again it is worth recalling the failure of Pardo Bazán to dramatise Carmen's 'prueba' in the earlier novel).

The device in chapter 1 of giving the reader direct information in Benicio's brief autobiographical sketch may make us apprehensive that he too is to be a mere *caso*. We recognise in the details he gives us a psychological make-up clearly akin to Julián in *Los pazos de Ulloa*, and a comparison of the treatment of the two characters is instructive. Julián is the major source of the astonishing vitality of the second half of that novel, yet for much of the time he is presented very obviously in response to a formula, that is, the contrast between his naive piety, insipidity and effeminacy and the aggressively masculine and savage environment in which he is placed. Only in the second half of the novel does he engage our interest as an individual.

The character of Benicio is based, as I have suggested, on a formula very similar to that on which Julián is based. He, like Julián, has a gentle, lymphatic personality and was brought up under the strong influence of his mother. He derived his strong sense of resignation to suffering from *The Imitation of Christ*, the work to which Julián constantly returns and a portion of which is reproduced, as he reads it, before the final climax of *Los pazos de Ulloa*. While not sharing Julián's effeminacy, Benicio has a submissiveness and passivity which make him describe himself as 'el hembro' (II, 413a), and, like Julián, he can explode into 'energías súbitas' (see II, 415a). I could continue the list (noting, for example, the strong paternal feeling in both), but it is not the similarities between the two characters that I wish to draw attention to so much as the contrast between their actual realisation. Benicio ceases after the first chapter (and even during it) to be a formula and is properly dramatised.

The way this is achieved through the language of the narration has already been dealt with. Here I shall examine two early examples of the way he is characterised by his interaction with others. The first example is chapter 3 where we are shown Benicio in the exclusively man's world of the Sociedad de Amigos. Like Julián, he stands apart from his fellows, but unlike him he is genuinely sociable and eagerly seeks out the amusing, lively company of the Sociedad de Amigos. This is an important distinction because, despite all his old-fashioned ideas of conduct subsumed under the word 'miramiento', it is impossible to regard him as priggish.

The main trait brought out is his ingenuousness in its various manifestations, and the vehicle is irony. We see it first at the end of the previous chapter where he confesses his fondness for cards as 'an evil habit, the only one, I believe, which has taken root in my soul' (II, 366a). This overscrupulousness is reinforced by further confessions at the beginning of chapter 3 about his habit of covering his losses without his wife's knowledge. In his explanation he inserts 'lo escribo con rubor' in parentheses, and from the fact of this very minor peccadillo (if it can be considered such at all) he concludes that it does not bear thinking about what he could have been capable of, if he had been dominated by less innocent passions (II, 366a). The irony lies in Benicio's innocent assumption that the reader will share his evaluation of his behaviour and will recognise the moral danger he is in.

But, more typically in this chapter, his naivety is presented through his reactions to his fellows and his delight in winning at cards. It is shown in the seriousness with which he takes their jokes about his supposed good fortune in love. It is shown in his child-like glee at his winning streak and in his motive for wanting to win – not for the money, but for 'the pure and ideal delight in victory', that is, to cut down to size those who mock him (II, 366b–7a). It is shown in his reluctance to leave the scene of his glory to go to his wife's side when she is in labour. It is shown when, not noticing the irony in his friend Primo Cova's praise of his versatility in cultivating 'all the forms of paternity', he proudly informs the company that they had even had a false pregnancy (II, 367b).

Benicio's ingenuousness is dramatised with particular force in his expression of emotion during the game. Again irony is the vehicle: Benicio is quite unaware that he is overreacting by any normal adult standards. For example:

Mi cara lo estaba proclamando a voces; mis ojos bailaban de gusto y mis manos temblaban ligeramente, estrujando contra el pecho el haz de cartas.

La placentera excitación que me obligaba a teclear sobre las cartas y sonreír de júbilo. (II, 366b)

Gané una jugada, y la satisfacción me puso más excitado. (II, 368a)

But these few examples of irony cannot fully account for the novelist's success in dramatising Benicio's ingenuousness: it is more properly her skill in rendering the whole atmosphere of the Sociedad de Amigos – the malicious banter and the increasing hilarity in response to Benicio's remarks – which brings him alive as he interacts with it.

A rather different perspective – at home with his wife Ilda and their neighbour, doña Milagros – on Benicio's passive personality is given in chapter 5. The shifting moods of each of the dramatic situations which fill this chapter, ranging from farce to tragedy, add complexity to our evaluation of that passivity. There are four situations in which Benicio is placed, and his horror and impotence as events overtake him typify his responses throughout the novel. The first of these situations puts him in unequal combat with his wife, Ilda, who, convalescing after the birth of the twins, fiercely resents what she considers to be Milagros's intrusion into the running of the household. Although created to set the very different character of Benicio at relief and therefore incidental to the main action of the novel, she is sketched with great economy and power. The economy is there from her introduction in chapter 1 where, as Benicio says, even her name, Ilduara, suggests noble severity and austere dignity, and where he compares her to the fortress of her native Montforte. The comparison perfectly delineates her as she relates to Benicio, and when on future occasions (II, 361a and 378b) he refers to her as 'el torreón', the 'straight line' of her face and her 'indomitable energy' are powerfully evoked. In addition, within the limitations of her conception and function, her speech characterises her very clearly in the irrational way she twists everything Benicio says about Milagros and in her unanswerable sarcasm. We can see this in chapter 4 and also here in chapter 5 in the heavy sarcasm of the repeated 'ciertas' (referring to Milagros) with which she silences and horrifies Benicio. In this episode, then, we see Benicio as the henpecked husband ('calzonazos' is what Ilda calls him on her death-bed), but this does not mean he is cast in the pathetically comic role normal for such a domestic phenomenon. There *is* an element of comedy in his helplessness before his wife, but what is brought more clearly to our attention is the misery of his married life and the calamity of a union between such an ill-matched pair.[13] Is it his fault if his personality does not conform to the accepted sexual stereotype? The same question could be asked of Ilda; indeed later in the novel we are probably less inclined to condemn her as both Moragas's remarks on Argos (II, 412a) and Feíta's assertion of her right to self-fulfilment invite us to ponder the deleterious effects the frustrations of the female social role can have on the personality of an energetic woman. The function of Ilda, then, in this first episode of chapter 5 as well as elsewhere, is to assist in the characterisation of Benicio.

The masterly transition between the first and second episodes exemplifies Pardo Bazán's skill at using the external world to convey inner psychological states. In the *galería* (where Benicio has taken refuge from his wife) the alternating colours of the glass through which he gazes at the port and mountains give us an insight into his vacillating nature. The 'land of gold' he sees through the yellow glass fills him with optimism and suggests simple solutions, while the 'funereal pallor' of the blue colours fills him with gloom and brings all the drawbacks and likely disasters to mind. In both cases, his state of mind is influenced from without and is therefore essentially passive.

Before he can decide what to do, we are into the second episode, which is even more traumatic for him than the first. A situation of great dramatic irony is created as Milagros, unaware of Ilda's violent hostility towards her and having ordered the twins to be brought in from the street, chides all present for allowing the babies out insufficiently protected against the weather. The irony is intensified as Milagros showers kisses onto one of the twins, and Rosa, seeing her mother 'como el torreón aquel' maintaining an ominous silence, tries to defend Milagros. The terrible scene which follows is impressively rendered in itself but its main purpose relates to the reactions of Benicio, caught between these two women, to both of whom in differing ways he is devoted. He does not dare interfere until directly challenged by Milagros to say whether or not she is 'una señora'. The 'impulso irresistible' which leads him to make that misjudged and ill-timed defence of Milagros earns him the contemptuous slap on the face from his wife which shows him again as both comic and tragic. But more important is the 'quijotismo' ('palabras quijotescas' is his phrase) which leaps out from his passivity here and increasingly throughout the novel as he defends Milagros from calumny and finally presents her with the twins. In his 'quijotismo' Benicio is related to Moragas and Salustio and like them he has an ambiguous moral status. Yet, as we shall see below, however ill-considered his actions may be (he hastens his wife's death and, in the sequel, kills a man), they are honourably motivated and spring from the heart, and that in a sense justifies them.

The two final episodes of this chapter need not be dwelt on, but it ought to be noted that the contrast between the farcical encounter with Milagros's 'animalazo barbudo' of a husband and the horrific torrent of abuse Ilda pours on Benicio in her delirium reinforces the sense of Benicio's being asked to cope with a wide range of emotional situations in quick succession. Ilda's death is certainly no Victorian death-bed scene and we cannot but feel for Benicio. Yet the incongruity of the final, laconic 'así me quedé viudo' after such an extraordinary string of events beautifully achieves Pardo Bazán's efforts to maintain a balance between comic and tragic in his character.[14]

This dual perspective is present throughout the novel, for example in chapter 11 when Benicio has a private interview with the Jesuit, Fr Incienso, to discuss Argos. Incienso's personality is quite opposed to Benicio's: he is manly, assured and majestic. His exasperation at Benicio's lack of paternal authority is understandable, because there is indeed something pathetic in Benicio's avowal that he can do nothing to curb Argos's excessive religious devotion. We cannot help registering Benicio's naivety and incompetence when he is astonished to hear from the Jesuit that it is not Argos but another of his daughters, Clara, who has decided to become a nun. Yet it is not entirely clear that the reader is intended to share Benicio's awe and respect for Incienso, whose very name smacks of irony. There is something disturbing, almost Satanic, about the pride of this 'arcángel muy casto . . y semirrebelde' (II, 409a). His concern is not for Argos, whose spiritual director he is, but for his own reputation, and his outburst against her and those who seek to besmirch his good name borders on the venomous. Benicio, on the other hand, displays during this interview not only his ineffectualness but also his genuine feeling and forbearance. He can hardly defend his daughter's behaviour in dogging the priest's steps, but he resists the notion that there is any malice in it. So our feelings towards him are inevitably mixed – no more so than at the end of this chapter when, having thought up on his way home furious entrances and stern philippics, on arrival he lamely asks: '"Hijas, ¿está la cena? Vengo muerto de debilidad."' In a moment, all the more touching for its brevity, Clara hangs on his neck, and he can do nothing more than exclaim: '" ¡Ay Clarita! ¿Que debía yo hacerte? ¿De cuándo acá a los padres los enteran los extraños?"' (II, 411a) He is not in control of the situation, but he gives and inspires affection.

The invitation to see his weakness as a kind of strength is repeated when we see him with Baltasar Sobrado. Benicio admires his landlord's experience of the world, yet Sobrado is cynical and contemptible, whereas Benicio's naivety is accompanied by integrity. Feíta, who in her shrewdness and energy is also contrasted to Benicio, puts the point most clearly when she murmurs, throwing her arms round her father's neck and kissing his moustache: '" ¡Papá del alma! [. . .] ¡Qué bonísimo, qué infeliz le hizo Dios! Por eso hay que quererle más."' (II, 420a)

I shall return to Benicio later, but it is impossible to give an adequate account of the treatment of his psychology without examining the character of Milagros. Like Argos and Benicio, she is a readily identifiable psychological case, that is, frustrated maternal instinct. This is a theme treated by Pardo Bazán in various short stories in the early 1890s.[15] In Milagros maternal frustration does not take the form of embittered repression (as it does in some of the short stories) but combines with her inherited Andalusian ebullience to result in an inexhaustible *cariño* ('affection' is too weak a word) and a desire to be helpful to a fault as illustrated in my discussion of chapter 5 above.

Her dynamic personality is well realised through external detail and speech, as she interacts with situations and other characters. Porfirio Sánchez has shown how the physical description given of her assists in her characterisation.[16] Equally revealing is the sound of her footsteps on the first occasion she appears in person: 'Al encontrármela yo en la escalera, doña Milagros subía con brioso taconeo, haciendo vibrar los peldaños, de prisa, como persona a quien no pesan aún la edad ni las carnes.' (II, 371b) Her energetic and determined steps define from the outset her own energy and determination always placed, as we see from the innumerable objects she is carrying, at the service of her neighbours, whether they want her help or not (this passage follows Ilda's complaint that Milagros gives unasked-for favours).

Other revealing details are given when Benicio is unable to contain his gratitude to her: 'Ella, no menos conmovida, quiso y pudo echarme un brazo al cuello, murmurando: —Cáyese usté. ¡Vaya unas bondaes, cristiano! ¡Ea!, cargue usté con este artilugio – y entregó la maquinilla –. Andando, andando, que no estamos pa paliques.' (II, 372a) We see in a nutshell Milagros as she appears in the rest of the novel: her affection in her attempt to embrace Benicio and hide her emotion by concentrating on practicalities; her good-natured tendency to take charge of every situation in the way she unloads the 'maquinilla' onto Benicio and hurries him along.

This extract also exemplifies the most important way in which her psychology is dramatised, that is, through her speech. She is Andalusian and has obviously lost none of the features of Andalusian speech. However, she is no uprooted *costumbrista* type, because she is established as a very definite individual. Many examples could be quoted, but Milagros's next appearance makes the point well enough. Benicio is pensively examining the twins, one in each arm, when Milagros enters: 'Entró en esto doña Milagros, y me las arrebató, y empezó a chillarles: —Monaas, tesoros, cominiyos, peasos de masapán . . . ¡ay, qué judiá, tenerlas así, en cuero, arresiditas de frío! ¡A ver, a ver, un capiyito, que la quiero vetir a esta emperatrís de la China!' (II, 372b) The overflowing maternal feeling of a childless woman is strikingly conveyed with the diminutives and apparently inexhaustible supply of terms of affection, and again her well-intentioned intrusiveness is apparent in the whole situation, particularly in the contrast between the single, restrained kiss Benicio gives the twins and the way Milagros snatches them from him and shrieks at them.

The intrusiveness I have mentioned is presented as the novel progresses as a spontaneous involvement in the lives of others and a completely generous self-giving, particularly with respect to Benicio. We see this in the unrestrained torrents of words (chapters 10, 14 and 16) she pours out to him, full of colourful comparisons, more or less popular wisdom, analysis of situations, and autobiography, which give the impression of being strung together as ideas come to her. It is impossible to illustrate the compelling energy of these speeches without quoting at length, but I refer briefly to chapter 16 where, having been banished from the presence of the twins, Milagros comes to beg Benicio to have compassion on her. Even with her spirits broken, her linguistic energy is unabated:

'Pero soy de esta hechura y no de otra; soy de la condisión de la hiedra, que se arrima, y se agarra y se abrasa, y no se pué apartar ya del árbol sin secarse ... Es una condisión mala, detestable, y daría argo porque me fabricasen un corasón de metal muy nuevesito y muy relusiente, que fuese a modo de reló, ¿comprende usté? de esos que se les da cuerda, y ya están en marcha para un año, sin discrepar ni un segundo. Eso me hase a mí farta; el relojiyo y no esta porquería de corasón de manteca, que se le sale el cariño por toós laos como harina por criba rota.' (ii, 433a)

Milagros, then, like Benicio but unlike Argos, is not a textbook psychological study. She is forcefully brought to life both in her reactions and in her speech. There remains, however, the question of her function in the novel. Why did Pardo Bazán import an Andalusian into a novel about Galician urban life? To answer this question we must return to Benicio.

In chapter 2 we are given a causal explanation of his psychological make-up (his gentleness and timidity), and the results of these traits are thereafter seen in his failure to control his own family situation. But there is another and related side to his personality, also stamped on him by his mother, that is, his old-fashioned values which, as he says, are quite unsuited to the age in which he lives. He stands aside from his environment with its petty materialism and lack of inner generosity. Ilda's determination to carry on a bitter family feud against his wishes is a case in point, as is his refusal to believe that Milagros is a woman of easy virtue. Milagros, on the other hand (the contrast is deliberate), comes from outside this environment both literally and metaphorically. She is from a country of warmth and sunshine and brings warmth and light to Benicio's life, as he explains in chapter 8: 'Como todas las personas de individualidad muy acentuada y típica, doña Milagros parecía crear vida alrededor de sí; diríase que la trama de la existencia diaria, tan pálida, vulgar y monótona, para ella estaba entretejida de hilos de color y de pajuelitas de oro. En mi casa hacía sol cuando entraba doña Milagros.' (ii, 393b–4a) Elsewhere, a contrast between Milagros and Ilda is made with this image. In chapter 9 when Argos insists on visiting the cemetery, Ilda's grim presence is implicitly associated with the nearby grim sea breaking against the rocks, while on the other hand Milagros and Benicio watch the setting sun spread ripples of gold and red over the ocean (II, 400b). In chapter 12 the blue glass of the *galería* summons up Ilda's face, 'irritada y fatídica, lívida de color', while Milagros appears in the yellow glass bathed in golden light (II, 412b). There are other associations of light and sun with Milagros (see II, 401b, 421b, 424b, 432b, 433a). The intention is clear: to associate Benicio and Milagros in their shared isolation from the immediate situation.

However, Pardo Bazán is not making an easy and therefore sentimental contrast. The relationship between Milagros and Benicio is the study of a delicate variation on the main theme of sexual attraction – delicate because of the spiritual nature of their love. By this I mean that their mutual attraction is not primarily physical. Despite his fit of jealousy in chapter 14, Benicio assures us that Milagros does not provoke in him 'sinful thoughts' and that he sees in her a friend in whom he can confide and to whom he can pour out his heart (II, 421a). Their relationship in the rest of the novel confirms this remark. In the same chapter doña Milagros expresses a similar view of the innocence of their love: '"Si todos los pecaos del mundo fuesen así . . . , ni agua bendita. Porque del modo que le quiero a usté . . . es una cosa tan bonita y tan inosente . . . que si Dió la pesca, dirá alla pa sí; 'Por esto no me atufo.'"' (II, 424a) Again, nothing in the novel contradicts this view. Although both of these remarks are taken from a fairly late chapter, the same kind of essentially innocent attraction is evident in the first encounter referred to above: Benicio is drawn to Milagros by her affectionate generosity and Milagros to Benicio by his gratitude. However, it is in the second half of the novel that the spiritual nature of their love is most developed, until each sees the other as a saint. In Milagros's case this is perhaps a conventional and characteristic hyperbole, so that when she calls him 'santo' (II, 424b) and 'santo varón' (II, 433a) she is referring simply to his meekness. In Benicio's case, however, the description applied to Milagros is put in explicitly hagiographical terms, particularly after Milagros has defended her honour from Vicente's attacks. Earlier in the novel she is already for Benicio an 'angel from heaven' but now he says of her: 'Su virtud, ya heroica, ya adornada con las palmas del martirio, era la forma en que correspondía a mi amante veneración.' (II, 441b–2a) We see here the association of heroism and sanctity typical of the Western hagiographical tradition. Benicio takes this up in an exaggeratedly exalted form, imagining Milagros ('la infeliz'), alone with Vicente ('el dragón furioso'), being saved only by divine intervention. Vicente's attempt both on Milagros's chastity and on her life is for Benicio a 'crown of glory placed on doña Milagros's brow' (II, 442b). This unexpected appearance of hagiography is an indication of the extent to which the novelist was preoccupied with the subject.

Now, it is difficult to know how far we are expected to accept Benicio's evaluation of Milagros. No definitive clue to her innocence is given, but it is at least open to doubt. As Sobrado and Moragas imply, Vicente's suicide strongly suggests that he was indeed having an affair with Milagros (II, 443ab). Given her affectionate and dynamic personality and her frank views on sex, there are no irresistible reasons for siding with Benicio against the experienced Sobrado and the respected Moragas. From the point of view of the novelist, however, the facts of the matter are less important than what they reveal about Benicio's psychology.

His feeling of 'alegría delirante, irracional, absurda' when he believes Milagros's reputation to be vindicated indicates how much he needs to believe in her innocence. However, the reason he gives for his euphoria is curious: it is not the joy of a lover whose jealousy is shown to be unfounded, but gratitude because she has preserved his cherished illusions and his ideal (II, 441b). He addresses himself to her with these words: '" ¡Ah doña Milagros! ¡Mujer soñada en mi juventud, bendita seas!"' (II, 442a) The word 'juventud' gives us a clue to the psychological basis of his Romanticism, which is made clear here, but is already apparent in his 'quijotismo'. It takes us back to his student days when he dreamed of married bliss (II, 357b), and beyond to his childhood, dominated by devotion to his mother and fear of his father. It is to motherhood that he returns now to describe his ideal of womanhood:

Porque en aquella ocasión lo veía claramente: la única persona que había realizado ante mis ojos el tipo de la bondad era doña Milagros. Pronta a sacrificarse por todos; con el sentimiento más hermoso y más santo en la mujer, que es la maternidad, tan poderosamente desenvuelto que absorbía los restantes; sencilla, humilde, mansa, desprendida, tierna, doña Milagros era la encarnación de *lo bueno femenino*. (II, 442a)

Now, although not all of these epithets are inappropriate to Milagros, taken as a whole they do not do justice to our picture of her. In particular, 'humilde' and 'mansa' seem out of place. The 'tipo de la

bondad' and 'lo bueno femenino' correspond much more closely to
Benicio's mother, as described in the first chapter. 'Industrious,
upright and Christian', 'despised and ill-treated', she devoted all her
affection to her son and instilled into him precisely those qualities of
meekness and humility which are lacking in Milagros. The idealised
nature of Benicio's love for Milagros results, then, from an identification of her in his mind with his venerated mother and a vision of
Milagros herself as the ideal of maternity, even though she is not a
mother in the physiological sense.

From this paradox of maternity without physical motherhood
springs the major theme of 'amor maternal electivo', that is,
Milagros's conviction that the twins are the spiritual progeny of
Benicio and herself. The idea is made explicit at the end of chapter 7
but is developed more fully in chapter 14. There she explains to
Benicio that she loves him because he is the father of the twins, and
that she thinks of herself as their mother:

'Me creo que soy la mamá de eyos, y que a Zita y Media las he dado a lus,
pasando los dolore, y las fatiga, y las aflisiones de las madre [...] me ha entrao
la manía de que es mentira que usté estuviese casao con . . . , con la difunta
[...], que con quien estuvo usté casao fue conmigo; que nos quisimo . . . allá en
tiempos; que tuvimos esas neniya . . . y que ahora todavía nos queremo, sí,
señó, nos queremo . . . de la entraña . . .; pero santamente, como los
hermanitos viejos, muy viejos . . . sin pecao ni malisia.' (II, 424a)

Milagros's 'manía'[17] illustrates a conviction also shared by Benicio:
that physiological phenomena are the mere letter of reality and may
conceal a deeper spirit. For example, he dismisses family kinship as
depending simply on 'formalidades externas' and the workings of
chance. Genuine kinship is *felt*: 'Nuestros parientes son los que nos
aman, los que nos auxilian, los que nos dan calor de afecto . . .' So he
can boast of being a very close relative of doña Milagros (II, 393a). By
the same token he contrasts the moral and the physiological in
declaring Milagros to be an exemplary mother: '¿Qué le falta para la
maternidad? Lo material y fisiológico: moralmente, ¡qué madre más
sublime! . . .' (II, 395a) Given this general frame of mind, it is not
unnatural that Benicio should finally consecrate Milagros's *idée fixe* by
presenting her with the twins. His description of them as he hands
them over as 'the two beings through whom and in whom we had
loved each other' (II, 446b) shows how he has come to accept her
belief. Having fulfilled the moral conditions of parenthood – mutual
love in and through the children – they are their mother and father,
despite the physiological facts.

It will be noted that the burden of this maternity motif is deliberately anti-positivistic in so far as the spirit of a situation is made to triumph over the dead letter of physiological and social fact. For the same reason in Benicio's mind the triumph is one of Romantic idealism over realism and logic. The gift of the twins is seen by him as a Romantic gesture when, for example, he swears to repay Milagros's heroism 'with some admirable deed, worthy of you and of me' (II, 442a), or when, in the final chapter, he conceives the idea of the gift as a 'great sacrifice, an offering' (II, 445b). The impulsiveness of this final gesture, the implications of which are subjected to no rational scrutiny, illustrates again the 'quijotismo' he has displayed earlier in defending Milagros. Benicio's 'quijotismo' is, as it has been through the novel, a defiant challenge to the hard-headed world of Marineda – realists like Sobrado and Moragas who, according to him, are morally and spiritually blind (II, 443b).[18]

But how is the reader to react to this grand gesture? I noted above that there is no conclusive evidence either for Milagros's innocence or for her guilt. However, there are powerful arguments advanced at the Sociedad de Amigos against her, and in her defence Benicio has nothing to offer but his own conviction, which, as the irony directed at his naivety throughout the novel suggests, is not necessarily reliable. Irony is indeed all-pervasive. Yet beside this irony stands the curious fact that Benicio is not ridiculous. The explanation is to be found in the way that the irony is largely neutralised by Benicio's very unsuitability as a victim for irony. Such a weapon is more appropriately aimed at the proud or self-righteous. His unpretentiousness disarms our criticism and his lack of priggishness removes any threat of moral censure his innocence might hold; his vulnerability to the irony of his fellows disinclines us to join in the general mirth. The effect at this point in the novel is that, however much the reader may believe Benicio to be deluded on an empirical level, emotionally he is with him and prefers to accept his vision of Milagros. If it is not true, it ought to be. As Pardo Bazán wrote to Santiago Rusiñol the year after the publication of Doña Milagros: 'Lo que existe con la grosera existencia llamada real sufre los accidentes del cambio y de la destrucción. Sólo lo que no existe no muere, no muere nunca.'[19]

If this is an accurate account of the way the reader's reactions are manipulated, we must recognise in it an example of narrative sleight of hand, whereby the novelist succeeds in reproducing in the reader her own ambiguous attitude towards the fact of nature. Are the delicate accompaniments of human love but a deceitful cloak for primitive animal instinct,[20] or are they the appropriate expression of a force which can civilise and elevate man and inspire the noblest deeds (the sentiment expressed in the second epigraph to the present chapter)?

The reader is prevented from leaning too far towards the latter alternative by the conclusion drawn from the episode which immediately follows the section we have been discussing. The elopement of Benicio's daughter Tula with a house-painter points to the supremacy of sexual instinct over all social laws: 'Bajo el impulso de esta necesidad apremiantísima; bajo la fuerza de esta ley, todo lo convencional desaparece, y sólo quedan en pie *Adán y Eva*, la primitiva pareja del Edén, el varón y la hembra atraídos el uno hacia el otro merced a instintos que a veces ni saben definir . . .' (II, 444a) This is Benicio's conclusion, and the reader is clearly intended to accept it; but there coexists with this conclusion the feeling that in the special case of Benicio and Milagros reproductive instinct is not predominant, since their attraction is not primarily physical but spiritual. So beside the theme announced by the general title *Adán y Eva* there is a strong resistance to the determinism which sees all relationships between the sexes as physical, and, in addition, more than an idea, an earnest desire to believe, that love can elevate as well as degrade human beings.

There is a paradox, however, in that although their relationship rejects one kind of determinism, it is explained by another. They love one another in the way they do because of their psychological make-up which has been determined by a combination of heredity (whether family or racial) and circumstances (upbringing in one case and childlessness in the other). I have observed a similar explanation of Romantic idealism in *Una cristiana–La prueba* and *La piedra angular*, but the explanation here is much more acceptable in a post-Freudian age then Pardo Bazán's idiosyncratic adaptation of instinct in those earlier works. Nevertheless, in all three works, by giving a psychological explanation, she is insisting, as she had insisted more explicitly ten years earlier,[21] that Romantic idealism is true in so far as it is part of life. Of course there is a distinction between admitting the existence of Romantic idealism and asserting its validity as a way of seeing the world. But the logical error only provides more evidence of Pardo Bazán's sleight of hand: a deliberate attempt to blur that distinction in order to justify and gain acceptance for the Romantic tendencies in her own sensibility. And this is no defect; one of the fascinations of

Doña Milagros is in witnessing, not a thesis being proved, but a dilemma being explored and woven into the very fabric of the text.

Doña Milagros represents a remarkable advance on *Una cristiana–La prueba* in the use of fictional autobiography as a vehicle for psychological analysis. This is true above all in the presentation of Benicio – Argos is lifeless, and Milagros, although well dramatised, is necessarily idealised. Benicio is satisfyingly established as a narrator, and as a character is treated with greater maturity than any of Pardo Bazán's earlier creations, including the related figure of Julián. The maturity lies in the fact that although like Julián Benicio is weak and naive, even perhaps stupid, unlike Julián he is never ridiculous. Pardo Bazán's detachment and clearsightedness, shown in the consistently concrete delineation of his psychology, go hand in hand with genuine understanding and compassion. The word 'compassion' bears some consideration. It was noted at the beginning of this chapter that Benicio's brief was to write an exemplary tale. But what exactly is the exemplum? How can there be any if, within the context of deterministic psychology, Benicio owes his personality to a combination of natural disposition and upbringing? He knows he ought to act differently but cannot.

The question is raised by the very last words of the novel, which describe the public's unfavourable verdict on Benicio: 'Yo era un mal padre . . . y además, un viejo chocho.' Even his sickness and premature ageing do not regain him the sympathy of his fellow citizens. It is a perplexing end to the novel because, although the *marinedinos'* judgement seems definitive and to all appearances justified, the reader must have difficulty in sharing it. As we have seen, the irony directed at those things found ridiculous by the town – his naivety, weak personality and 'quijotismo' – is self-defeating. It wins us over and prevents us, as the text here seems to enjoin, from condemning him. To find an issue from this impasse, the reader must turn back to the 'Prólogo en el cielo', where he learns, as he has already in *La piedra angular*, that a superficial, uninformed judgement is unlikely to be fair. The Voice of the Spirit implies that what may seem a failure in worldly terms, in spiritual terms may be no such thing. The fact that, strictly speaking, Benicio is a murderer is dismissed on the grounds that external events are merely the shell of inner reality: 'El hecho descarnado nada significa para Mí. Mi justicia no se parece a la que tú conociste allá en el mundo [. . .] Intenciones, motivos, pensamientos . . . Hechos, no. El hecho no existe en estas regiones. El hecho es la cáscara de la realidad.' (II, 353b) He is also told that he is forgiven because of his great love. Here is another manifestation of Pardo Bazán's distrust of the Positivistic confidence in empirical fact. It is also present in the curious letter to Santiago Rusiñol I quoted from above: 'No puedo transigir [. . .] con que sólo los modernistas y los partidarios del "arte por el arte" posean la llave del sueño y la coraza contra el positivismo que domina (¿hoy solamente?) en nuestra sociedad; somos tantos los que no nos tenemos por modernistas y vivimos y hemos vivido de esas aspiraciones.'[22]

There is in *Doña Milagros*, then, a contrast between the tribunal of public opinion, which judges only on the basis of external fact, and the judgement of God, just as there is by implication in the epilogue of *La piedra angular*. The important point for the reader is that he is privileged to share the divine judgement, because he has precisely the kind of infallible insight into Benicio's motives that with non-fictional people is the prerogative of God alone. He can penetrate beyond the letter of Benicio's situation to the spirit and, understanding, have compassion. This is one consideration the word 'compassion' leads us to.

But there is another, depending on the first, which concerns Pardo Bazán's increasing interest in psychology; a mind which values the spirit more than the letter is unlikely to remain a *colorista*, content to render the external appearance of reality. Moreover, the novel's prologue suggests that the sympathy with which she treats individual psychology and situations owes something to a Christian world-view – a world-view which involves respect for the injunction 'Judge not, that ye be not judged.' The implication of this is that, however much Pardo Bazán may have been influenced by Bourget and Russian writers, her turn towards the psychological novel was a natural, if not inevitable, response to her own Christian beliefs.

7

Memorias de un solterón

'We are often mastered by a feeling which has already struck firm roots in our inmost being without suspecting it, and suddenly, on some occasion or other, there fall, as it were, scales from our eyes.' E. von Hartmann, *Philosophy of the Unconscious* (London, 1893), I, 259

The second part of the *Adán y Eva* cycle, *Memorias de un solterón*, was published two years after *Doña Milagros*, also in *La España moderna*, between January and May of 1896, and then in book form in the same year.[1] Although (unlike *Una cristiana–La prueba*) the two novels can be read independently, *Memorias* continues the account of Benicio Neira's family life, but with Mauro Pareja as the narrator. Through Mauro's eyes we see the disorder in Benicio's household, particularly the flirtations of Rosa with Benicio's landlord, Sobrado (Amparo's seducer in *La Tribuna*), and Argos with the Civil Governor, Mejía. Both girls are dishonoured and Benicio, with typical impetuosity, runs Mejía through with a sword.

The contrast between the narrator of this novel and that of *Doña Milagros* is striking. Benicio is weak-willed, whereas Mauro is a man of strong resolution; Benicio is steeped in traditionalist ideas and attitudes, Mauro is *au fait* with the most modern tastes and ideas; Benicio had married as soon as he possibly could, Mauro intends to avoid marriage altogether. Consequently, the impression we receive of Benicio's family is not quite the same as that in *Doña Milagros*. Apparently, then, *Memorias* is a continuation of the story of Benicio and his family, but told from a different point of view.

However, on closer inspection we see that the novel revolves around two centres of interest – Mauro's observation of the Neira family but, more important, his observation of his own emotional life, in particular his involvement with another of Benicio's daughters, Feíta. These two threads are carefully interwoven. In the first four chapters Mauro describes his self-sufficient way of life; chapters 5 to 10 contain his observations on the Neira family; chapters 11 to 15 bring the narrator back to himself with the intrusion of Feíta into his life. Chapter 16 contains a stocktaking by Mauro and is, as we shall see below, the novel's central point. The second half of the novel can be divided broadly into three sections: the first, chapters 17 to 21, deals with the development of Mauro's relationship with Feíta; the second, chapters 22 to 25, deals with the events surrounding Neira's two daughters, Rosa and Argos; finally, the two threads are pulled together in chapter 26 with an account of the family situation after Neira's death and the engagement of Feíta and Mauro. This, as I have said, is only a broad schema; the two threads are not clearly distinguishable because Feíta is a feature of both. For example, the meeting of Mauro and Sobrado's illegitimate son, *el compañero Sobrado*, belongs to the observation of the Neira family since Mauro's ostensible aim is to help Neira with his family problems. But it also belongs to the observation of Mauro's emotional life, since his real motive is to satisfy the demands of jealousy. The greater part of the novel deals with Mauro himself (only ten chapters centre directly on Neira) and indeed it is one of the ironies of the work that Mauro, the detached observer, protected by his egoism or *filaucia*, is increasingly drawn into the situation and becomes himself the object of scrutiny.

Mauro is aware of the ambiguity of his position as a narrator and in the pivotal chapter 16 he tries to answer the reader's possible objections to the way he is telling his story. The reader demands to know whether it is his own story he is telling or that of the Neira family. Is he really a confirmed bachelor protected from women by the cult of his own self, or does he in fact fall for every girl who crosses his path? He defends himself by arguing that if he were to restrict himself to telling the story of his own life, it would not be worth the telling. On the question of the subject of his story he explains that our lives only acquire meaning as they come into contact with other lives: 'Donde no hay lucha no hay drama, y donde no hay drama no hay emoción. Diríase que nuestra propia existencia, si se considera aislada y disgregada de las demás, carece de sentido, y sólo lo adquiere al relacionarse con otras, al producirse ese oleaje y ese hervidero de sentimientos que determina el contacto con seres humanos.' (II, 493a) The novel is indeed his own story, but, despite his original intention, his story is one of relationships and must necessarily involve the lives of others.

The novel's structure, juxtaposing and interweaving Mauro's experience with that of others, is obviously appropriate to Pardo Bazán's purposes, not least for the irony it generates at Mauro's expense. In this chapter I shall examine first Pardo Bazán's use of the first-person narration as a vehicle for psychological analysis and then each of the novel's two threads in turn.

THE FIRST-PERSON NARRATIVE METHOD

Memorias is another fictional memoir, dealing, like *Doña Milagros*, with only a short but critical episode in the life of the narrator. If the earlier novel centred on the relationship between Benicio and Milagros, *Memorias* centres on the relationship between Mauro and Feíta. Benicio's motives for writing are clear, and so, ostensibly, are Mauro Pareja's. He explains in the first paragraph how what he writes is a personal apologia: 'Para vindicarme ante la posteridad, referiré, sin quitar punto ni coma, lo que soy y cómo vivo, y daré la clave de mi filosofía peculiar y de mis ideas.' (II, 448ab) In reality the novel is anything but a vindication of Mauro's 'filosofía peculiar' as outlined in the opening chapters. It begins as such, but by the end he has abandoned the attitude to life he set out to justify. The narrator is not, therefore, looking back at events from a fixed point in time after they have occurred; neither is his narration informed by hindsight. Needless to say, the discrepancy between the professed aim of the memoir and the eventual end-product is not an oversight: it is an important tactic in the study of the way an individual can move from self-deception to a new self-awareness and a consequently greater self-fulfilment. So the narrator changes as his memoir progresses and he lets his story lead him where it will, being no less surprised than the reader at his final destination. Obviously hindsight would detract from this effect since the transformation in Mauro would be far less impressive if he did not argue so persuasively at the beginning for the ideas he renounces at the end.

As in *Doña Milagros*, Pardo Bazán plays with the ironies of fictional conventions, but more blatantly. At the beginning of chapter 22 Mauro focuses attention away from himself to don Baltasar and his natural son, *el compañero Sobrado*, and in so doing he conveys information he could not possibly possess, even though he claims to have discovered it by means which, in order not to bore the reader, he will not go into. Here he confronts one of the limitations of the first-person narrative technique, but he overcomes it simply enough by doing the impossible: he assumes the guise and attributes of an omniscient narrator: 'Opto [. . .] por imitar a los novelistas, que no dan razón de cómo se las compusieron para averiguar los íntimos pensamientos [. . .] de sus héroes.' (II, 511a) In using this device Pardo Bazán is not only introducing a burlesque note, but also raising the question of why she should be restricted by the demands of plausibility when the very act of writing novels, however objective the method, is based on a set of implausible conventions: 'Y aunque pertenezcan los susodichos novelistas a la escuela llamada del documento humano, la verdad es que jamás nos presentan comprobantes y justificantes de sus profundas y sutiles observaciones.' (II, 511ab) Mauro resumes the narration in the first person fairly emphatically at the beginning of the final chapter.

This recourse to Romantic irony,[2] with its clearly practical aim, needs no justification as it contributes to the ironic tone of Mauro's narration. Nevertheless, Pardo Bazán uses the device discreetly. The four chapters of detached omniscient narration, from which Mauro's reactions of discomfort are excluded, obviously differ from what has gone before, but as this section contains the very dramatic climax to Benicio Neira's story, the reader will probably forget the change (just as he does in Galdós's *La de Bringas*). He is helped by the fact that Mauro slyly resumes the narration in the first person at the end of chapter 23 before unobtrusively slipping back to his omniscient role at the beginning of the following chapter.

As far as the feasibility of Mauro's authorship of the memoirs is concerned, Pardo Bazán solves the problem without using the ghost-writer convention she had in the previous novel. She makes Mauro an avid reader of novels and, moreover, precisely the kind of novels she herself admired. He describes himself as a 'devoted reader of those great foreign novelists who expertly delve into the hidden places of the soul' (II, 458a), and refers on two occasions to Bourget as being among his particular favourites. Not only is he an admirer of Bourget, but he also has the inquisitive mind and eye of a novelist (II, 462b). So although Mauro is not a novelist by profession, it is not at all strange that he should be writing his memoirs with the skill of a novelist.

In addition, Pardo Bazán alleviates her problems by giving him tastes similar to her own in other things apart from reading matter, notably a liking for bric-à-brac. His room is decorated with porcelain, watercolours, Impressionist landscapes, photographs, pieces of tapestry, an oriental sabre and the like (II, 450a). As he has a similar range of interests to the novelist herself, she can give him a voice similar to her own without his becoming inconsistent in the way Salustio does in *Una cristiana–La prueba*.

However, despite these coincidences of author and narrator, there is an important difference which results from the epic situation itself – the fact, that is, that Mauro intends his memoirs to be a vindication of his philosophy of life. Such an intention gives his narration a tone at once self-satisfied and defensive. The self-satisfaction is evident in the description of his orderly life and in his conviction that he sees life with a clearer vision than most. The defensiveness is less obvious but no less present. It is there, for example in the first paragraph where he rejects the implications of his nickname *Abad*. Most obviously it is there in his direct address to the reader. The reader is implicitly brought in by the questions in the first paragraph ('¿Qué intentan significar con esto de *Abad*?') but is explicitly referred to at the beginning of the third paragraph: 'No crean, señores, que me acicalo por afeminación.' Here and in the other quite frequent examples he attempts to explain and justify his attitudes and conduct. He foresees the reader's assumptions and objections and takes it for granted that he must share the disapproval of the *marinedinos*; but, as he proceeds, he looks to the now more understanding reader for approval:

¿No es cierto, señores, que mi pueblo peca de injusto y de poco reflexivo al excomulgarme por actos en el fondo tan inofensivos y tan defendibles? (II, 456a)

Comprendes ahora, lector delicado, lector psicólogo, poeta lector, por qué, aparte de todo egoísmo, me infunde horror [. . .] la santa coyunda? (II, 459b)

Mauro is given a personal voice, then, in the tension between his apparent self-satisfaction and this need to justify himself, in the impression he gives of constantly looking over his shoulder to see the reader's reaction. The latter is an important trait because the psychological study of Mauro starts from the premiss that he is the victim of his own self-deceit. In other words, he is, like Benicio, an unreliable narrator. As we shall see below, he is mistaken first in thinking that he is indifferent to Feíta, and then, having admitted his love for her, he takes it to be spiritual rather than physical. Narrative procedure then is essential to the novel's psychological analysis.

THE PSYCHOLOGICAL NOVEL

Pardo Bazán's by now familiar approach to the psychological novel is present in the attitude of her narrator, whom she has given the inquisitive mind of a novelist, to the Neira family. He claims (we learn later that he is mistaken in his motives) to be attracted to the Neira *tertulia* for its potential psychological interest: 'Me condujo el interés por el estudio de las miserias de la paternidad y la sospecha de que algún drama fértil en peripecias y en lances hondos iba a representarse en aquel hogar tranquilo en la superficie, pero interiormente trabajado por las pasiones y los anhelos de mujeres jóvenes, bellas y sedientas de vivir.' (II, 462b) Well-versed as he is in contemporary theories (he would have found them in his favourite *Revue des deux mondes*), he personifies the Neira family, endowing it with both a conscious ('superficie') and unconscious ('interior') life, and like Pardo Bazán he implies that he is drawn to the greater dramatic interest which the Unconscious gains from its mysteriousness. However, in Mauro's story of the Neiras, the Unconscious remains only a metaphor for drama and mystery, whereas in the autobiographical sections it is presented literally. I shall deal first with the Neira family, beginning with Benicio.

Mauro tells us that he cultivates the friendship of Benicio ('el caso más caracterizado de paternidad') to protect himself from the temptation of matrimony, since his example demonstrates that marriage is incompatible with men's dignity (II, 460a). To justify this assertion he has to do little more than maintain the picture of Benicio the reader has brought from *Doña Milagros*. For example, we see Benicio's familiar ingenuousness when he misses the irony in Mauro's description of his daughters as 'superiores' and smiles with pleasure at the epithet, as he does when he describes with childish satisfaction his daughter Clara's success as a nun (II, 461a). Or again, we are shown his utter despondency in the picture of him, having told the story of his daughter Tula's married life with her painter, staring at the toes of his shoes (II, 461b).

The tragi-comic light in which Benicio is seen in *Doña Milagros* reappears here in Mauro's evaluation of him: his weakness as a father is to be smiled at, but at the same time he is Mauro's 'old friend', a good man whose calamitous circumstances cause his friend genuine distress and concern. In addition, there is in Mauro's account the same psychological phenomenon of the weak, pacific man who reacts with 'energías súbitas' or sudden outbursts in extreme situations and, as in the previous novel, he is never just a formula. In the climactic scene with Mejía the novelist is at pains to dramatise Benicio's specific feelings in his specific situation, for example, his inability to speak when overcome with indignation or the premonition that he will emerge from the interview humiliated: 'Antes que Mejía la lanzase escuchaba su carcajada mofadora, soportaba sus insolentes negativas, tragaba el alcíbar de su desprecio y se veía saliendo de allí burlado, con las orejas gachas, porque hay en el mundo ciertas grandes iniquidades que inclinan al suelo para siempre, no la cabeza del que las comete, sino la del que las padece y llora . . .' (II, 522a) Here the general truth to which Benicio's case is related is neither pedantic nor intrusive because the metaphor precisely defines Benicio's sense of definitive shame and grief. The implications of his situation bow him down further as he learns that his honour is irretrievably lost, realises that death is near without his having provided for his daughters in any way, and is finally humiliated by Mejía, as anticipated. Benicio's inner feelings are presented with such clarity and understanding that the two tears which appear in his eyes are not a piece of sentimentality: they are an appropriate response to his situation.

Mauro's case against marriage is perhaps weakened by the fact that the example he chooses is particularly unsuited to the trials of married life and indeed of life in general. At the beginning of *Doña Milagros*, Benicio has told us that events thwarted his natural inclination to be a humble country priest, and later he envies the peace of the friar in his convent (II, 395b). He repeats this yearning in *Memorias* (II, 462a) and we are told that he would have been happier if he had been born two centuries earlier and been able to shut himself up in a convent where nobody has to create his own destiny because it has already been laid down by the Rule of the order (II, 518a). Mauro goes further and describes him as 'predisposed to sanctity' (II, 526a). In another context his meekness, simplicity and utter lack of malice could have become a form of sanctity. This view of Benicio as a saint *manqué*, representing as it does an unexpected reappearance of the hagiographical pattern I have noted in Pardo Bazán's work, is yet another indication of the extent to which the novelist was preoccupied with the lives of the saints.

From Benicio we pass to Rosa and Argos. The presentation of the two sisters is similar to that of Argos in *Doña Milagros*, that is, neither of them is seen except from the outside. The one exception is in chapter 24 where Rosa's cold personality is warmed into life by her father's sudden change from anger to affection. For this short scene her reactions have a genuinely human complexity, as she hints at Argos's guilt, tries to retract, considers and rejects the possibility of falsely denouncing Feíta, hesitatingly gives Benicio the bare facts and finally pours out detail upon detail of Argos's affair with Mejía, all – it is the motive that rings most true – to turn her father's anger away from herself towards her sister. For the rest of the novel, however, she is seen, like Argos in *Doña Milagros*, as a case-study. Her obsession with clothes is not studied from within; instead we are shown her vacuous beauty, her poor reputation among the pious ladies, her provincial dress-sense, and her position as the local leader of fashion. In short, the study of her character tells us more about Marineda than about her own psychology.

The same is true of Argos, whose portrait centres largely on her suitor, the young musician, León Caballero (possibly an allusion to the operatic composer Ruggiero Leoncavallo, 1858–1919). The account of León's career, a lively and ironical tale interpolated in the narrative, has little to do with the rest of the novel's action, since Argos soon ends her association with him. Its function is to help establish the novel's provincial context. León is the local boy made good, whose talent is lost on his philistinic countrymen. The adulation he receives changes to enmity when financial interests become involved ('cuando los intereses se ponen en juego, no hay tigres ni panteras comparables en su furor a los marinedinos' – II, 467b). So the portraits of both Rosa and Argos are directed towards a picture of the provincial attitudes of Marineda, against which the strange behaviour of Mauro and Feíta must be seen.

Their personalities are also important because of the events they lead to, that is, seduction and murder. These, together with *el compañero Sobrado*'s blackmail, are examples of the popular novelist's stock-in-trade and, as such, point to the contrast between the two threads of the novel. Side by side in *Memorias* there are two entirely contradictory conceptions of the novel – on the one hand, a story full of striking events, and, on the other, a study of psychic phenomena in which plot counts for little. The tension between the two contradictory threads is justified because it pinpoints the tension in Mauro between the regularity of his chosen life and the chaotic world outside into which he is increasingly drawn.

To complete this survey of Mauro's observation of the Neira family we turn to Feíta, the discussion of whom has been postponed because, significantly, Mauro finds it impossible to encapsulate her in a neat descriptive analysis: '¿Cómo te haría yo comprender bien, ¡oh sesudo y morigerado lector!, lo que era la tal Feíta, en lo físico, en lo moral, en lo intelectual? Cien pliegos de papel no basta para retratar a este curioso personaje.' (II, 468b) His attempt to describe her by combining description and dialogue gives the impression that her outrageous personality dominates him and forces him out of his attitude of ironic detachment ('—Por Dios, Feíta . . . ¡Qué cosas dice usted! Que no la oigan, al menos . . .' – II, 471a). The physical description he gives of her is intended to reveal moral characteristics: 'Sus ojos son chicos, verdes, de límpido matiz, descarados, directos en el mirar, ojos que preguntan, que apremian, que escudriñan, ojos del entendimiento.' (II, 468b) The repetition of the subject ('ojos') together with the accumulation of adjectives and verbs conveys the restless energy which accompanies Feíta's intelligence.[3] Her irrepressible ebullience is emphasised in the whole portrait, most aptly in a topical metaphor applied to her hair: 'Su pelo vive en perpetua insurrección; es el mambís [a Cuban rebel] más rebelde que conozco.' (II, 469a)

But, most characteristically, Feíta is dramatised in her speech – her engaging impertinence to Mauro and her frank and sometimes outrageous expression of feminist views. We note, for example, her response to Mauro's defence of her brother Froilán's prior claim to an education because he is a man: '"¿Froilán hombre? Froilán jumento – respondía perentoriamente e imitando el habla de los negros, la diabólica."' (II, 470a) Or her suggestion, the boldness of which alarms Mauro, that for a man it is easy to enjoy the advantages of marriage without facing its responsibilities (II, 471a).

The presentation of her character, so vigorously begun, gains momentum as the novel proceeds, particularly in the element of pathos which creeps into it. I use the word 'pathos' advisedly because there is no trace of sentimentality in her character. On the contrary, the pathos is conveyed through the humour of Feíta's singlehanded crusade against social attitudes. An example of this is in chapter 12 when she takes Primo Cova aback by demanding that he tell her all the things he is intending to spread around about her. The preemptive strike wins her a lasting ally, but the fact remains that she *will* be talked about and she *will* be censured. The paradox is that the more she defies society and proclaims her independence, the clearer it is that she cannot possibly win her battle. This is most obvious in chapter 21 where Feíta's assertion of independence is countered by Mauro's predictions about the sufferings which await her. The pathos generated by the contrast between her determination and her vulnerability reveals, more than anything else, how much of herself Pardo Bazán put into this character. Unlike Argos and Rosa whom the novelist views only from the outside, Feíta is a character whose struggle and situation she fully understands. It is therefore no accident that Feíta is one of Pardo Bazán's most living and deeply felt creations.

So Mauro is apparently attracted to the Neira *tertulia* because in the behaviour of these three daughters he finds an interesting situation ('los derroches de Rosa, las novelerías de Argos y las inauditas excentricidades de Feíta' – II, 469a), the likely developments of which present a challenge to his powers of observation. Obviously Feíta is the most interesting of the three and the one who plays the most important part in the novel. Because of this and because of Feíta's feminism, some critics have supposed that this is primarily a novel about feminism.[4] Now it is perfectly true that Feíta's challenge to social attitudes towards her as a woman is important in the novel. Indeed, Maryellen Bieder is surely correct when she suggests that Feíta is intended as a counterweight to the eponymous heroine of Galdós's *Tristana*.[5] But in my view it is not accurate to describe *Memorias* as a feminist novel. Gómez de Baquero in an early review writes: 'Diré primeramente que lo principal, a mi entender, de esta novela, es lo *psíquico*, la intensa vida interior de los personajes.'[6] This is a point I wish to insist on: this novel is about two people (Mauro and Feíta) of advanced and unconventional ideas within a certain social context, but it is the confrontation of the two individuals which is the stuff of the novel. Of course, in the process of describing this confrontation Pardo Bazán makes an unanswerable case for the rights of women to self-fulfilment, but she makes a similar case on behalf of men. The male characters' lives have been trivialised by social prejudices as much as the female characters' lives, and Mauro, as much as Feíta, struggles to find his dignity as an individual in a society which frowns on such an enterprise. In other words, the feminist argument is part of a broader argument.

This is a novel, then, about a confrontation, even though, as we have seen, confrontation is the last thing Mauro intends: his interest in the Neira family is, from his point of view, purely academic. Yet, after the description of the three daughters, when he is ready to set in motion the process of his careful observation, he becomes increasingly involved in the family's problems. Having allowed himself to become Benicio's confidant, he soon finds himself offering him help in protecting his daughters' honour. Then, as the hoped-for drama in the family develops, far from delighting in the details Primo Cova gives him, he is alarmed and begs his friend not to gossip about the family. He becomes more materially involved by agreeing to help

Benicio find out about *el compañero Sobrado*. It is Mauro whose quick thinking saves Benicio from a criminal charge and it is finally he who takes over responsibility for the family and marries Feíta. What brings about this change from detachment to involvement? As we must expect in this cycle and as Mauro explains, the villain of the piece is love: '¿Quién (preguntáis) me obligó a intervenir en el conflicto [. . .]? ¡Bah! De sobra habéis adivinado el móvil que me dictaba rasgos de tan inverosímil abnegación y daba al traste con el bien cimentado edificio de mi sosiego. Ya estabais enterados de que me había cogido entre uñas el misterioso duende que desde el origen de los tiempos juguetea con la Humanidad.' (II 524a) This ironic reversal in Mauro is the final outcome of the second and more important thread in the novel. It is here that there appear signs of Pardo Bazán's contact with contemporary ideas on psychology, particularly the concept of the Unconscious.

The composition of *Memorias* is based on the contrast between the rational conscious self and the irrational Unconscious, explicitly at times, as the following extracts show:

La antipatía que al pronto creí sentir hacia ella no era sino la atracción del abismo, *la negra magia de lo desconocido*, contra la cual parecemos indignarnos *mientras nuestro espíritu en secreto la sueña y la busca*, obedeciendo al impulso que lleva al hombre al progreso, aunque parezca repugnarlo. (II, 494a)

Era mi yo verbal y superficial el que condenaba a la innovadora, mientras *mi yo esencial y profundo, desde lo más secreto de la conciencia*, abrazaba sus teorías, la aclamaba, la colocaba en un trono. (II, 494b–5a)

Apenas articulé estas palabras decisivas, cuando se me figuró que las había pronunciado otro, *una persona desconocida que estaba allí, dentro de mí, agazapada en lo profundo de mi ser*, pero que no era yo mismo, sino más bien *mi antagonista, un espíritu hostil*, alguien que procuraba mi daño y mi muerte. (II, 507b)

La idea de tener por compañera a Feíta había cristalizado ya, sin que yo mismo lo notase, *en lo más hondo de mi espíritu*, allí donde radican y perseveran las ilusiones invencibles, las ilusiones amadas, las que tienen el bello color de la esperanza y el ardiente color del deseo. (II, 508b)

The phrases in italics (mine) surely refer to the Unconscious, as Pardo Bazán understood it. Its use here suggests that she may have taken the idea not directly from Schopenhauer, Hartmann or Taine, but from Bourget, the idea for whose *L'irréparable* (1884) was taken from Taine's *De l'intelligence* and Ribot's *Les maladies de la mémoire*.[7] In *L'irréparable* we find the following passages:

Non, la personne humaine, la personne morale, celle dont nous disons *moi*, n'est pas plus simple que le corps lui-même. Par-dessous l'existence intellectuelle et sentimentale dont nous avons conscience, et dont nous endossons la responsabilité, peut-être illusoire, *tout un domaine s'étend, obscur et changeant*, qui est celui de notre vie inconsciente. Il se cache en nous une créature que nous ne connaissons pas, et dont nous ne savons jamais si elle n'est pas *précisément le contraire de la créature que nous croyons être*. De là dérivent ces volte-face singulières de conduite qui ont fourni prétexte à tant de déclamations des moralistes . . . Nous dépensons toute notre activité à poursuivre un but dont nous imaginons que dépend notre bonheur, et, ce but atteint, nous nous apercevons que nous avons méconnu les véritables, *les secrètes exigences de notre sensibilité* . . . (My italics)

Quelles mystérieuses métamorphoses de l'âme traversent un être humain que s'éprend d'un autre? Quelles·influences, impossibles à décomposer dans leur menu détail, déterminent cette invasion de notre vie par un sentiment qui se glisse en nous minute à minute, et que nous reconnaissons alors seulement que nous sommes incapables de le chasser?[8]

Bourget calls the phenomenon he is describing 'la dualité de notre être', a phrase which equally well defines the psychological development of Mauro Pareja. It will be noticed that there are various reminiscences of Bourget in the quotations from *Memorias* above: 'tout un domaine s'étend, obscur et changeant' – 'la atracción del abismo, la negra magia de lo desconocido'; 'Il se cache en nous une créature que nous ne connaissons pas' – 'una persona desconocida que estaba allí, dentro de mí, agazapada en lo profundo de mi ser'; 'précisément le contraire de la créature que nous croyons être' – 'no era yo mismo, sino más bien mi antagonista, un espíritu hostil'; 'les secrètes exigences de notre sensibilité' – 'mientras nuestro espíritu en secreto la sueña y la busca'. It seems at least likely that Pardo Bazán is following Bourget here (a copy of *L'irréparable* was in her private library). This probable influence is in itself interesting; more interesting still is the fact that, as I shall suggest below, Pardo Bazán's novel is quite different from Bourget's.

The 'dualité' which Mauro Pareja slowly discovers inside himself is clear enough. On the conscious level, he is a man who by a rational process has decided that he does not wish to marry, least of all Feíta; on the unconscious level, he is a man who needs to love and be loved and whose longed-for companion is the same Feíta. As the novel proceeds, the Unconscious imposes itself on the conscious self to such an extent that by the end it has entirely supplanted it.

In the first four chapters Mauro presents his conscious self to the reader, as he defends himself from the supposed charge that he is a 'slave to the least spiritual pleasures', by showing that his way of life is based on a moral stance. Observation of life in Marineda, centred, as it is, on the institution of marriage, has led him to want nothing of it; he will not marry. Instead he prefers to order his life in a peaceful and aesthetic way, according to his own wishes and not 'según las exigencias, siempre algo prosaicas, de la vida de familia' (ii, 450b). These words illustrate the impulse in Mauro towards the poetic and the elevated, and it seems that, in the absence of anything nearer at hand, he takes his model for life from the books, particularly the French books, he so avidly reads. In them he finds the Decadent enthusiasm for the refinements of civilisation – '*confort*, bienestar, pulcritud, decoro' – the cult of things English (the anglophilia of Mauro's landlady, doña Consola) and the typically Decadent figure of the dandy.[9] He does not explicitly claim the title of dandy but his 'cult of his own person' or *filaucia* strongly recalls it. Apart from the great care he takes with his dress and personal hygiene, and the delight in surrounding himself with exquisite objects of superior taste, he scrupulously avoids love ('pasión') and active benevolence towards others ('altruísmo').[10]

Having withdrawn from life, he satisfies his affective needs with books and his 'idilios' (his deliberately inconclusive courtships), themselves 'novelitas cortas y del más calificado idealismo' (ii, 455a). Novels are for him a means of escape from the real world:

Y ya me tienen ustedes lejos del mundo real, en grato coloquio con damas espiritadas y neuróticas, con maniáticos donosos [. . .] con damas parisienses vestidas por Worth y que exhalan perfumes de gardenia y de verbena blanca, con heroínas emancipadas y que huyen de su hogar batiendo las puertas, con caballeros de trusa y garzota . . . En fin, con una cohorte de seres extraños, fantásticos, pero de vida más intensa y ardiente que la de los hombres y mujeres de carne y hueso que recorren las calles de Marineda. (ii, 454a)

In authentic Decadent manner, Mauro's esoteric tastes are an expression of his inner dissatisfaction with the colourless world of Marineda.[11]

This, then, is the person Mauro believes himself to be: a man whose superior intelligence, sensibility and legitimate pride lead him to remain detached from the normal life of men, and, in particular, to resist marriage. But what are we to make of his self-portrait and apologia? It is as well to approach the question bearing in mind the conflict between the Catholic view of marriage as central to human society and certain misogynistic and anti-matrimonial tendencies in nineteenth-century Rationalist thought.[12] Within this polemical context, it would be difficult to convince the average middle-class Catholic reader (in the absence of any firm evidence we must assume that the majority of Pardo Bazán's readers would fall into this category) of the validity of confirmed bachelorhood, especially if Pereda's hard line in *El buey suelto* was typical.[13] On the other hand, the same middle-class reader would probably see truth in Mauro's description of the economic trials of married life, with all their distasteful side effects. Equally he would probably accept Mauro's claim (he could not decently do otherwise) that his 'idilios' are preferable to the activities of the adulterer, seducer or slanderer. Certainly there is no indication in what Mauro says that the novelist intends us to disagree with him. Indeed it is important that we should assent to his clear and logical arguments in these early chapters if we are to follow with interest and sympathy the course of his psychological development in the rest of the novel.

Nevertheless, there is a sense in which the very qualities of clarity and logicality undermine his position. He asserts, for example, that in rejecting marriage and fatherhood, he is loving his non-existent wife and children more than any husband or father could love their actual spouse or offspring, and he supports this with 'solid arguments'. But his logic excludes the possibility that he may one day experience a love more genuine than that which inspires his 'idilios sosos'. He assumes, that is, that he will always keep a rational hold on his life. There is a similar reductive attitude to life in his praise of egoism: 'Consejero prudente sentado a nuestra cabecera y consagrado a reprimir nuestros caprichos sentimentales, nuestros arrechuchos, nuestras vehemencias, él es quien nos manda no alterar la paz del hogar ajeno, no meter la hoz en la mies del vecino, no revolver el cotarro, no buscar quimera, rehuir la acción y evitar el interés y la lucha, fuente de todo disgusto.' (II, 451a) A first reaction to these Schopenhauerian approaches to *ataraxia* may be to regard them as impossible, but a more serious objection would be that, in his efforts to avoid unhappiness, Mauro is depriving himself of anything one might call fulfilment. We can surely appreciate what Benicio means when, with all his misfortunes, he tells Mauro that he himself has known pleasures which a bachelor could not even guess at (II, 460b). So although the reader can see the logic of Mauro's position, he must have doubts about his wisdom.

Sympathy with reservation is also evoked by Mauro's final and, he claims, most subtle reason for remaining unmarried. The psychological study of a girl at a ball who, rejected by the man she admires, in pique accepts another, rings true, as does Mauro's fear of being accepted in marriage in similar circumstances.[14] But how can the reader not react against him when he explains that he has very special motives ('móviles altos, quintaesenciados y sublimes'), incomprehensible to the herd, because he is a 'refined man of his times' and a reader of foreign psychological novels? Quixote-like, he has allowed his reading to go to his head and the reader may well suspect that in this particular section at least Mauro has simply been tilting at windmills. Of course, on a second reading all these problems have disappeared and these early chapters take on great irony.

So his conscious self is undisturbed for the first eight chapters of the novel, but after this it is possible to trace the successive stages of his growing awareness of the unwelcome presence of his unconscious self. One can identify seven stages: 1. The moment when Mauro becomes Benicio's confidant. 2. The dream in chapter 11. 3. The arrival of Feíta at his house. 4. The point at which his jealousy makes him realise the true nature of his feelings towards Feíta. 5. The attempt at a cure. 6. The unexpected visit of Feíta, during which he realises that he is completely in love and proposes. 7. His final admission that he has been deceiving himself and that the real motive for his interest in the Neira family is simply the operation of sexual instinct. His psychological development, which I shall now consider, is conveyed by his reactions to people and events, and by his (often devious) musing on his own reactions.

The first stage of this development is contained in chapters 9 and 10. As we have seen, Mauro prides himself on his detachment from his fellow men. In chapter 8 he reaffirms this: 'Entre las enseñanzas de mi santo egoísmo contaba la de no tener amigos íntimos, ni pecho abierto para persona alguna.' (II, 472a) However, his behaviour during the conversation with Benicio which follows immediately after belies this affirmation. At first he laughs inwardly at Benicio and goads him into expressing his disapproval of Feíta, but as Benicio alludes to the Civil Governor's recent display of interest in the girl, Mauro, sensing the danger to which she is exposed, feels a sudden interest in her – 'un deseo de contribuir a salvarla, que me impulsó a decir a Neira: — Cuente usted conmigo . . .' (II, 474a) Despite himself, as the word 'impulsó' indicates, Mauro has broken his golden rule and allowed himself to become involved. He immediately repents of this indiscreet attack of altruism, the more so as it provokes Benicio to open his heart more than he has ever done. A relationship of intimacy has been established between them, and Mauro has become Benicio's confidant. The same pattern of detachment and involvement is repeated: Mauro finds himself reassuring and advising Benicio, reacting against this involvement when called upon to take an active part in solving his problems, but finally giving way before Benicio's unaffected gratitude. There appear phrases such as 'a pesar mío', 'me conmoví' and 'sin reflexionar' which point to the irrational nature of Mauro's response. The lifestyle chosen by his conscious self is based on his reason, the control of which his unconscious self is now escaping.

At this stage, Mauro is barely aware of this process, but the dream which follows the conversation between Benicio and himself (stage 2) makes it clear to the reader. The context of the dream is a revealing example of Mauro's tendency to self-deception. He consoles himself with the fact that his involvement with Neira was motivated simply by friendship: 'No estando interesado mi corazón por ninguna de las hijas de don Benicio, y sintiendo, en cambio, una afición nobilísima hacia el buen padre, no entrañaba verdadero peligro mi injerencia en los asuntos de la casa.' (II, 477a) The nightmare of the serpent intruding into his bed represents his Unconscious, and forcefully contradicts Mauro's sanguine view of his situation. The dream itself is a curious mixture of the scientific and the symbolic. It is scientific in so far as it is given a rational explanation – the serpent is a transformation of Mauro's cat who sleeps at the end of his bed. The common features of both are their sinuous backs and their glinting eyes. The fact that Mauro has eaten some shell-fish that night also helps to explain the dream.[15] The reader, however, is unlikely to be content with such an explanation and will probably be more inclined to notice that Mauro compares the serpent to Eve's tempter in the Garden of Eden ('el maldito ofidio, el que causó en el Paraíso la pérdida de nuestro padre Adán y de toda nuestra estirpe, sentenciada a la concupiscencia y al dolor' – II, 477b). The novelist is giving us a definite clue that her narrator has been moved at the level of his sexual instinct without being, or wishing to be, aware of it.[16] All that he is sure of, on awaking, is that the innocent pleasures of his peaceful life have lost their appeal and that he is left uneasy and listless.

It is with him in this state of mind that the third stage of his development begins (the arrival of Feíta to use doña Consola's library). In chapters 11 and 12 Pardo Bazán shows Mauro taken off guard for the first time and losing control of the situation. The undoubted humour of chapter 11 results from the contrast between Mauro's overreaction to Feíta's presence – his 'sorpresa', 'asombro', 'incredulidad' – and Feíta's impatience with him. He is further disconcerted when his landlady, doña Consola (a rather Dickensian character), grandly contradicts him and defends Feíta's behaviour. Ironically, one of the mainstays of his *filaucia* has been turned against him.

Mauro's discomfiture is compounded with the arrival in chapter 12 of Primo Cova, Marineda's leading gossip-monger. Again the irony is directed at Mauro's superior pose: he values Cova's visits as a means of finding out about the activities of the Neira daughters, but now he himself is frightened of providing material for Cova's tongue. The humour of this chapter lies in Mauro's attempt to recapture the initiative in order to prevent Cova from gaining the wrong impression – 'Usted lo acierta—exclamé, acogiéndome a la hipótesis como el náufrago al palo flotante. Un capricho de esta señorita, que nos ha de volver locos a todos.' (II, 480a) Excluded from the conversation by Feíta and Cova, he tries to force his way back to explain Feíta's behaviour, only to be cut short by Cova who knows the explanation already. Beleaguered, bewildered and deflated, Mauro hands the keys over to Feíta and flees with Cova. The confrontation of these four contrasting characters – Feíta, Mauro, Cova and doña Consola, produces a scene of great humour which brings alive, more than anything else in the book, the personality of Feíta and the change taking place in Mauro. Previously, Mauro was detached and in control, presenting his own personal analysis of Feíta; now the impression is given that this analysis has escaped his control because it is presented by events themselves, that is, the presentation is dramatic.

From drama we return to reflection at the beginning of the following chapter (13) where Mauro considers his attitudes towards his new situation. As in the previous reflective passage (the dream) the reader is given more of an insight into the narrator's feelings than he has himself. This is achieved by the discrepancy between Mauro's interpretation of his emotional state and what he does and says. He states emphatically that he cares not one bit for Feíta: 'A mi parecer, ni se me importaba un bledo del marimacho, ni al marimacho se le daba de mí un ardite. ¿Yo querer a semejante mascarón?' (II, 485a) But if this is indeed the case, his behaviour is singular, to say the least.

Why should he avoid the Neira *tertulia* and even Benicio himself? The reason he gives – his embarrassment that Feíta's first show of emancipation has taken place in his house – hardly convinces. Equally, why should he be so distressed at Feíta's presence in the same house? He tells us that she upsets his routine; but he never sees her, neither does she make any attempt to disturb him. His reaction, therefore, is out of all proportion to the stimulus of her presence: 'Me alteraba, me desazonaba, me trastornaba, destruía mi dulce paz.' (II, 484a)

He offers as a further explanation the fact that his vanity is wounded by the near presence of a woman who is quite oblivious of him. Again he implies that Feíta, as an individual, means nothing to him, since any woman in the next room would have affected him in the same way. He is betrayed, however, by his final reason, which is not given precisely as a reason but as a rather baffled observation. This bafflement, this admission of a factor beyond his control, makes his final reason more convincing to the reader. It takes the form of a metaphor used to express the effect Feíta's proximity has on him. It is like the fear, he tells us, of going into a darkened room and realising that someone is there: 'Aunque tengamos motivos para suponer que ese alguien no quiere hacernos ningún daño; aunque nos conste que el individuo allí agazapado nos tiene miedo a su vez . . . no somos dueños de reprimir un intenso escalofrío, una especie de horror misterioso, que no procede de la persona oculta por las tinieblas, sino de lo desconocido, de una aprensión sin objeto, casi sobrenatural . . .' (II, 484b) The intensity of feeling contained in the metaphor (resulting largely from the syntactic accumulation leading up to the final epithet) must prompt us to question again Mauro's professed indifference for Feíta. But the details of the metaphor suggest that it is not Feíta as such who disturbs him – not the person in the dark – but a mysterious force associated with her. Mauro himself cannot explain his irrational alarm but the reader has been given sufficient clues to identify it with sexual passion.

In case he fails to do so, a further indication is given immediately after as Mauro makes an indirect reference back to the give-away dream in chapter 11. In expressing his fear that Feíta might get into his room ('la lectora *se me colase en la habitación*') he lets slip a verbal reminiscence of the dream ('*se me colaba dentro de la alcoba* una serpiente' – II, 484b, my italics in both cases) and follows this with a simile about a cat, which reinforces the reminiscence. It seems as if

Mauro is unconscious of the identification of Feíta with the tempting serpent, but it is there, and, if registered, strengthens the superior understanding the author and reader have of his feelings.

Again the narrative moves from reflection to drama, with Mauro's decision to bring the situation to an end by talking to Feíta. Here we reach the fourth stage of his development. As before, Mauro is thrown off balance, this time by Feíta's irritated welcome. He makes his response 'algo confuso' and thereafter never regains the initiative. Feíta finally leaves before he has time to broach the subject which is the reason for his visit. There are three points relevant to our reconstruction of his emotional development. First, Mauro finds Feíta physically attractive for the first time and in her face he notices an inexplicable change. Now, it seems clear from the context that Feíta has objectively become more attractive, blossoming out as a woman in her new-found liberty. Nevertheless, that Mauro should notice this and dwell on it at some length is an indication that there is a change of attitude on his part towards her. This is on the physical level: the second point concerns the moral level. Mauro is astonished to hear Feíta enunciating a view of life identical to his own – his egocentric theory of *filaucia*: 'La cosa que más me interesa a mí es Feíta Neira, y a usted, Mauro Pareja' and 'el deber supremo es para con nosotros' (II, 487a). No more can he dismiss her views and personality as merely eccentric.

The third point is the introduction of the major factor in Mauro's development: his jealousy. This phenomenon is already present in *Doña Milagros* when Benicio's jealousy of Vicente teaches him that he loves Milagros, but it is much more important here.[17] We are given the first indication of Mauro's jealousy when Feíta implies that she has a suitor. This is Mauro's reaction: '—¿Quién, quién? Feíta, hónreme usted con su confianza —supliqué, lleno de inexplicable afán.' (II, 489a) The repeated 'quién' and the 'supliqué' betray the intensity of Mauro's interest, and the word 'inexplicable' shows that he is still unaware of his feelings. In the following chapter (15) he becomes aware of his jealousy and realises the danger he is in, when Cova mentions *el compañero Sobrado*. Mauro's own reaction takes him by surprise: 'Sentí un choque raro y desagradable, una especie de malestar violento y repentino, una repulsión.' (II, 492ab) A notable feature of his reaction is that for the first time in his life a moral sensation is accompanied by a physical image of the person who has caused it. The fact that the image he has of *el compañero Sobrado* is attractive and therefore potentially attractive to Feíta causes him 'a great sorrow, an intense pain'. He takes due warning from this response and sees the relevance of his dream: ' ¡Mis presagios, mis presagios! ¡La serpiente!' (II, 492b) The novelist no doubt intends the reader to smile at Mauro's backwardness in understanding his own feelings.

Chapter 16 is the centre of the novel, because in it Mauro wrestles with himself, trying to understand his situation; he is in love and he is jealous, although even now he is unhappy about stating it unequivocally ('*casi* prendado y *casi* celoso' – II, 493a, my italics). The greater part of the chapter Mauro devotes to an inquiry into the origin of his sickness ('enfermedad' is his word). Having decided that Feíta lacks all the qualities necessary to appeal in the normal way either to his senses or to his feelings, he isolates imagination as the cause of his complaint. His 'curiosidad moral' has been aroused by Feíta's very strangeness and his original antipathy to her was simply 'la atracción del abismo, la negra magia de lo desconocido' (II, 494a). If we extend and update Mauro's own metaphor, we can say that although he is immune to women in general, Feíta is a new form of virus against which he is quite unprotected. She is everything the subjects of his previous 'idilios' had not been – independent in mind and action, guardian of her own dignity. Consequently, she inspires in him feelings of respect and esteem. In other words, he is resisting the idea that his attraction to Feíta is sexual. There is in him a typically Decadent aversion to the natural processes which, in Schopenhauerian terms, work in favour of the species but without thought for the individual.

However, despite this resistance to the truth, in this central self-analysis Mauro is struck by the strangeness of the human mind and its capacity for self-deception and recognises the existence of an unconscious self in complete contradiction to his conscious rational self. From now on the interest for the reader lies not in Mauro's ignorance of his unconscious desires but in his struggle against them, and in his continuing belief that these desires are not sexual.

Now that Mauro has reached this measure of self-knowledge, we arrive at the fifth stage of his development. He is as yet unprepared to accept the demands of his unconscious self and attempts to cure himself of his sickness by avoiding Feíta at all costs. However, this treatment, far from remedying his condition, simply aggravates the symptoms, intensifying his jealousy and leaving him dissatisfied with all the pleasures of his bachelor life. This is a measure of the transformation love has worked in him. Mauro, the dandy of the beginning of the novel, would have been horrified to hear himself utter these words: 'Que no se puede ser impasible; que necesitamos sentir, aunque el sentir nos atormente, y que ciertos estados de alma no piden retraimiento, piden guerra y conflicto . . .' (II, 496a)

The final long encounter between Mauro and Feíta (chapters 19 to 21) during which the proposal of marriage is made (the sixth stage), is among the most vigorous and yet most delicate pieces of writing in the novel, arguably indeed in the whole of Pardo Bazán's *œuvre*. In it the novelist presents in a kind of counterpoint the separate inner conflicts of Mauro and Feíta. For Mauro, there is the struggle with love, jealousy and suspicion; for Feíta, the struggle to rise above the limitations and degradations of her social and family situation. Mauro's feelings pass back and forth between complete infatuation, doubts and jealousy; in Feíta we see righteous indignation, heroism, tenderness and vulnerability.

At this stage, although Mauro admits his love for Feíta, he cannot rid himself of his suspicions of her motives, deriving as they do from his suspicions of women in general. As soon as she confides in him he suffers a reaction, just as he did with her father in similar circumstances: 'Noté una especie de frío moral repentino, y acogí receloso las confidencias de Feíta, precisamente cuando éstas llegaban al grado de mayor intimidad y abandono [. . .]. Sentí que me ponía en guardia y me pareció que de pronto mi cariño se sumía como agua en arenal.' (II, 504a) However, the sincerity of her indignation at the behaviour of her two sisters dispels his doubts entirely ('disipadas mis sospechas enteramente'). Or so it seems. Further on he contradicts this: 'Mis desconfianzas, *ya que no muertas*, reposaban adormecidas por la magia de aquella bravía veracidad.' (II, 506b-7a, my italics) But this contradiction well expresses his inner vacilation. Just before this passage Mauro presents us with a very immediate account of his traumatic transformation in his reaction to Feíta's heroic intention to seek her own fortune in Madrid:

Me levanté sin contestar, y comencé a pasear por el reducido espacio del cuchitril. Una lucha se verificaba en mi alma. Las palabras de Feíta, su modo de pensar y sentir [. . .] habían acrecentado y desatado, con reacción violenta, mi entusiasmo, actuando sobre mi imaginación, realzando su figura, obligándome, casi a la fuerza, sin acquiescencia de mi voluntad, a estimarla como nunca, y a postrarme rendido a sus pies. (II, 506b)

The reference to the smallness of the room in the opening sentence (in this context 'cuchitril' has no derogatory connotations) is not gratuitous, as it suggests the intensity of Mauro's agitation. This, together with the mounting tension of participial clauses and adverbial phrases (in the third sentence), leading to the definition of his final mental state (itself rising in intensity – 'estimarla [. . .] postrarme rendido') attests to Pardo Bazán's sureness in the use of language for the concrete evocation of psychological states. We notice that, as before, Feíta appeals to his imagination and that his esteem for her grows without the control of his will, or rather, his conscious self. The transformation is now complete: he is in love, and glories in the fact:

Sentíame arrebatado, conquistado, enamorado a todo trapo, de veras, y un transporte inexplicable llenaba mi pecho, como si aquel sentimiento singular, que pocos días antes ni sospechaba, fuese para mí una patente de juventud, de salud moral, de energía, la potencia germinativa del alma, conservada en mí y atrofiada antes bajo la plancha de acero del egoísmo. Sí; lo más extraordinario es que me regocijaba de sentirme en poder de la pasión. Juraría que había crecido. Mi pulso se apresuraba, mis venas hervían, mi cuerpo era ligero y ágil como cuando respiramos inhalaciones de éter. ¡Sensación extraña! En aquel instante me parecía volar . . . No quería combatir: ansiaba entregarme; rabiaba por dar salida a las palabras que se agolpaban a mis labios y desahogo a la plenitud de mi corazón. (II, 507a)

Comment is hardly necessary on a passage which, given Mauro's former deviousness, is startlingly explicit. His *egoísmo*, or *filaucia*, far from enlarging him spiritually, had diminished him as a human being. For the first time he gives himself over to the plenitude of human emotion.

But even in the proposal of marriage which Mauro then makes, Pardo Bazán still wants to convey the violent oscillation of feeling which characterises his *volte-face*. The strong sense of alienation he experiences is described thus: 'Apenas articulé estas palabras decisivas, cuando se me figuró que las había pronunciado otro, una persona desconocida que estaba allí, dentro de mí [. . .] pero que no era yo mismo, sino más bien mi antagonista, un espíritu hostil, alguien que procuraba mi daño y mi muerte.' (II, 507b) Mauro feels himself split in two and his conscious self – the personality created by his will and his reason – now views with terror the unconscious self he had just welcomed so wholeheartedly. His ascent to the heights of emotion is dismissed as a sentimental impulse. He himself puts his terrified reaction down to celibacy and an 'inveterate fear of the great madness' (marriage). But, ever volatile, he promptly lurches back into his rapture, grasping Feíta's proffered hand. The utter confusion inside him during his encounter with Feíta is conveyed by the accumulation of unfamiliar and contradictory experiences. Here, as he takes her hand, he feels an electric shock which tells him clearly for the first time (the reader has long been aware of it) that Feíta appeals as much to his senses as to his imagination; he has to admit at last that his attraction is sexual. A little awkwardly, Pardo Bazán cannot resist showing her hand by reminding the reader that this is a more subtle analysis than that offered by the simplistic certainties of Positivist psychology: 'En esto del análisis amoroso siempre nos aguarda sorpresas, porque no hay instrumentos para pesar y aislar los sentimientos y las sensaciones.' (II, 508a) The novelist cannot quite resign herself to the rule that art conceals art. This is, however, a lapse rare in the treatment of these two characters.

With admirable control, Pardo Bazán extends the effects of Mauro's transformation and brings the encounter between the couple to a climax by reversing their situations. Aware that he is playing for the highest stakes, Mauro risks all in a display of uncommon eloquence. For the first time in the novel he publicly drops his mask of detachment and impassiveness ('Si parezco enigma, este enigma tiene solución, tiene clave') and admits that his continued bachelorhood is a sign of weakness rather than strength. Countering Feíta's assertion of her right to individual self-fulfilment, he points out the realities of her situation, the suffering and disillusion which must accompany her schooling in the way of the world. Since his arguments are so convincing, he assumes moral strength in relation to Feíta. She, on the other hand, shows and admits her weakness, while still clinging to her own search for personal dignity. It is difficult to describe the genuine pathos of this section without quoting at length, but Feíta's simple, heroic response to Mauro's picture of her future in a hostile society and his noble offer of himself is some indication:

'Piénselo usted, niña mía ..., loquita mía ... Le ofrezco a usted la libertad ... dentro del deber ..., y con el amor de propina ... Me parece que no hay motivo para que usted vuelva la cara. ¿Que dice usted? ...
—Que deseo recorrer la senda de abrojos, Mauro amigo —respondió conmovida a pesar suya la muchacha. (II, 510b)

Here, as throughout these chapters, it is the shifting complexity of Mauro's emotions that the text conveys. Having risen to the heights of generous feeling, he descends suddenly to base suspicion and jealousy and throws the name of *el compañero Sobrado* in Feíta's face. The chapter ends with characteristic control of emotional impact and psychology. Feíta brings the conversation to an abrupt end by resuming control, as Mauro, by showing jealousy, loses his moral authority. The final exchange presents most dramatically her complex personality:

—¿Me escribirá usted? ¿O tampoco . . . quiere usted escribirme?
—¡Escribir! ¡Yo lo creo! ¿No le he dicho a usted que es usted mi mejor amigo? ¿A quién quiere usted que cuente mis esperanzas, mis batallas, mis triunfos, toda mi historia? ¡Ya verá usted cómo mis cartas le aburren y cómo no me las devuelve después! Adiós, Pareja, adiós . . .; no quiero enternecerme; necesito ánimos . . . Gracias . . ., perdóneme usted . . . ¡No, no me acompañe; ya sé la casa! (II, 511a)

There could be no better example of the way Feíta is characterised by her speech; the emphatic manner of expression and its lively familiarity. Here the reader is shown the strength of her personality, her ebullience, her tenderness, loyalty and practicality. Unlike earlier assertions of independence, her final words here have a certain tragic quality in the light of what precedes them. They exemplify her avowed determination to 'tread the path of thorns'. We are presented at this point with the depths of not only the narrator's soul, but also Feíta's: a glimpse is given of the pressures to which she is subjected and we realise that the strong exterior hides a tortured personality trying to retain her dignity as a person. She is, then, far more complex than she may seem and her eccentricity now appears as a cry for freedom of spirit. We have already seen in Mauro a parallel desire to escape social limitations.

By this stage in the novel the process of Mauro's psychological development is complete and the final chapter (chapters 22 to 25 complete the other thread in the novel) adds little except to show how Mauro has accepted the change in himself with equanimity and even satisfaction (the seventh stage): 'Había desertado tan resueltamente de mis banderas, que llegué a dudar si el Mauro Pareja cauto, precavido y cuerdo de las primeras páginas de estas *Memorias* sería el mismo que sólo vivía para tomar como cosa propia aquellos cuidados ajenos que, según el proverbio, matan al . . . ¡No escribiré el poco halagüeño sustantivo!' (II, 524b)[18] Mauro is referring directly to the transformation I have been describing here. He had mistakenly believed that it was possible to resist the demands of nature and that submission to these demands would inevitably lead to a loss of fulfilment. Now he knows that both these beliefs are untrue. Not that the conclusion of the novel suggests the kind of argument in favour of the institution of marriage found in Pereda's *El buey suelto*: the union of Mauro and Feíta is clearly exceptional in the context of Marineda. Their criticisms of the normal, conventional manner of contracting marriages and the hollowness of what follows remain valid.

So out of the psychological study of Mauro there emerges an affirmation of life, a middle way between the constraints of provincial attitudes and the emotional atrophy of a self-absorbed aestheticism. In her last three published novels, Pardo Bazán was to take up again the search for an alternative to these two extremes, but the Christian solution offered there differs radically from the secular common-sense of *Memorias*.

CONCLUSION

As an aid to understanding the kind of novel *Memorias* is I have mentioned its probable debt to Bourget. Certainly that can help us to identify the particular nature of Pardo Bazán's interests as a psychological novelist: the mysterious activities of the human mind as described by contemporary psychologists. But another parallel can be drawn with Jane Austen. The comparison suggests itself in the first place because of the resemblances between *Memorias* and *Pride and Prejudice*. Mauro, like Darcy with Elizabeth Bennet, thinks Feíta beneath his notice as a woman, and, again like Darcy, entirely revises his opinion. Feíta, although not prejudiced against Mauro, nevertheless refuses his offer of marriage and then, like Elizabeth, changes her mind. So the situational irony of both novels is similar. However, I offer the comparison, not on account of these fortuitous resemblances (there is no evidence that Pardo Bazán had read *Pride and Prejudice*), but because it helps to set at relief the humour which is a common characteristic of both *Pride and Prejudice* and *Memorias*, and which is signally lacking in Bourget's work. In the novels of the French writer the point of departure and ultimate destination is pessimism about a human wretchedness which is not even a cause for laughter. Jane Austen's view of humanity, on the other hand, itself scarcely rosy, is consistently humorous: the Collinses and Mrs Bennets condemn themselves by their utterances to derision, and the mistaken judgements of Elizabeth and Darcy provoke a gentler and more sympathetic form of mirth.

It is to this latter variety that Pardo Bazán approaches in *Memorias*, notably with Mauro's ignorance of the activities of his unconscious self. He is like the pantomime character who, warned by his youthful audience of the presence of some menace, always refuses to look in the right direction. Yet, despite the similarity between the two novels, there is a radical difference in the underlying causes of the comic situation. In *Pride and Prejudice* the mistake is accidental, depending on partial understanding of the circumstances and people involved. In *Memorias* the mistaken judgement of Mauro and Feíta about themselves and their way of life has social roots. Mauro imagining that he can withdraw from life and Feíta that she can take her full part in it are comic, but in their delusion they compel our sympathy because both, in ways only apparently opposed, are attempting to preserve their dignity in a hostile social context. As in *Doña Milagros*, there appears that maturity which can combine both irony and clarity of vision with understanding and compassion.

I wish to go further and argue that *Memorias* represents an advance on *Doña Milagros* in the central matter of psychology. I am not concerned with the concrete presentation of the characters' personalities (the study of Benicio in the first novel is equally as satisfying as that of Mauro in the second) but rather with the kind of subject Pardo Bazán chooses to treat. Benicio and Milagros are case-book studies in so far as the novelist's attention is drawn to them because they are in some sense abnormal. Milagros is an Andalusian (with the psychological characteristics attributed by Pardo Bazán to her race) and childless, and Benicio is a man lacking in masculine aggression. Mauro and Feíta, on the other hand, do not exemplify any particular psychological phenomenon; they are, as we see once their superficial eccentricities have been abandoned, perfectly normal, intelligent people. In fact they are successfully established as a norm against which society itself is judged to be eccentric. As a result we cannot distance ourselves from them as we might from Benicio and Milagros: they challenge us more directly. *Memorias* has, then, deeper resonances than *Doña Milagros*. Pardo Bazán was, of course, writing in the 1890s, when the extreme individualism of aestheticism and a certain kind of feminism may have seemed to some (at times, indeed, to the novelist herself) an appropriate response to the depersonalising effects of contemporary society. But this does not mean that *Memorias* is dated; in so far as conflicts between individuals and social norms continue to exist, the deeper resonances remain.

So *Memorias de un solterón* is for me one of Pardo Bazán's most significant novels. The energetic and quite unsentimental presentation of the genuinely profound emotional processes of Mauro and Feíta, as these characters relate to society, attests to the high quality of Pardo Bazán's achievement in this novel. It is therefore all the more unfortunate for her reputation that this should be one of the least read and commented on of her works.

Conclusion

I began by saying that Pardo Bazán has hitherto been regarded first and foremost as a Naturalist. I hope it is clear by now that such a view needs to be modified. I hope it is also clear that the almost universal acceptance of *Los pazos de Ulloa* as her finest work undervalues her achievement as a novelist. That novel, I have suggested, represents not a pinnacle, but a turning-point. In it she begins to move away from the attempt (inspired by the Goncourt brothers) to render 'la visión lúcida de las cosas exteriores' towards the exploration of the human mind. In the presentation of Julián we see for the first time the probing irony which characterises her mature work. Her increasing interest in psychology was undoubtedly encouraged by the examples of experimental psychology on the one hand and the Russian novelists and Bourget on the other. Yet her growth as a novelist was not just the assimilation of sources, whether scientific or literary: the novels examined above have a very individual flavour, deriving from a blend of ironic detachment and sympathy and involvement, as well as a sense of the complexity of human motivation.

In *Insolación* Pardo Bazán scrutinises Asís's bewilderment with an irony which is often comic but never sneering, because Asís's self-deception is an understandable response to her contradictory feelings. The question of whether she is a victim or beneficiary of love is left open; but if it is the former we feel for her, and if the latter we share her happiness. The narrator's detachment is the detachment of doubt, not of indifference. The same is true of *Morriña*, where the impertinence of simple explanations of human behaviour is exposed and where the dual perspective on the characters warns us to be circumspect in our judgement of them.

Una cristiana–La prueba is marred by the preconceived idea which informs it: it is not the 'experiment in life' (to use George Eliot's phrase) that *Insolación* is. The affirmative tone adopted by the novelist to defend an extreme Catholic view of life is unconvincing because it is difficult for the reader to transfer his sympathy from Salustio, the freethinker, to Carmen, the saint–heroine. But even this failure is an indication of the positive quality of Pardo Bazán's mature work, that is, an awareness of the complexity of moral judgements. Such an awareness creeps in despite the simple solution the novel suggests. How can we categorically condemn Salustio's love and wholeheartedly applaud Carmen's sacrifice? Moreover, Salustio's frailty as he struggles to reconcile his Positivism and deep-seated Romanticism provides a more persuasive critique of Positivist certainties than Carmen's triumph over human nature. Pardo Bazán does not, as Pereda would have done, make her freethinker totally misguided. In fact her sympathy for him is so great that she fails to make him the unreliable narrator he is apparently intended to be.

In *La piedra angular* Pardo Bazán's clearsightedness is not obstructed by a preconceived idea and, as in *Insolación*, she stands back in order to see more clearly into a complex moral case to which she is obviously not indifferent. Moragas's philanthropy and *quijotismo* are admirable when compared with the smallmindedness of the *marinedinos*, but his self-indulgent *campaña redentorista* appears trivial beside the suffering of Rojo. The executioner's legalism is obtuse and inhuman when compared with Moragas's spontaneous concern for the condemned criminals, yet at the same time he is a victim both of the society which needs him and of Moragas's megalomania. In this novel there is no overt Christian thesis, but Pardo Bazán suggests indirectly that a compassionate understanding of an individual's situation is of more value than formal religious observances.

Like *Insolación*, *Doña Milagros* deals with two opposing views of love, but the dual perspective here derives from the irony not of the omniscient narrator but of the unreliable first-person narration. Through his quixotic attitude to Milagros Benicio expresses forcefully an idealistic view of love, yet his comic naivety suggests that the cynicism of others is perhaps more justified. Nevertheless by making him the narrator and by implying that his weaknesses are in fact strengths, Pardo Bazán silently invites us to prefer his Romantic idealism, not because it is necessarily valid, but because it gives meaning to life. This advocacy of the *mentira vital* reminds us of the Unamuno of, for example, *San Manuel Bueno*. So although we are still faced with the ambiguity found in *Insolación*, we sense more clearly where Pardo Bazán's sympathies lie.

In *Memorias* the dialectic between detachment and involvement is at its most intriguing. Feíta and Mauro are both part of Pardo Bazán herself. Feíta's feminism is clearly shared by the novelist, and Mauro's escape into art is a temptation which she herself faced. Yet there is no sentimental identification of author and characters. Mauro's rejection of human involvement in favour of idealised *idilios* and Feíta's brave attempt to gain her own dignity singlehanded, although treated sympathetically, are shown in the end to be misguided. The novel's dénouement is not, however, reductive: it does not imply the Naturalist thesis that fundamentally we are no more than animals. The ideals which lie behind Mauro's and Feíta's delusions are not discredited. Mauro accepts the existence of his sexual nature and Feíta her need for others, but their marriage is not a capitulation. The respect they offer each other enhances their dignity and is the basis of a creative engagement with the situation they have been thrust into. So the ambiguities of the previous novels find their resolution in an affirmation of the value of life. But even here the solution is not absolute: the open-ended final sentence, where Mauro suggests that he might write his *Memorias de un casado*, warns us against imagining that the couple's life will be without its problems.

The story of the making of Pardo Bazán the novelist is of a journey, which begins with a rendering of the external world and ends with a telling and touching account of a search for meaning. Like the mature works of Galdós (to which in the end Pardo Bazán's novels of the 1890s bear most resemblance) the novels discussed here are characterised above all by ambiguity and moral complexity. In their obstinate idealism they are quite unlike Zola's novels and approximate more not only to Galdós but also to Pardo Bazán's younger contemporary, Unamuno. The comparison is not as absurd as it might seem and I offer it in order to underline what I hope the preceding pages have shown: that Pardo Bazán is a considerably more intelligent and significant novelist than is generally supposed.

Appendix 1
A biographical sketch

Emilia Pardo Bazán was born on 16 September 1851 in La Coruña, the principal town of Galicia. She was the only child of comfortably-off, broadminded parents who encouraged her intellectual interests from an early age. She was educated privately in La Coruña and also for three years in a French school in Madrid, and this early introduction to French culture may account for her lifelong francophilia. In 1868, when aged sixteen, she married José Quiroga, a law-student belonging to one of the most important families in Galicia and therefore a highly suitable match for Emilia. In the following year her father, a former Carlist, was elected to the Cortes as a Progressive deputy, so the family moved to Madrid where doña Emilia gained her first experience of high society. With the election of Amadeo de Saboya as king, her father, now disillusioned with Progressive politics, thought it prudent for the family to leave the country. Between 1871 and 1874 Pardo Bazán visited Paris, Vienna, Venice, Verona, Geneva and London, on the first of her many travels round Europe. In 1876 her first child, Jaime, was born; Blanca was born in 1879, Carmen in 1881. During these years doña Emilia was also occupied with the study of philosophy, theology and the natural sciences, and was greatly influenced by the educationalist Francisco Giner de los Ríos. Although she did not sympathise with the Krausist philosophy of Giner and his associates, she greatly admired their integrity and intellectual seriousness. Her first notable publications were a prize-winning essay on the Enlightened eighteenth-century Galician Benedictine, Feijóo (1876), articles on heat, light and electricity (1876), and studies of Dante, Milton and Darwin (1877). Although her first novel (*Pascual López*, 1879) is a relatively light-weight piece, her novels of the 1880s are informed by the seriousness of these early publications. Inspired by the example of French novelists such as Balzac, the Goncourt brothers and Zola, she set out to write novels based on the careful observation first of the external world and later of human psychology. In 1882, for example, she spent some time in a cigarette factory in La Coruña gathering documentary information for her third novel, *La Tribuna*. In the late 1880s and the 1890s her novels deal less with external reality and more with individuals' self-deception and inner conflicts. Her last three published novels, *La quimera* (1905), *La sirena negra* (1908) and *Dulce dueño* (1911) are influenced by *modernismo* and explore the psychology of religious experience. Pardo Bazán published nineteen novels, as well as twenty-one *novelas breves*. She was also the most prolific short-story writer in nineteenth-century Spain, publishing at least 579 short stories.

She was a woman of great energy who wrote, apart from fiction, much important literary criticism. She edited a monthly literary review (*Nuevo teatro crítico*, 1891–3) which was written entirely by herself, contributed numerous articles on a variety of subjects in periodicals on both sides of the Atlantic, and published several travelogues and even two cookery books. She was deeply involved in the intellectual life of

163

Madrid (where she lived for half the year) and frequented the Ateneo, the literary section of which she became the first woman president of in 1906, and occupied the Chair of Romance Literature at the Central University of Madrid from 1916.

She was a highly controversial figure, particularly in the 1880s and 1890s, not only because of the *succès de scandale* enjoyed by her study of Naturalism (*La cuestión palpitante*, 1883), but also because of her pronouncements on politics and religion, and her militant feminism. She wrote frequently about the state of women in Spain, edited a collection of books entitled *La biblioteca de la mujer*, and tried unsuccessfully to be admitted to the all-male Real Academia de la Lengua. Pardo Bazán, like other writers at the turn of the century, was dissatisfied with the state of Spain, but in politics she was fundamentally conservative and did not believe that democracy was the answer to Spain's problems.

Her zest for polemics was not a search for notoriety (although her husband's belief that this was the case contributed to the separation of the couple in 1885): she was very much alive to the age in which she lived and her combativeness was motivated by a desire to contribute to the rebirth of Spanish intellectual life. Nevertheless, she was jealous of her literary reputation and the honours bestowed on her gave her great satisfaction. She was particularly proud when in 1908 Alfonso XIII converted her papal title, inherited from her father, into a Castilian title.

The last decade of her life was devoted largely to lecturing at the Central University and publishing short stories and *novelas breves* (although she wrote another full-length novel entitled *Selva*, as yet unpublished, probably around 1914). She retained her legendary good health and continued writing until the end of her life. Her last article, on Juan Valera, was published in *ABC* on 13 May 1921, the day after her death.

Appendix II
Some French works in
Pardo Bazán's personal library

Pardo Bazán's private library was, at the time of my visit (1970), still in her former residence, the Pazo de Meirás. At the time of writing, it has been moved to the recently opened Pardo Bazán museum, located in her house in La Coruña, and belonging to the Real Academia Gallega, where it is being catalogued. The information below is taken from Pardo Bazán's own card-index catalogue and the presence of a particular title does not necessarily imply that that work is still in the collection. The original dates of publication or the Spanish translation (where I have been able to ascertain them) are enclosed in square brackets. All other details of publication, as well as subheadings, are taken from the catalogue. In some cases the catalogue includes a detailed list of contents. This information has been omitted.

Barbey d'Aurevilly (Jules Amédée)

Crítica literaria
L'Esprit de . . . – Dictionnaire de pensées, traits, portraits, et jugements tirés de son œuvre critique [1908]
Le roman contemporain [1902]
Les poètes [Published in two series, 1862 and 1889]
Les bas-bleus [1878]

Novelas y cuentos
Las diabólicas [*c.* 1890]
Una historia sin nombre [1909]
La hechizada [1910]
Venganza de una mujer
L'ensorcelée [1854]
Une histoire sans nom [1882]
Les diaboliques [1874]
Le chevalier des Touches [1844]

Obras varias
Lettres de . . . à Léon Bloy [1902]
El dandismo y Jorge Brummell [1891]

Baudelaire (Charles)

Curiosités esthétiques [1868]
L'albatros[1]

Poemas fantásticos: camino del infierno
Los paraísos artificiales [*c.* 1890]
Elevación[2]
Les fleurs du mal [1857][3]
L'art romantique [1868]
Lettres. 1841–1866 [1906]

Bloy (Léon)

Les dernières colonnes de l'Eglise [1903]
Pages choisis. 1884–1905

Bourget (Paul)

Filosofía
Essais de psychologie contemporaine [1883]
Nouveaux essais de psychologie contemporaine [1885]

Novelas y cuentos
André Cornélis [1887]
Un cœur de femme [1890]
Complications sentimentales [1898]
Cosmopolis (1894)
Cosmopolis (Edición definitiva) [1902]
Cruelle énigme [1885]
Les détours du cœur [1908]
Le disciple [1889]
Un divorce [1904]
L'eau profonde (sin fecha) [1904]
Id. (en un volumen con otra obra)
Drames de famille [1900]
L'étape [1902]
Le fantôme [1901]
Id. (Edición distinta a la anterior)
Un homme d'affaires [1900]
Une idylle tragique (mœurs cosmopolites) [1896]
L'irréparable [1884]
Un fugador
Le justicier [1919]
Mensonges [1887]
Monique–Les gestes–Reconnaissance–Trois récits de guerre [1902]
Les pas dans les pas [1904]
Pastels. Dix portraits de femmes [1889]
Nouveaux pastels. Dix portraits d'hommes [1891]
Recommencements [1897]
La terre promise [1892]

Poesía
Rebeldía–Tarde de verano–La capilla

Obras diversas
Etudes et portraits [1900]

Outre-mer (Notes sur l'Amérique) [1895]
Un remords[4]

Oratoria
Discours de réception a l'Académie Française [1895]

Gautier (Théophile) ('Edgard de Mulham')

Crítica literaria
Portraits et souvenirs littéraires (París, 1881)
Nerval y Baudelaire [1912]
Madama Girardin y Balzac [1912]

Crónicas
Tableaux de siège – Paris 1870–1871 [1871]
Bajo las bombas prusianas (París sitiado) [1910]

Semblanzas
Portraits et souvenirs littéraires (París, 1885)

Novelas y cuentos
Mademoiselle de Maupin (París, sin fecha, 2 tomos)
Id. (París, 1882, 1 tomo)
Le roman de la momie [1858]
Historia de una momia (Madrid) [1868]
Id. (Valencia) [*c.* 1900]
Spirite (Nouvelle fantastique) [1866]
Espírita [Two translations, 1866 and 1894]
Avatar [1857]
Les jeunes-Frances [1833]
Contes humoristiques[5]
Cuentos [*c.* 1915]

Miscelánea literaria
La croix de Berny. – (En colaboración con Mme Emile de Girardin, con Jules Sandeau
y con Méry y bajo el seudónimo 'Edgard de Mulham') [1846]

Poesías
Poesías de . . . [1875–6]
Emaux et camées (52 composiciones) [1852]
El obelisco de la Plaza de la Concordia[6]

Viajes y descripción de países
Voyage en Espagne (tra los montes) [1843]
Voyage en Russie [1867]
Constantinople [1853]

Goncourt (Edmond et Jules de)

Feminismo
La femme au dix-huitième siècle [1862]

Historia
Histoire de la société française pendant la Révolution [1854]
Historia de María Antonieta, reina de Francia
La du Barry [1860]
Sophie Arnould, d'après sa correspondance et ses mémoires [1857]
Historia de la Pompadour
Histoire de la société française pendant le Directoire [1855]

Literatura en general
Journal des . . . Mémoires de la vie littéraire [1887–96]
Pages retrouvées [1886]
Un premier livre. En 18 . . [1851]
Idées et sensations [1886]
Id.

Novelas y cuentos
Germinie Lacerteux (París, 1888)ʾ
Id. (París, 1889)
Id. (España moderna) [1892]
Madame Gervaisais (París, 1887)
Id. (París, 1882)
La señora Gervaisais (España moderna)
Manette Salomon (París, 1881)
Renée Mauperin (París, 1890)
Renata Mauperin (España moderna) [c. 1892]
Sœur Philomène (París, 1877)
Id. (París, 1899)
Charles Demailly (París, 1877)
Quelques créatures de ce temps [1876]

Goncourt (Edmond de)

Chérie (París, 1884)
Querida (España moderna)
La fille Elisa (París, 1880)
Id. (París, 1891)
La Elisa (España moderna)
La Faustin (París, 1882)
Id. (España moderna)
Les frères Zemganno (París, 1879)
Germinie Lacerteux (Adaptación escénica de la novela) [1888]

Huysmans (Joris-Karl)

Sac au dos [1880]
Là-bas [1891]
A va-l'eau [1882]
A rebours [1884]
La cathédrale [1898]
Mochila al hombro

Chronological list of works by Pardo Bazán

This list includes only works published in book form. Where reference has been made to any edition other than the first or the three volumes of the Aguilar *Obras completas*, the date has been added in square brackets.

Novels

1879 *Pascual López*
1881 *Un viaje de novios*
1883 *La Tribuna*
1885 *El Cisne de Vilamorta*
1886 *Los pazos de Ulloa*
1887 *La madre naturaleza*
1889 *Insolación*
1889 *Morriña*
1890 *Una cristiana–La prueba*
1891 *La piedra angular*
1894 *Doña Milagros*
1896 *Memorias de un solterón*
1897 *El tesoro de Gastón*
1897 *El saludo de las brujas*
1899 *El niño de Guzmán*
1903 *Misterio*
1905 *La quimera*
1908 *La sirena negra*
1911 *Dulce dueño*

Short stories and *novelas breves*

1885 *La dama joven*
1891 *Cuentos escogidos*
1892 *Cuentos de Marineda*
1894 *Cuentos nuevos*
1894 *Cuentos de Navidad y Año Nuevo*
1895 *Arco iris*
1895 *Novelas ejemplares*
1898 *Cuentos de amor*
1899 *Cuentos sacro-profanos*
1900 *Un destripador de antaño*

1901   *En tranvía, cuentos dramáticos*
1902   *Cuentos de Navidad y Reyes; cuentos de la patria; cuentos antiguos*
1907   *El fondo del alma*
1909   *Sud-exprés, cuentos actuales*
1912   *Belcebú, novelas breves*
1913   *Cuentos trágicos*
1923   *Cuentos de la tierra*
1925   *Cuadros religiosos*

Poetic, critical and general works

1877   *Estudio crítico de las obras del padre Feijóo*
1881   *Jaime* (collection of poems)
1882   *San Francisco de Asís*, 2 vols [1941]
1883   *La cuestión palpitante*
1884   *El folklore gallego*
1887   *La revolución y la novela en Rusia*
1887   *La leyenda de la pastoriza*
1888   *Mi romería* [4th ed., 1909]
1888   *De mi tierra*
1889   *Al pie de la Torre Eiffel*
1889   *Los pedagogos del Renacimiento. (Erasmo, Rabelais y Montaigne)*
1890   *Por Francia y Alemania*
1891   *El P. Luis Coloma, biografía y estudio crítico*
1892   *Los franciscanos y Colón*
1892   *Alarcón, estudio biográfico*
1892   *Polémicas y estudios literarios*
1893   *Campoamor, estudio biográfico*
1895   *Por la España pintoresca*
1895   *Los poetas épicos cristianos*
1896   *Hombres y mujeres de antaño*
1896   *Vida contemporánea*
1899   *La España de ayer y la de hoy*
1899   *Discurso inaugural en el Ateneo de Valencia*
1900   *Cuarenta días en la Exposición*
1901   *Discurso leído en los juegos florales de Orense*
1902   *Los franciscanos y el descubrimiento de América*
1902   *Por la Europa católica*
1902   *De siglo a siglo*
1905   *Discurso a la memoria de Gabriel y Galán*
1905   *Goya y la espontaneidad española*
1906   *Lecciones de literatura*
1908   *Retratos y apuntes literarios*
1910   *La literatura francesa moderna: I. El romanticismo*
1911   *La literatura francesa moderna: II. La transición*
1912   *La quimera, conferencia*
1913   *La cocina española antigua*
1914   *La literatura francesa moderna: III. El naturalismo*
1914   *Hernán Cortés y sus hazañas*
1916   *La cocina española moderna*
1917   *El porvenir de la literatura después de la guerra*
1923   *El lirismo en la poesía francesa*

Unpublished correspondence

Instituto Municipal de Historia, Barcelona, thirty-two letters from Emilia Pardo Bazán to Narciso Oller, 1883–90, Epistolario de Narciso Oller y Moragas, N.O.–I–1135–66. Fourteen of these letters were published by Oller in his *Memòries literàries* (Barcelona, 1962), but the transcriptions are not always accurate.
Real Academia de la Historia, sixty-two letters from Emilia Pardo Bazán to Francisco Giner de los Ríos, 1877–1909, Papeles de Giner, cajas 2–14.

Notes

Introduction

1. C. A. Longhurst, *Pío Baroja*, 'El mundo es ansí' (London, 1977), pp. 15 and 24.
2. Among the first group are César Barja, *Libros y autores modernos: siglos XVIII y XIX*, 2nd edn (New York, 1964), p. 317; Fernando J. Barroso, *El naturalismo en la Pardo Bazán* (Madrid, 1973), p. 147; E. Correa Calderón, 'La Pardo Bazán en su época' in *El centenario de Emilia Pardo Bazán* (Madrid, 1952), pp. 9–56 (pp. 43–4); A. González Blanco, 'Juicio crítico de la condesa de Pardo Bazán', *La novela corta*, IV, no. 286 (4 June 1921); D. L. Shaw, *A Literary History of Spain: the Nineteenth Century* (London, 1972), p. 157. Among the second group are Eduardo Gómez de Baquero (*Andrenio*), *El renacimiento de la novela en el siglo XIX* (Madrid, 1924), p. 72; Domingo Pérez Minik, *Novelistas españoles de los siglos XIX y XX* (Madrid, 1957), p. 124; Guillermo de Torre, *Del 98 al barroco* (Madrid, 1969), p. 261.

1. The development of Pardo Bazán's ideas on the novel in the 1880s

1. See Albert Cassagne, *La théorie de l'art pour l'art en France chez les derniers romantiques et les premiers réalistes* (Paris, 1906).
2. For other examples see III, 635a, 643a, 761a, 946b; *Lecciones de literatura* (Madrid, 1906), p. 40; *José María Gabriel y Galán* (Madrid, 1905), p. 41 (the relevant extract does not appear in the version of this essay published in vol. III of the Aguilar *Obras completas*); *La quimera, conferencia* (Madrid, 1912), pp. 25–6.
3. There is a notable similarity between Pardo Bazán's comments on Zola's didactic pretensions quoted above and the following remarks of Victor Cousin and Théophile Gautier respectively: 'Le seul objet de l'art est le beau. L'art s'abandonne lui-même dès qu'il s'en écarte.' 'De l'art et du beau', *Revue des deux mondes*, XI (1845), 773–811 (p. 804); 'Tout artiste qui se propose autre chose que le beau n'est pas un artiste à nos yeux.' Quoted by Cassagne, p. 137.
4. *Histoire du romantisme*, new edn (Paris, 1901), pp. 18–19.
5. *Mademoiselle de Maupin* (Paris, 1930), p. 255. In the catalogue of Pardo Bazán's library in the Pazo de Meirás there were two copies of this work, one undated, the other dated 1882. See Appendix II.
6. 'Notice' to Charles Baudelaire, *Les fleurs du mal* (Paris, 1868), p. 46.
7. RAH, Giner, caja 3, 25 January 1882.
8. Antonio Jaén Morente, *Juan Montalvo y Emilia Pardo Bazán, diálogo epistolar* (Quito, 1944), p. 21.
9. 'Literatura y otras hierbas', *Revista de España*, CXVII (1887), 133–45 (p. 133).
10. See III, 711b and 719a. Pardo Bazán had already read some of Zola's work (see III, 717b), and in a letter to Giner written before she set off for Vichy she refers to

Zola's technique in some detail, delighting in her own boldness: 'Supongo que V. no se escandalizará si cito a este autor *fuerte*.' In the same letter she expresses some reservations about the French Realists: 'Yo no me afilio así, sin más ni más a la escuela realista, y menos con esos patrones *non sanctos* que le han salido.' RAH, Giner, caja 3, 17 May 1880.

11. Her first novel, *Pascual López* (1879), was regarded at the time as Realist because of its self-consciously picaresque treatment of student life in Santiago de Compostela. But this novel, with its fundamentally Romantic plot and linguistic archaisms, owes little or nothing to contemporary Realism.

12. See Cassagne, ch. 4, 'L'art pour l'art et la science'.

13. Compare this remark in a letter to Menéndez Pelayo, dated 29 September 1882: 'Es en mí cosa inevitable, condición de mi temperamento, ver antes que todo el color. Se reiría Vd. si le comunicase algunas de mis impresiones *crómicas*. [...] Me han traído ahora de Tánger una gumía árabe, cuya coloración es por todo extremo grata, una combinación de plata oxidada, cobre y seda carmesí: pues a veces estoy leyendo y suelto el libro para recrearme en mirar la gumía. [...] El sentido del color impera en mí hasta un grado que parecerá inverosímil al que no sepa lo que se afinan y excitan los sentidos por la contemplación artística. De tal manera me parece característico este modo de sentir las diversas vibraciones luminosas, que se me figura que siempre mis escritos de resentirán de esta excesiva sensibilidad de mi retina, como se resentían los de Teófilo Gautier. (Siempre hay que compararse con algo bueno.)' Carmen Bravo-Villasante, *Vida y obra de Emilia Pardo Bazán* (Madrid, 1962), pp. 80–1. In a review of *La Tribuna* Alas wrote: 'De todos los novelistas del naturalismo, son los Goncourt los que más pintan y los que más enamorados están del color. La señora Pardo Bazán es de todos los novelistas de España el que más pinta: en sus novelas se ve que está enamorada del color y que sabe echar sobre el lienzo haces de claridad como Claudio Loreno.' *Sermón perdido* (Madrid, 1885), p. 113. See also Mary E. Giles, 'Impressionist Techniques in Descriptions by Emilia Pardo Bazán', *Hispanic Review*, xxx (1962), 304–16, and Clémessy, pp. 704–10.

14. *Correspondance* (Paris, 1908), pp. 19–20.

15. *Nueva campaña (1885–86)* (Madrid, 1887), p. 225.

16. 'Estudios de literatura contemporánea: Pérez Galdós', *Revista de Galicia*, no. 20 (25 October 1880), 350–3 (p. 351).

17. Prologue to *La Gaviota* (Madrid, 1856), pp. v–vi.

18. See *Clarín*'s review in Sergio Beser, *Leopoldo Alas, teoría y crítica de la novela española* (Barcelona, 1972), p. 275, and the introduction to Mariano Baquero Goyanes's edition of *Un viaje de novios* (Barcelona, 1971). Pardo Bazán expressed her view of the critical reaction to this novel in a letter to Narciso Oller, dated 25 February 1883: '¡Conque ha estado usted en Vichy! Entonces comprendo que leyese con gusto aquellas descripciones por otra parte difusas y quizás inoportunas que hay en mi libro. Digo *quizás* porque a mí se me figuró aplicar el principio realista de los *medios ambientes* y estudiar el desarrollo de una pasión romancesca en el alma de Lucía, pasión provocada por el espectáculo de la naturaleza (que tiene tan decisivo influjo en esos casos) y por el aislamiento en que la dejaba la sociedad. Los críticos, tratando de innecesarias (aunque con el paliativo de *bellas*) a mis descripciones, me dieron a entender que o mi idea era mala, o no supe darle forma conveniente. La verdad es que, por otra parte, la crítica española no se quiebra de sutil. ¡Dónde están aquellos críticos franceses, que penetran en el espíritu del artista, se adaptan a su pensamiento y sorprenden la gestación de sus ideas!' N.O.–I–1136.

19. See *Un viaje de novios*, ed. Baquero Goyanes, pp. 29–30.
20. Pardo Bazán contrasted so-called fluidity with precision of style when she praises in *La cuestión palpitante*, amongst other features of the style of Flaubert, the fact that it lacks 'esa vaguedad en las expresiones que suele llamarse fluidez' (III, 609a).
21. *Sermón perdido*, p. 115. For other unfavourable views of the characterisation of Amparo see Barja, p. 314, and D. F. Brown, *The Catholic Naturalism of Pardo Bazán* (Chapel Hill, North Carolina, 1957), p. 81. Subsequent references to the latter work are given in the text.
22. From a letter to Narciso Oller, dated 15 November 1883. N.O.–I–1141.
23. Referring to *La Tribuna* Pardo Bazán wrote: 'El verdadero infierno social a que puede bajar el novelista, Dante moderno que escribe cantos de la comedia humana, es la fábrica, y el más condenado de los condenados, ese ser convertido en rueda, en cilindro, en autómata.' (II, 725b) See also the novel itself, II, 127a.
24. Walter T. Pattison, *Emilia Pardo Bazán* (New York, 1971), p. 47.
25. See Alas's review in *Obras selectas* (Madrid, 1947), pp. 1208–11.
26. See Mario Praz, *The Romantic Agony*, called 2nd edn, but in fact 3rd edn (London, 1970), pp. 29–30 and 40–5.
27. A letter to Narciso Oller, dated 12 October 1886, suggests that she had reached the stage of planning the Russian lectures as early as March 1886, just after the completion of *Los pazos de Ulloa*: 'Estoy en el corazón de Rusia. Quiero hacer un estudio sobre esa extraña y curiosa literatura, como ya he dicho a V. creo que en París [i.e. in March 1886].' N.O.–I–1155.
28. See A. E. Carter, *The Idea of Decadence in French Literature, 1830–1900* (Toronto, 1958).
29. Robert M. Scari in 'El regionalismo de *Morriña*', *Hispanófila*, XIX (May 1976), 47–55 (p. 52) sees *Morriña* primarily as a psychological novel and a sign of Pardo Bazán's response to the reaction against Naturalism. See also his 'Aspectos distintivos del lenguaje de *Morriña*', *Cuadernos hispanoamericanos*, no. 313 (July 1976), 191–9. H. L. Kirby discusses both *Insolación* and *Morriña* as psychological novels in 'Evolution of Thought in the Critical Writings and Novels of Emilia Pardo Bazán' (Unpublished Ph.D. thesis, Illinois, 1963), pp. 116–21.
30. See P. Martino, *Le naturalisme français (1870–95)*, 4th edn (Paris, 1945), pp. 189–206; J.-H. Bornecque and P. Cogny, *Réalisme et naturalisme* (Paris, 1958), pp. 160–77; R. Ternois, *Zola et son temps* (Paris, 1961), especially chs 4 and 5; Richard Griffiths, *The Reactionary Revolution: The Catholic Revival in French Literature (1870–1914)* (London, 1966). See also Walter T. Pattison, *El naturalismo español. Historia externa de un movimiento literario* (Madrid, 1965), ch. 19, and Clémessy, part I, ch. 8.
31. Vte E. M. de Vogüé, *Le roman russe* (Paris, 1886), p. xxiv.
32. *Là-bas* (Paris, 1908), reprinted 1960, pp. 4 and 5.
33. See 'La banqueroute du naturalisme', *Revue des deux mondes*, LXIX (1887), 213–24.
34. See Griffiths, pp. 4–8.
35. *Al pie de la Torre Eiffel* (Madrid, 1889), p. 286. Subsequent references to this work are given after quotations in the text. The chapter on *Le disciple* was omitted from later editions.
36. Pardo Bazán expressed more fully her reservations about the spiritual and moral element of Spiritual Naturalism in a study of Edouard Rod, published between 1897 and 1898. See III, 1202a–3a.

37. E. Sánchez Reyes, 'Centenarios y conmemoraciones, cartas de Da. Emilia Pardo Bazán a Menéndez Pelayo', *Boletín de la Biblioteca de Menéndez Pelayo*, XXIX (1953), 120–44 (p. 138).
38. See also *Nuevo teatro crítico*, no. 6 (June 1891), 60 and 63; III, 952b, 956b, 1146b, 1199b–1200a; *La literatura francesa moderna*, III, *El naturalismo*, p. 329; *La literatura francesa moderna*, II, *La transición*, pp. 50, 80 and 150 (these three extracts first published in *La España moderna* in December 1901, January 1902 and December 1908 respectively). Subsequent references to the three volumes of *La literatura francesa moderna* will give only the title of the relevant volume.
39. See Michel Mansuy, *Un moderne, Paul Bourget: De l'enfance au disciple* (Paris, 1968), pp. 319–51 and 401–3.
40. Paul Bourget, *Oeuvres complètes (romans)*, II (Paris, 1901), 460.
41. *La transición*, p. 48 (first published in *La España moderna*, December 1901).
42. *El naturalismo*, p. 119.

2. *Los pazos de Ulloa*: Naturalism and beyond

1. This chapter and the one that follows have benefited from discussion with students of the Spanish Department of Exeter University, particularly Mercedes Catton, Laura Corob, Liz Evora, Belinda Fischel and Frank McQuade.
2. See my article 'Grace, Nature, Naturalism, and Pardo Bazán', in *Forum for Modern Language Studies*, XVI (1980), 341–9.
3. James Sully, *Illusions*, 2nd edn (London, 1882), p. 142. Subsequent references to this work are given in the text.
4. Albert Fouillée, 'La survivance et la sélection des idées dans la mémoire', *Revue des deux mondes*, LXVII (1885), 357–89.
5. For two other readings of this dream see Carlos Feal Deibe, 'Naturalismo y antinaturalismo en *Los pazos de Ulloa*', BHS, XLVIII (1971), 314–27, and Robert E. Lott, 'Observations on the Narrative Method, the Psychology, and the Style of *Los pazos de Ulloa*', *Hispania* (U.S.A.), LII (1969), 3–12.
6. See the article 'Temperamento' in the Espasa-Calpe *Enciclopedia universal ilustrada*.
7. J.-L. Brachet, *Traité de l'hystérie* (Paris, 1847), pp. 101, 104 and 278. Although Brachet identified the 'boule' on the basis of many case-studies, the *globus hystericus* had long been regarded as a symptom of what eventually became known as hysteria. See Ilza Veith, *Hysteria, the History of a Disease* (Chicago, 1965).
8. See Robert Ricatte, *La création romanesque chez les Goncourt* (Paris, 1953), pp. 296–7. In 1891 Pardo Bazán described the eponymous heroine of *Germinie Lacerteux* as 'un caso patológico' and 'la infeliz histérica protagonista' (III, 960ab). For a discussion of the presentation of hysteria and other neuroses by the Goncourt brothers and Alas, see Noël Maureen Valis, 'Leopoldo Alas y los Goncourt: el alma neurótica', *Hispanic Journal*, I (1979), 27–35.
9. See N.O.–I–1147, where Pardo Bazán writes: 'Ahora al leer el segundo tomo de la *Regenta*, me he encontrado yo con un cura enamorado de una dama: esto mismo, aunque en bien distinta forma y modo, danza en la novela que traigo entre manos.'
10. See Lott, 5–6 for a slightly different interpretation of these references to the Virgin Mary.

3. *Insolación* and *Morriña*

1. Pattison, *Emilia Pardo Bazán*, p. 61.
2. 'Emilia Pardo Bazán y sus últimas obras', in *Folletos literarios*, VII (Madrid, 1890), 51–88; Matías Montes Huidobro, 'Emilia Pardo Bazán: niveles técnicos y temáticos de su determinismo' in *Superficie y fondo del estilo* (North Carolina, 1971), pp. 69–81 (p. 69). Subsequent references to these works will be included in the text.
3. See Emilia Pardo Bazán, *Cartas a Benito Pérez Galdós (1889–90)*, ed. Carmen Bravo-Villasante (Madrid, 1975), p. 17.
4. See Pattison, *Emilia Pardo Bazán*, p. 59, R. E. Osborne, *Emilia Pardo Bazán, su vida y sus obras* (Mexico, 1964), p. 72, and Brown, p. 107.
5. Galdós, in his description of the house of the three señoras de Porreño y Venegas (*La Fontana de Oro*, ch. 15), included a clock which had stopped at the last moment of the eighteenth century, but the indirectness and ambiguity of Pardo Bazán's use of the stopped clock is far removed from Galdós's obvious (if witty) symbolism.
6. See Montes Huidobro, p. 73.
7. Ruth A. Schmidt, 'A Woman's Place in the Sun: Feminism in *Insolación*', *Revista de estudios hispánicos* (VIII) (1974), 69–81 (p. 73).
8. For a Jungian interpretation of Asís's mental processes see Mary E. Giles, 'Feminism and the Feminine in Emilia Pardo Bazán's Novels', *Hispania* (U.S.A.), LXIII (1980), 356–67.
9. For a different approach to this novel see Robert M. Scari, 'La presentación del personaje en *Morriña*', *Romanistisches Jahrbuch*, XXII (1971), 297–305.
10. See Ian Watt, *The Rise of the Novel* (London, 1957), pp. 9–34.

4. *Una cristiana – La prueba*

1. *Cartas a Galdós*, p. 57.
2. See *Mi romería* (Madrid, 1888), and *El eco de Galicia*, XII, 13 July 1889, 6.
3. *El eco de Galicia*, XII, 5 October 1889, 6.
4. L. L. Whyte in his work *The Unconscious before Freud* (London, 1960) shows that the idea of the Unconscious has a history going back at least to the eighteenth century.
5. See Albert Réville, 'Un nouveau système de philosophie allemande, M. von Hartmann et la doctrine de l'inconscient', *Revue des deux mondes*, V (1874), 511–51 (p. 521), and Whyte, p. 328.
6. Sherman H. Eoff, *The Modern Spanish Novel* (New York, 1961), p. 92.
7. *Philosophy of the Unconscious*, tr. W. C. Coupland (2nd edn, London, 1893), I, 114.
8. See Réville, p. 521.
9. See Whyte, pp. 163–4, and Eoff, p. 91. U. González Serrano speaks of the great popularity of Hartmann's *Philosophy of the Unconscious* in Spain. See his 'La psicología contemporánea', *Revista de España*, LXVIII (1879), 481–97 (p. 488). Some remarks of the early 1890s show that Pardo Bazán had at least some knowledge of the ideas of Schopenhauer and Hartmann. In 1891 she wrote: 'Si por *instinto* quiere Campoamor significar esa inspiración o actividad de algo sobrehumano, distinto del individuo, que llama Schopenhauer representación *independiente del principio racional*, entonces convendré en que el prosista escribe por instinto.' (III, 948a) See also *Nuevo teatro crítico*, no. 24 (December 1892), 79; III, 1336a and 1198ab. The as yet incomplete catalogue of Pardo Bazán's library, now in the Real Academia Gallega, La Coruña, contains Schopenhauer's *Essay on Free Will* and *The Foundations of Morality* (Paris, 1887 and 1879 respectively).

10. Brian J. Dendle, in 'The Racial Theories of Emilia Pardo Bazán', *Hispanic Review*, XXXVIII (1970), 17–31, assumes that Pardo Bazán shared Salustio's anti-semitism, overlooking the fact that Salustio himself regards it as indefensible in a rational man (I, 548a). This is a view Pardo Bazán herself held (see *Nuevo teatro crítico*, no. 6 (June 1891), 89). Dendle's case is based on quotations which in their context are not at all anti-semitic. For example, Pardo Bazán's remarks on lack of hygiene and prevalence of leprosy are a general comment on the condition of nomadic races, not simply on the Jews. She goes on to say that when the Jews became more sedentary, leprosy decreased and they took pleasure in bathing (*De siglo a siglo* (Madrid, 1902), p. 258).

11. David Torres, 'Veinte cartas inéditas de Emilia Pardo Bazán a José Yxart', *Boletín de`la Biblioteca de Menéndez Pelayo*, LIII (1977), 383–409 (pp. 395–6); N.O.–I–1144.

12. See Clémessy's remarks on Pardo Bazán's use of the first-person narration, pp. 672–3.

13. *Studies in the Narrative Technique of the First-Person Novel* (Stockholm, 1962).

14. The movement from the general to the particular seen in the examples quoted here and usually introduced, as in these cases, by a demonstrative adjective is characteristic of Pardo Bazán's third-person omniscient narrative style. See Clémessy, pp. 664–7, and Mariano Baquero Goyanes, 'La novela naturalista española: Emilia Pardo Bazán', *Anales de la Universidad de Murcia*, XIII (1954–5), 157–234, 539–639 (ch. 4).

15. See Correa Calderón, pp. 43–4.

16. See my article referred to in ch. 2, note 2 above.

17. *Emilia Pardo Bazán*, p. 69.

18. *La catéchisme positiviste* (Paris, 1852), p. 135.

19. Grace, according to St Augustine, is 'the sum total of God's free gifts, the purpose of which is to make man's salvation possible in the state of fallen nature'. Etienne Gilson, *The Christian Philosophy of Saint Augustine* (London, 1961), p. 152. See this work, part II, ch. 3 for the effects of grace on the human will.

20. Richard Griffiths, in his study of French Catholic writers of this period (p. 157), emphasises the importance of the voluntary acceptance of suffering: 'In the case of all these forms of expiation, an essential element is the free will of the sufferer [...] even if it is God who sends the suffering to the chosen one, that person must both understand the cause of this suffering and willingly accept it, for the suffering to be in any way valid.' The operation of grace is a much disputed question and is part of the wider issue of free will and predestination which was at the centre of the controversy between the Jesuits and the Jansenists. Gilson tells us that 'grace can be irresistible without being constraining, because it is either suited to the free choice of those it has decided to save, or, by transforming from within the will to which it is applied, it causes it to delight freely in things it would otherwise find repugnant' (pp. 155–6). In ch. 6 of *Los pazos de Ulloa* the local clergy argue about this very issue.

21. See the article on Pedro de Rivadeneira in the Espasa-Calpe *Enciclopedia universal ilustrada*. *Año cristiano* is a generic term referring to a devotional work containing the lives of the saints arranged according to their feasts throughout the year. Rivadeneira's *Flos sanctorum* (1599–1601) was the most important of these in Spain and went through many editions. In the eighteenth century it was augmented by the *Année chrétienne* of Jean Croisset, translated by P. José Francisco de Isla. The collated version became so large that another *Año cristiano* was published by Lorenzo Villanueva in 1790 (see the *Obras escogidas* of Rivadeneira (Madrid, 1952), p. vii). Croisset's work went through various

editions (it had reached its ninth edition by 1877) in up to as many as eighteen volumes. It is this work that Julián reads in *Los pazos de Ulloa* (see I, 234ab).

22. There are numerous references to the lives of the saints in her critical and journalistic writings. See for example *Mi romería*, pp. 104–5; *Nuevo teatro crítico*, no. 5 (May 1891), 24; *La ilustración artística*, no. 988 (3 December 1900), 778; *Por la Europa católica* (Madrid, 1902), pp. 247–50. Pardo Bazán shows her love of the lives of the saints in this remark to Narciso Oller: 'Celebro que mi San Francisco le haya aficionado a V. un poco a los Santos. La vida de estos es un tesoro de ternura, gracia, sentido histórico y otras mil cosas buenas. Ardo en deseos de hablar algún día de dos Santos españoles: Santa Teresa y San Juan de la Cruz. – Veremos si Dios me da vida para esta y otras muchas tareas que me he propuesto llevar a cabo.' N.O.–I–1141, 18 November 1883.

23. *The Russian Religious Mind* (Cambridge, Massachusetts, 1966), II, 110.

24. *El Naturalismo*, p. 112.

25. Pedro de Rivadeneira, *Flos sanctorum*, I (Madrid, 1717), i–ii and iv–v. For the Western tradition of martyr heroes see H. Delehaye, *Les origines du culte des martyrs*, 2nd edn (Paris, 1933), p. 1.

26. See Fedotov, pp. 99 and 105.

27. See E. Behr-Sigel, *Prière et sainteté dans l'église russe* (Paris, 1950), ch. 6, and Fedotov, ch. 12.

28. For 'divine folly' see St Paul, 1 Corinthians 1.18–31, 3.18–19 and 4.10. This last is quoted by Pardo Bazán in her discussion of the Franciscan, Brother Juniper (see note 29 below). For St John of God see Behr-Sigel, p. 93.

29. *San Francisco de Asís*, vol. I, 220. In the same work she describes the childlike behaviour of Brother Juniper and says that in him 'llegó a su colmo la sublime insensatez de la Orden nueva, y se cumplió la enseñanza de Jesús, viéndose al hombre vuelto parvulillo para conquistar el reino de los cielos' (p. 176).

30. Pardo Bazán's remarks on *The Idiot* follow Vogüé closely (see *Le roman russe*, pp. 257–60). Vogüé mentions Myshkin's epilepsy as well as the fact that he is intended by Dostoyevsky to acquire 'les proportions morales d'un saint'. As *The Idiot* was not translated into French until 1887, Pardo Bazán is unlikely to have read it before the composition of *La revolución y la novela en Rusia*. For our purposes, then, what Dostoyevsky wrote is less significant than Vogüé's account of his work.

31. See III, 984a–95b.

32. Alas complained that the characterisation of Carmen was too physical: 'El mérito del artista no aumenta por la magnitud de las hazañas que relata, y la Pardo Bazán, excusándose de estudiar y pintar a su cristiana por dentro y de hacernos ver el conflicto espiritual, no deja de huir las dificultades de su aunto, por muy a lo vivo que nos describa las lacerías bíblicas del leproso y la fuerza de estómago de su legítima esposa.' *Clarín, obra olvidada*, ed. Antonio Ramos-Gascón (Madrid, 1973), p. 86. See also Francisco Pérez Gutiérrez, *El problema religioso en la generación de 1868* (Madrid, 1975), p. 365.

33. *Clarín, obra olvidada*, p. 91.

34. See Clémessy, pp. 553–4, and *Un viaje de novios*, ed. Baquero Goyanes, pp. 39–45.

35. See my article 'The Religious Content of Pardo Bazán's *La sirena negra*', *BHS*, XLIX (1972), 369–82.

5. *La piedra angular*

1. See Brown, pp. 122–9, and Pattison, *Emilia Pardo Bazán*, p. 75.
2. Osborne, p. 106.

3. Although I know of no evidence that Pardo Bazán read this work by Ribot, she mentions him in *Al pie de la Torre Eiffel* (1st edn, p. 280), as one of the influences on Bourget. It has been shown that Bourget did indeed draw on Ribot and that *Les maladies de la mémoire* was used in the composition of *L'irréparable*. See Mansuy, pp. 360-3. At all events, in the chapters here under discussion there are a number of reminiscences of Ribot. For example, the suggestion that a fresh supply of blood finally made Moragas remember Rojo's identity echoes Ribot's theory that the working of memory is dependent on the circulation of blood in the brain. See Théodule Armand Ribot, *Les maladies de la mémoire*, 12th edn (Paris, 1898), p. 159. Another example is Rojo's sense of *déjà vu* in chapter 5 which recalls Ribot's 'fausse mémoire' (pp. 149-51).
4. Gustav Fechner, *Elements of Psychophysics*, tr. H. E. Adler (New York, 1966), p. 7.
5. Pattison, *Emilia Pardo Bazán*, p. 75.
6. See F. F. Villegas (*Zeda*), 'La piedra angular', *La España moderna*, January 1892 (no. 37), 177-82 (p. 179); Emilio González López, *Emilia Pardo Bazán, novelista de Galicia* (New York, 1944), p. 170; Brown, pp. 49 and 128; Osborne, p. 106; Clémessy, pp. 515 and 524. For details of the contemporary debate on capital punishment and the sources Pardo Bazán used, see Clémessy, pp. 219-23 and 515-30, and Benito Varela Jácome, *Estructuras novelísticas de Emilia Pardo Bazán* (Santiago de Compostela, 1973), pp. 133-7. Also Lily Litvak, 'La sociología criminal y su influencia en los escritores españoles de fin de siglo', *Revue de littérature comparée*, XLVIII (1974), 12-32. For Pardo Bazán's views, see her review of César Silió y Cortés's book *La crisis del derecho penal* (Madrid, 1891), in *Nuevo teatro crítico*, no. 7 (July 1891), 94.
7. See *Nuevo teatro crítico*, no. 9 (September 1891), 95-6.
8. Varela Jácome, p. 134.
9. The reporting of crime in the Spanish press at the time was (as it tends to be anywhere and at any time) decidedly novelistic, particularly when a woman was involved. Pardo Bazán may have had in mind in writing *La piedra angular* the murder of don Felipe Conesa who was reported to have been killed in Zaragoza on 30 December 1890 by a man hired by his wife and her lover, who had already tried to poison him. The murder and police investigation were covered in some detail in, for example, *El imparcial* at the beginning of January 1891, until displaced as the centre of interest by a General Election campaign. That the reaction towards a reprieve (*indulto*), as described in *La piedra angular*, is not fantastic is shown by the following report published in *El eco de Galicia* on 12 December 1888 (p. 4), under the heading 'El indulto de un reo': 'El reo Nieto Abeijón, condenado a la última pena por la Audiencia de Santiago, ha obtenido de S. M. La Reina la gracia de indulto. Cuando circuló la noticia en aquella ciudad, el entusiasmo público fue indescriptible, arrebatándose de mano de los vendedores los números de la *Gaceta de Galicia*, en que se publicó. El alcalde acudió a la cárcel y notificó la gracia de que había sido objeto el reo, originándose con este motivo una escena en extremo conmovedora. La prensa prepara un banquete en celebridad del suceso. [...] Un periódico de la localidad refiere que cuando el reo recibió la noticia de labios del alcalde, Nieto, con las lágrimas en los ojos, se prosternó de rodillas ante él, intentando besarle los pies.' Public enthusiasm in Santiago (as far as I can see, the *indulto* went unnoticed in the Madrid press, apart from the official announcement in *La gaceta de Madrid*) mirrors that in *La piedra angular*, and the sensational treatment of the condemned man's reactions recalls the treatment of those of the condemned woman. Luis Taboada wrote a witty, if hawkish, piece in *El imparcial* on 21 April 1891 entitled 'Filantropía', in which he satirises the frequent calls for clemency on behalf of

convicted murderers under sentence of death. He points out, amongst other things, how, during the trial, the accused is vituperated, only to become an object of pity after having been sentenced to death.

10. RAH, Giner, caja 6, n.d. [January, 1892].
11. See Bravo-Villasante, p. 186, Clémessy, p. 223, and Varela Jácome, p. 133.
12. See Ronald Hilton, 'Doña Emilia Pardo Bazán, Neo-Catholicism and Christian Socialism', *The Americas*, xi (1954), 3–18.
13. *Emilia Pardo Bazán*, p. 75.
14. Gustave Flaubert, *Correspondance* (Paris, 1927), iii, 61–2.

6. *Doña Milagros*

1. At the same time as Pardo Bazán was writing *Una cristiana–La prueba* and *La piedra angular*, she was preparing another novel to be called *Propiedad y familia* which was never published, possibly because it referred to real people and she was afraid of scandal (see *Nuevo teatro crítico*, no. 9 (September 1891), 94) or simply because the labour of editing the *Nuevo teatro crítico* left her no time. J. P. Criado y Domínguez, in his *Literatas españolas del siglo XIX, apuntes bibliográficos* (Madrid, 1889), announced *Propiedad y familia* as 'novela en preparación', and José Lázaro Galdiano in 'Nuevas publicaciones de la Sra. Pardo Bazán' (*La España moderna*, June 1889 (no. 6), 180–1) includes the projected novel among works either completed or nearly completed. It may be that it finally emerged as *Doña Milagros* in 1894 because it was to have taken place in Marineda (like *La Tribuna* and *La piedra angular*) and, to judge from the title, was to deal with middle-class domestic life. Froilán, Benicio Neira's son, is one of the boys who stone Telmo in ch. 3 of *La piedra angular*, which may mean that *Doña Milagros* or another work (possibly *Propiedad y familia*) had already been planned in 1891. *Doña Milagros* first appeared in *La España moderna* between January and May of 1894 in the following order: chs 1–5 in January; chs 6–10 in February; chs 11–14 in March; chs 15–16 in April and chs 17–18 in May. It is described as the 'primera parte' of *Adán y Eva*.
2. Among the 'libros nuevos' in the February 1893 number of *Nuevo teatro crítico* (no. 26) there appears E. Caro's *El pesimismo en el siglo XIX* (Leopardi–Schopenhauer–Hartmann), Madrid, n.d.; and in November 1893 (no. 29) *Estudios escogidos* by Schopenhauer, Madrid, n.d.
3. See Romberg, p. 95.
4. The Galdosian irony I am thinking of particularly appears in *La de Bringas* where the narrator is both a minor character in the novel and omniscient. See P. A. Bly, 'The Use of Distance in "*La de Bringas*"', *Modern Language Review*, lxix (1974), 88–97. The Romantic irony in the epic situation of *Doña Milagros* looks back to *El amigo Manso*.
5. A similar description of the *Soledad* procession appears in an article entitled 'Semana santa', in *La ilustración artística*, no. 744 (30 March 1896), 242.
6. Again we are reminded of Galdós's *El amigo Manso* where, for example, eleven of the chapter titles are exclamations.
7. Barcelona, 1896. There are four studies, all published originally in *Nuevo teatro crítico* in 1892 or 1893: 'Quevedo', 'Juana la loca', 'Episodio de la vida de la Dubarry' and 'La venerable de Agreda'. Subsequent references to this work will be given in the text.
8. F. F. Villegas (*Zeda*), 'Doña Milagros', *La España moderna*, May 1894 (no. 65), 202–3 (p. 203).
9. See Veith, p. 231.

10. See the article 'Stigmatisation' in the *Dictionnaire de théologie catholique*.
11. Bleeding was still recommended as a treatment for hysteria in the nineteenth century. See Brachet, pp. 159, 161 and 180.
12. This story was published in *El Liberal* on 11 February 1894 while *Doña Milagros* was coming out in instalments in *La España moderna*.
13. In an early letter to Giner, Pardo Bazán expresses her reservations about the marriage bond: 'Recién nacido Jaime, y en el primer júbilo maternal recuerdo que le escribí "cásese a toda costa". Pero después, reflexionando, comprendí que el matrimonio, si no se realiza en condiciones de probabilidades de armonía, es una temeridad espantosa. Cadena que no puede romperse, hay que mirar cómo se suelda. Por lo demás, la ida de Augusto [Linares] a París, me parece muy bien. Quizás en el extranjero, en donde hay más mujeres educadas e instruidas, halle Augusto algo a su medida. En España, a no intervenir la casualidad, me parece, querido Paco, dificilísmo.' RAH, Giner, caja 3, 19 September 1879.
14. The emphatically unsentimental death-bed scene is probably what Valera was referring to when, having read this chapter, he wrote to Menéndez Pelayo: 'Hasta ahora no he leído más del primero número de la nueva y reformada *España Moderna* que la novela de doña Emilia Pardo Bazán, de la que mucho me he maravillado. El diablo de la mujer tiene singular y muy raro talento; su espíritu es una máquina fotográfica que afea las cosas en vez de hermosearlas. Aquello es la verdad, pero ¿qué verdad? Lo soez, lo vulgar, lo villano y lo sucio, no superficial y alegremente pintado para hacer reír, sino pintado con delectación morosa y dispuesto de manera que se combine con lo trágico y lo pesimista. Y con todo, la novela interesa y no se suelta hasta que se lee. Creo que – dentro de esta perversión del gusto, del sentido moral y de la teodicea – doña Emilia es toda una novelista.' *Epistolario de Valera y Menéndez Pelayo*, ed. M. Artigas Ferrando and P. Sainz Rodríguez (Madrid, 1946), p. 479. Letter dated 10 January 1894, the month in which the first five chapters of the novel were published.
15. *En el nombre del Padre, Nuevo teatro crítico*, no. 11 (November 1891) (*Cuentos de Marineda*); *La estéril, El imparcial*, 25 December 1892 (*Cuentos de Navidad y Año Nuevo*); *Vida nueva, El Liberal*, 1 January 1893 (*Cuentos de Navidad y Año Nuevo*); also a later story *Leliña, El imparcial*, 2 February 1903 (*El fondo del alma*). The novelist's own deep maternal feelings are evident from her letters to Giner. For example: 'Si V. presumiera los abismos de amor que hay en un hijo! [. . .] Todo es seco, todo es árido, comparado con esta efusión. Se vuelve uno tonto a fuerza de cariño.' RAH, Giner, caja 2, 21 March 1877.
16. 'Emilia Pardo Bazán: a Contrast Study between the Novelist and the Short-Story Writer' (Unpublished Ph.D. thesis, U.C.L.A., 1964), pp. 148–9.
17. The resemblance between this *manía* and Fortunata's and Jacinta's strange ideas about their marital and maternal status is unmistakable. Milagros's conviction that she is Benicio's wife recalls Fortunata's 'ideíta', and her belief that she is the mother of Ilda's twins recalls Jacinta's idea that Fortunata's son is her own. There is a verbal reminiscence in the beginning of the passage quoted above (describing the pains of childbirth) of a similar passage in *Fortunata y Jacinta*, see Benito Pérez Galdós, *Obras completas*, Aguilar, v, 5th edn (Madrid 1967), 544.
18. Benicio's condemnation of the Positivist frame of mind in the name of 'quijotismo' is reminiscent of the Unamuno of for example *Vida de don Quijote y Sancho* (1905). The two writers certainly knew each other in the year after the publication of *Doña Milagros*. In a letter dated 22 May 1895 Unamuno writes: 'Pasé unas tres horas charlando con Da. Emilia Pardo Bazán [. . .] en la tertulia del Ateneo.' *Cartas inéditas de Miguel de Unamuno*, ed. Sergio Fernández Larraín

(Santiago de Compostela, 1965), p. 227. In a letter to Giner dated 16 September 1905 Pardo Bazán wrote: 'Ya lo creo que le habrá gustado mucho Unamuno a Cossío. Es hombre interesantísimo, original, bueno, y su casa y su familia, muy graciosas y muy castizas a pesar de todas las novedades que lleva Unamuno en la cabeza, que no son pocas. La gente, que se empeña en cortar por patrón, critica a Unamuno y le cree empeñado en hacerse el raro. Yo estoy aburrida de la uniformidad; Unamuno me entretiene y se me figura que a él le pasa conmigo lo propio. Su artículo [on *La quimera*] es leal, y yo se lo he agradecido. Confiesa que coincidimos en muchos pensares, y esto, en él, indica estimación intelectual.' RAH, Giner, caja 12. J. Rubia Barcia in his article 'La Pardo Bazán y Unamuno', *Cuadernos americanos*, CXII (1960), 240–63, suggests an influence of Pardo Bazán's late novels (*La quimera* and *La sirena negra*) on Unamuno, but, as this passage suggests, it is more likely to be a case of coincidence than influence. Unamuno, of course, treats the theme of spiritual maternity in *Dos madres* and *La tía Tula*. See Clémessy, p. 621.

19. Miguel Utrillo, 'Las espinas de Doña Emilia Pardo Bazán', *La estafeta literaria*, 5 April 1944, 17.
20. The extent of Pardo Bazán's pessimism about love in the 1890s is made clear by Thomas Feeny in 'Pardo Bazán's Pessimistic View of Love as revealed in *Cuentos de amor*', *Hispanófila*, XXII (September 1978), 6–14.
21. See Prologue to *La dama joven*, III, 669b.
22. Utrillo, 17.

7. *Memorias de un solterón*

1. *Memorias* (as it will hereafter be referred to) appeared in *La España moderna* of 1896 in the following order: chs 1–5 in January; chs 6–12 in February; chs 13–20 in March; chs 21–6 in May.
2. 'Romantic Irony is the irony of a writer conscious that literature can no longer be simply naive and unreflective but must present itself as conscious of its contradictory, ambivalent nature.' D. C. Muecke, *Irony* (London, 1970), p. 78.
3. Mary E. Giles comments on the same passage, drawing attention to its rhythmic quality. See 'Pardo Bazán's Two Styles', *Hispania* (U.S.A.), XLVIII (1965), 456–62 (pp. 457–8).
4. See, for example, Bravo-Villasante, p. 197, and Teresa A. Cook, *El feminismo en la novela de la Condesa de Pardo Bazán* (La Coruña, 1976), pp. 131–51.
5. 'Capitulation: Marriage not Freedom. A Study of Emilia Pardo Bazán's *Memorias de un solterón* and Galdós' *Tristana*', *Symposium*, XXX (1976), 93–109.
6. '*Memorias de un solterón*', *La España moderna*, August 1896 (no. 96), 106–13 (p. 109).
7. See Mansuy, pp. 360–5.
8. *L'irréparable* (Paris, n.d. [1901]), pp. iv–v and 88.
9. For the importance of the dandy figure to the Decadents see Carter, ch. 12, Charles Dédéyan, *Le nouveau mal du siècle de Baudelaire à nos jours* (Paris, 1968), pp. 306–9, and Noel Richard, *Le mouvement décadent, dandys, esthètes et quintessents* (Paris, 1968), p. 253.
10. 'The decadent is like the dandy: he refuses to be embroiled in human relationships.' G. R. Ridge, *The Hero in French Decadent Literature* (Atlanta, Georgia, 1961), p. 49. In *El lirismo* (p. 348) Pardo Bazán wrote: 'El *dandismo* es una forma de superioridad y toda superioridad es distanciación.'
11. This characteristic Decadence shared, of course, with Romanticism. However, it

is the modernity of Mauro's tastes that marks them out as Decadent. See Ridge, pp. 105–8. Mauro's dissatisfaction with Marineda and his escape into fiction recall Pardo Bazán's dissatisfaction with the contemporary world and her escape into art.

12. This misogyny probably stemmed from Schopenhauer. See Dédéyan, pp. 166–7. For the Decadents also, woman was a malevolent force. See Ridge, ch. 8, 'Metamorphoses of the Vampire: Modern Woman and the *Femme Fatale*'.

13. In *El buey suelto* (1878), Pereda illustrates the supposedly disastrous consequences of bachelorhood. A remark Pardo Bazán made to Giner in the year of the completion of *El buey suelto* suggests that Pereda's attitude was not untypical: 'Y no porque yo participe de la idea de que *los solterones* son unos egoístas y duros: al contrario: dos amigos solterones tengo, uno aquí y el otro en La Coruña, a los cuales debo un afecto muy tierno y delicado, que solo puede venir de un alma buena.' RAH, Giner, caja 2, Pontevedra, 14 August [1877]. Nicolás de Díaz de Benjumea's *El solterón o el gran problema social* reached at least a fifteenth edition (Sevilla, 1888).

14. This story bears a strong resemblance to the ball scene in Tolstoy's *Anna Karenina*, part I, chs 22–3.

15. See Sully, pp. 139 and 146.

16. A similar use of a dream appears in *La Regenta* (1884–5). See John Rutherford, *Leopoldo Alas: La Regenta*' (London, 1974), p. 15.

17. Pardo Bazán may conceivably have taken her cue from Bourget's *Le disciple* (1889), where one of the two principles from Adrien Sixte's treatise on love is the following: 'C'est que la jalousie peut très bien exister avant l'amour, par suite, elle peut quelquefois le créér, de même qu'elle peut souvent lui survivre.' *Oeuvres complètes (romans)*, III (Paris, 1901), 134. Although this is not precisely the same phenomenon as that in *Memorias*, they are closely related. Bourget, who deals at length with jealousy in his *Physiologie de l'amour moderne* (1891), is probably the 'favourite author' who helped Mauro to realise how fundamental jealousy was to relationships between the sexes (II, 495a). Jealousy had, in any case, already been used by Jane Austen to show the eponymous heroine of *Emma* (ch. 48) that she is in love.

18. The proverb Mauro is referring to appears in *Don Quixote*, II, ch. 13: 'Cuidados ajenos matan al asno.'

Appendix II   Some French works in Pardo Bazán's personal library

1. Here follow the titles of ten other poems from *Les fleurs du mal*. I have been unable to trace such a collection.

2. Here follow the Spanish titles of six other poems (five, like the first, from *Les fleurs du mal*). I have been unable to trace such a collection.

3. The list of contents given in the catalogue indicates that this is the 1868 edition which contained the 'Notice' by Gautier.

4. I have been unable to trace this work, but it may be *Un scrupule* (1893).

5. This is presumably *Les Jeunes-France, suivis de contes humoristiques* (1875).

6. Here follow the Spanish titles of five other poems by Gautier. I have been unable to trace such a collection.

Bibliography

Alas, Leopoldo (*Clarín*), *Clarín, obra olvidada*. Ed. Antonio Ramos-Gascón. Madrid, 1973.
—'Emilia Pardo Bazán y sus últimas obras' in *Folletos literarios*. VII. Madrid, 1890.
—*Nueva campaña (1885–86)*. Madrid, 1887.
—*Obras selectas*. Biblioteca nueva. Madrid, 1947.
—*Sermón perdido*. Madrid, 1885.
Artigas Ferrando, M. and Sainz Rodríguez, P. (eds), *Epistolario de Valera y Menéndez Pelayo*. Madrid, 1946.
Baquero Goyanes, Mariano, 'La novela naturalista española: Emilia Pardo Bazán', *Anales de la Universidad de Murcia*, XIII (1954–5), 157–234, 539–639.
Barja, César, *Libros y autores modernos: siglos XVIII y XIX*, 2nd edn. New York, 1964.
Barroso, Fernando J., *El naturalismo en la Pardo Bazán*. Madrid, 1973.
Behr-Sigel, E., *Prière et sainteté dans l'église russe*. Paris, 1950.
Beser, Sergio, *Leopoldo Alas: teoría y crítica de la novela española*. Barcelona, 1972.
Bieder, Maryellen, 'Capitulation: Marriage not Freedom. A Study of Emilia Pardo Bazán's *Memorias de un solterón* and Galdós' *Tristana*', *Symposium*, XXX (1976), 93–109.
Bly, P. A., 'The Use of Distance in "La de Bringas"', *Modern Language Review*, LXIX (1974), 88–97.
Bornecque, J.-H. and Cogny, P., *Réalisme et naturalisme*. Paris, 1958.
Bourget, Paul, *L'irréparable*. Paris, n.d. [1901].
—*Oeuvres complètes*. II and III. Paris, 1901.
Brachet, J.-L., *Traité de l'hystérie*. Paris, 1847.
Bravo-Villasante, Carmen, *Vida y obra de Emilia Pardo Bazán*. Madrid, 1962.
Brown, D. F., *The Catholic Naturalism of Pardo Bazán*. Chapel Hill, North Carolina, 1957.
Brunetière, Ferdinand, 'La banqueroute du naturalisme', *Revue des deux mondes*, LXIX (1887), 213–24.
Carter, A. E., *The Idea of Decadence in French Literature, 1830–1900*. Toronto, 1958.
Cassagne, Albert, *La théorie de l'art pour l'art en France chez les derniers romantiques et les premiers réalistes*. Paris, 1906.
Clémessy, Nelly, *Emilia Pardo Bazán, romancière (la critique, la théorie, la pratique)*. Paris, 1973.
Comte, Auguste, *Le catéchisme positiviste*. Paris, 1852.
Cook, Teresa A., *El feminismo en la novela de la Condesa de Pardo Bazán*. La Coruña, 1976.
Correa Calderón, E., 'La Pardo Bazán en su época', in *El centenario de Emilia Pardo Bazán*. Madrid, 1952.
Cousin, Victor, 'De l'art et du beau', *Revue des deux mondes*, XI (1845), 773–811.

Criado y Domínguez, J. P., *Literatas españolas del siglo XIX, apuntes bibliográficos.* Madrid, 1889.

Dédéyan, Charles, *Le nouveau mal du siècle de Baudelaire à nos jours.* Paris, 1968.

Delehaye, H., *Les origines du culte des martyrs.* 2nd edn. Paris, 1933.

Dendle, Brian J., 'The Racial Theories of Emilia Pardo Bazán', *Hispanic Review*, XXXVIII (1970), 17–31.

Dictionnaire de théologie catholique. Ed. A. Vacant, E. Mangenot and E. Aman. Paris, 1903–50.

Enciclopedia universal ilustrada. Espasa-Calpe. Madrid. 1908–75.

Eoff, Sherman H., *The Modern Spanish Novel.* New York, 1961.

Feal Deibe, Carlos, 'Naturalismo y antinaturalismo en *Los pazos de Ulloa*', *BHS*, XLVIII (1971), 314–27.

Fechner, Gustav, *Elements of Psychophysics.* Tr. H. E. Adler. New York, 1966.

Fedotov, G. P., *The Russian Religious Mind.* Cambridge, Massachusetts, 1966.

Feeny, Thomas, 'Pardo Bazán's Pessimistic View of Love as revealed in *Cuentos de amor*', *Hispanófila*, XXII (September, 1978), 6–14.

Fernán Caballero, *La Gaviota.* Madrid, 1856.

Fernández Larraín, Sergio, *Cartas inéditas de Miguel de Unamuno.* Santiago de Compostela, 1965.

Flaubert, Gustave, *Correspondance.* III. Paris, 1927.

Fouillée, Albert, 'La survivance et la sélection des idées dans la mémoire', *Revue des deux mondes*, LXVII (1885), 357–89.

Gautier, Théophile, *Histoire du romantisme.* New edn. Paris, 1901.

—*Mademoiselle de Maupin.* Paris, 1930.

—'Notice' to Charles Baudelaire, *Les fleurs du mal.* Paris, 1868.

Giles, Mary E., 'Feminism and the Feminine in Emilia Pardo Bazán's Novels', *Hispania* (U.S.A.), LXIII (1980), 356–67.

—'Impressionist Techniques in Descriptions by Emilia Pardo Bazán', *Hispanic Review*, XXX (1962), 304–16.

—'Pardo Bazán's Two Styles', *Hispania* (U.S.A.), XLVIII (1965), 456–62.

Gilson, Etienne, *The Christian Philosophy of Saint Augustine.* London, 1961.

Gómez de Baquero, Eduardo (*Andrenio*), '*Memorias de un solterón*', *La España moderna*, August 1896 (no. 96), 106–13.

—*El renacimiento de la novela en el siglo XIX.* Madrid, 1924.

González Blanco, A., 'Juicio crítico de la condesa de Pardo Bazán', *La novela corta*, IV, no. 286 (4 June 1921).

González López, Emilio, *Emilia Pardo Bazán, novelista de Galicia*, New York, 1944.

González Serrano, U., 'La psicología contemporánea', *Revista de España*, LXVIII (1879), 481–97.

Griffiths, Richard, *The Reactionary Revolution: The Catholic Revival in French Literature (1870–1914).* London, 1966.

Hartmann, E. von, *Philosophy of the Unconscious.* Tr. W. C. Coupland, 2nd edn. London, 1893.

Hemingway, Maurice, 'Grace, Nature, Naturalism, and Pardo Bazán', *Forum for Modern Language Studies*, XVI (1980), 341–9.

—'The Religious Content of Pardo Bazán's *La sirena negra*', *BHS*, XLIX (1972), 369–82.

Hilton, Ronald, 'Doña Emilia Pardo Bazán, Neo-Catholicism and Christian Socialism', *The Americas*, XI (1954), 3–18.

Huysmans, J.-K., *Là-bas.* Paris, 1908. Reprinted 1960.

Jaén Morente, Antonio, *Juan Montalvo y Emilia Pardo Bazán, diálogo epistolar.* Quito, 1944.

Jiménez Fraud, Alberto, 'Jaime, doña Emilia y don Francisco', *Papeles de son armadans*, XXVI (1962), 171–82.

Kirby, H. L., 'Evolution of Thought in the Critical Writings and Novels of Emilia Pardo Bazán' (Unpublished Ph.D. thesis, Illinois, 1963).

Lázaro Galdiano, José, 'Nuevas publicaciones de la Sra. Pardo Bazán', *La España moderna*, June 1899 (no. 6), 180–1.

Litvak, Lily, 'La sociología criminal y su influencia en los escritores españoles de fin de siglo', *Revue de littérature comparée*, XLVIII (1974), 12–32.

Longhurst, C. A., *Pío Baroja, 'El mundo es ansí'*. London, 1977.

Lott, Robert E., 'Observations on the Narrative Method, the Psychology, and the Style of *Los pazos de Ulloa*', *Hispania* (U.S.A.), LII (1969), 3–12.

Mansuy, Michel, *Un moderne, Paul Bourget. De l'enfance au disciple*. Paris, 1968.

Martino, P., *Le naturalisme français (1870–95)*. 4th edn. Paris, 1945.

Montes Huidobro, Matías, *Superficie y fondo del estilo*. North Carolina, 1971.

Muecke, D. C., *Irony*. London, 1970.

Oller, Narcís, *Memòries literàries*. Barcelona, 1962.

Osborne, R. E., *Emilia Pardo Bazán, su vida y sus obras*. Mexico, 1964.

Pardo Bazán, Emilia, *Cartas a Benito Pérez Galdós (1889–90)*. Ed. Carmen Bravo-Villasante. Madrid, 1975.

—'Dos sacerdotes se matan', *La ilustración artística*, no. 988 (3 December 1900), 778.

—'Estudios de literatura contemporánea; Pérez Galdós', *Revista de Galicia*, no. 20 (25 October 1880), 350–3.

—'Literatura y otras hierbas', *Revista de España*, CXVII (1887), 133–45.

—*Nuevo teatro crítico*. Madrid, 1891–3.

—*Obras completas*. Aguilar. I and II, ed. Federico Carlos Sainz de Robles, 3rd edn. Madrid, 1957 and 1964. III, ed. Harry L. Kirby Jr, Madrid, 1973.

—'Semana santa', *La ilustración artística*, no. 744 (30 March 1896), 242.

—*Un viaje de novios*. Ed. Mariano Baquero Goyanes. Barcelona, 1971.

Pattison, Walter T., *Emilia Pardo Bazán*. New York, 1971.

—*El naturalismo español. Historia externa de un movimiento literario*. Madrid, 1965.

Pérez Galdós, Benito, *Obras completas*. Aguilar. V. 5th edn. Madrid, 1967.

Pérez Gutiérrez, Francisco, *El problema religioso en la generación de 1868*. Madrid, 1975.

Pérez Minik, Domingo, *Novelistas españoles de los siglos XIX y XX*. Madrid, 1957.

Praz, Mario, *The Romantic Agony*. Called 2nd edn, but in fact 3rd edn. London, 1970.

Réville, Albert, 'Un nouveau système de philosophie allemande, M. von Hartmann et la doctrine de l'inconscient', *Revue des deux mondes*, V (1874), 511–51.

Ribot, Théodule Armand, *Les maladies de la mémoire*. 12th edn. Paris, 1898.

Ricatte, Robert, *La création romanesque chez les Goncourt*. Paris, 1953.

Richard, Noel, *Le mouvement décadent, dandys, esthètes et quintessents*. Paris, 1968.

Ridge, G. R., *The Hero in French Decadent Literature*. Atlanta, Georgia, 1961.

Rivadeneira, Pedro de, *Flos sanctorum*, I. Madrid, 1717.

—*Obras escogidas*. Ed. Vicente de la Fuente. Madrid, 1952.

Romberg, Bertil, *Studies in the Narrative Technique of the First-Person Novel*. Stockholm, 1962.

Rubia Barcia, J., 'La Pardo Bazán y Unamuno', *Cuadernos americanos*, CXII (1960), 240–63.

Rutherford, John, *Leopoldo Alas: 'La Regenta'*. London, 1974.

Sánchez, Porfirio, 'Emilia Pardo Bazán: a Contrast Study between the Novelist and the Short-Story Writer' (Unpublished Ph.D. thesis, U.C.L.A., 1964).

Sánchez Reyes, E., 'Centenarios y conmemoraciones, cartas de Da. Emilia Pardo Bazán a Menéndez Pelayo', *Boletín de la Biblioteca de Menéndez Pelayo*, XXIX (1953), 120–44.

Scari, Robert M., 'Aspectos distintivos del lenguaje de *Morriña*', *Cuadernos hispanoamericanos*, no. 313 (July 1976), 191–9.

—'La presentación del personaje en *Morriña*', *Romanistisches Jahrbuch*, XXII (1971), 297–305.

—'El regionalismo de *Morriña*', *Hispanófila*, XIX (May 1976), 47–55.

Schmidt, Ruth A., 'A Woman's Place in the Sun: Feminism in *Insolación*', *Revista de estudios hispánicos*, VIII (1974), 69–81.

Shaw, D. L., *A Literary History of Spain: the Nineteenth Century*. London, 1972.

Sully, James, *Illusions*. 2nd edn. London, 1882.

Taboada, Luis, 'Filantropía', *El imparcial*, 21 April 1891.

Ternois, R., *Zola et son temps*. Paris, 1961.

Torre, Guillermo de, *Del 98 al barroco*. Madrid, 1969.

Torres, David, 'Veinte cartas inéditas de Emilia Pardo Bazán a José Yxart', *Boletín de la Biblioteca de Menéndez Pelayo*, LIII (1977), 383–409.

Utrillo, Miguel, 'Las espinas de Doña Emilia Pardo Bazán', *La estafeta literaria*, 5 April 1944, 17.

Valis, Noël Maureen, 'Leopoldo Alas y los Goncourt: el alma neurótica', *Hispanic Journal*, I (1979), 27–35.

Varela Jácome, Benito, *Estructuras novelísticas de Emilia Pardo Bazán*. Santiago de Compostela, 1973.

Veith, Ilza, *Hysteria, the History of a Disease*. Chicago, 1965.

Villegas, F. F. (*Zeda*), '*Doña Milagros*', *La España moderna*, May 1894 (no. 65), 202–3.

—'La piedra angular', *La España moderna*, January 1892 (no. 37), 177–82.

Vogüé, Vte E. M. de, *Le roman russe*. Paris, 1886.

Watt, Ian, *The Rise of the Novel*. London, 1957.

Whyte, L. L., *The Unconscious before Freud*. London, 1960.

Zola, Emile, *Correspondance*. Paris, 1908.

Index